macOS Sierra

CHRIS KENNEDY

Questing Vole Press

macOS Sierra
by Chris Kennedy

Editor: Bill Gregory
Proofreader: Pat Kissell
Compositor: Birgitte Lund
Cover: Questing Vole Press

Contents

macOS Basics

On your Apple Mac computer, macOS 10.12—better known as Sierra—is the software that controls:

The user interface
macOS manages the appearance, behavior, and interaction of the windows, buttons, icons, folders, cursors, menus, pointers, and other visual elements on your screen, either directly or indirectly through another program.

Storage
macOS's file system allocates space for and gives access to files—programs and documents—stored on drives or in memory.

Other software
macOS is a launching platform for programs. Word, iTunes, The Sims, and all Mac programs rely on the services and building blocks that macOS provides for basic operations such as drawing a user interface, saving files, and sharing hardware.

Peripheral devices
macOS controls or syncs with peripheral hardware such as your mouse, keyboard, trackpad, display, printer, scanner, external drives, digital camera, ereader, smartphone, iPhone, iPad, and iPod.

Networks and security
macOS controls the interaction of a group of computers and peripheral devices connected by a communications link such as Ethernet or wireless. macOS also protects your system and data from harm or loss.

System resources
macOS handles the allocation and use of your computer's low-level hardware resources such as memory (RAM) and central processing unit (CPU) time.

Task scheduling
macOS acts like a traffic cop, setting priorities and allocating time slices to the processes running on your machine.

Tip: OS stands for "operating system". macOS was formerly called OS X.

About This Book

This book is for you if you're new to macOS, you're upgrading from an earlier version of macOS, or you need a quick reference at hand. It's organized, linked, and cross-referenced to help you find things fast.

Conventions

A shorthand instruction to navigate to a nested folder or to choose a command looks like this:

Choose > System Preferences > Dock > Position on Screen > Left.

Each name between the > symbols refers to an icon, folder, window, dialog box, menu, button, checkbox, option, link, or pane; just look on the screen for a matching label. The refers to the Apple menu (page 27), in the top-left corner of the desktop.

Keyboard shortcuts (Chapter 12) are given in the form "Shift+Command+N".

Default Settings

macOS's **defaults** are Apple-defined settings shipped with the product. In some cases, someone else—an administrator or whoever set up your computer—will have changed some defaults, so your initial setup might look or behave a little differently than I describe.

Paths

A **path** specifies the unique location of a file or folder on a drive or network. A slash (/) separates folder and file names. A path that begins with a slash starts from the **root** (topmost) level of the drive. The path to Disk Utility, for example, is /Applications/Utilities/Disk Utility. A tilde (~) denotes your home folder. For a user named tom, for example, the paths ~/Library/Fonts and /Users/tom/Library/Fonts are equivalent.

Tip: To copy a file or folder path to the clipboard (for later pasting), right-click the file or folder icon, hold down the Option key, and then choose Copy as Pathname.

What's New

Sierra's new features include:

Siri (page 56)

Siri is a voice-controlled personal assistant that can answer questions, make recommendations, and complete common tasks. Siri for the Mac works like Siri for the iPhone and iPad, but with additional macOS-specific features (including most Spotlight search features). You can speak to Siri to open apps, find files, send messages, make FaceTime calls, search the web, get travel directions, report the weather, make restaurant reservations, set reminders, and much more.

Continuity (page 169)

Use the universal clipboard to copy and paste content between Macs and iOS devices. Unlock your Mac automatically when you're wearing your Apple Watch. Use Apple Pay to make purchases on participating websites.

iCloud Desktop and Documents (page 78)

Back up all the files in your Desktop and Documents folders to iCloud. Your files are stored and updated (synced) automatically in iCloud Drive so that you can access them on your iOS devices or another Mac.

Optimized Storage (page 190)

Optimized Storage analyzes your drive and offers suggestions for decluttering your Mac. You can make room for new files by storing older ones in the cloud. Or you can delete obsolete or redundant files that you'll never need again: used app installers, duplicate downloads, caches, and logs.

Tabs

All multiwindow applications now support tabs, including third-party applications (no developer modifications are required). Maps, Pages, Numbers, and Keynote, for example, now support tabbed documents. To create a new tab, press Command+T. To manage tabs, use the Window menu. To set systemwide tab preferences, choose > System Preferences > Dock > "Prefer tabs when opening documents".

Picture in Picture (page 138)

Safari and iTunes support Picture in Picture (PiP). To use this feature, click the Picture-in-Picture button 🖳 at the bottom of a video. A small, borderless, floating video window pops out of the page and hovers over all other windows and apps (including full-screen apps). You can drag the PiP video to any corner of the screen, drag its edges to resize it (within limits), or point to it to use its playback controls. Click the

Picture-in-Picture button again to return the video to its original page. If the Picture-in-Picture button doesn't appear on a video (on YouTube, for example), right-click the video *twice* and then choose Enter Picture-in-Picture.

Finder (page 88)

You can now Command-drag third-party menu extras to reposition icons on the right side of the menu bar. Three new preferences are available in Finder > Preferences > Advanced: "Show warning before removing from iCloud Drive", "Remove items from the Trash after 30 days" (for people who don't empty the Trash until they run out of space), and "Keep folders on top when sorting by name" (a gift to Windows users).

System Preferences (page 61)

In Keyboard preferences, you can choose to capitalize words automatically or end a sentence with a period by double-tapping the spacebar. Dictation & Speech preferences is gone; Dictation has moved to Keyboard preferences and Speech has moved to Accessibility preferences. Accessibility preferences offers Dwell Control for controlling the mouse. Language & Region preferences lets you choose Celsius or Fahrenheit temperature. Dock preferences lets you choose when to open documents as tabs rather than as new windows.

System changes

Sierra drops support for Macs from 2007, 2008, and 2009. The Mac operating system is now named macOS (formerly, it was named OS X). This rebranding fits better with the names of Apple's other operating systems: iOS, watchOS, and tvOS. Otherwise, Sierra looks and feels like its predecessor, El Capitan. The Sierra installer (~5 GB) is smaller than the El Capitan installer (~6 GB).

Messages (page 132)

Insert oversized emoji. Tapback (reply) to a message quickly with a heart, thumbs up, thumbs down, and more. View inline video playback and link previews. View (but not send) handwritten messages, invisible-ink messages, and touchscreen drawings.

Odds & ends

In Photos, the Places album maps photos geographically, the Faces album identifies people, and the Memories album creates short videos that are set to music and based on people, places, dates, scenes, topics, and moods. In Notes, invite people to collaborate on notes in real time. In Mail, click the funnel icon at the top of a message list to filter messages quickly. In Contacts, the contact buttons are front-and-center at the top of cards. In Disk Utility, the Partition page is less confusing. Notification Center always shows dark text on a light background, even if you have the dark theme enabled in General preferences. Console has been redesigned. Apple Music inside iTunes has been slightly redesigned.

New Features from El Capitan

Sierra inherits the following new features from El Capitan (OS X 10.11):

Split View (page 49)

Split View places two full-screen apps side by side, divided by a vertical line that can be dragged to resize the windows.

Mission Control (page 50)

Thumbnail previews of your desktop windows arrange themselves in a single layer, maintaining their relative sizes and positions, with nothing stacked or hidden. Spaces, full-screen apps, and Split Views appear as text labels at the top of the Mission Control screen and turn into thumbnail previews when you point to them. Drag a window to the top edge of the screen and hold the pointer there for a moment to open Mission Control, then drop the window to create a new space, move it to an existing space, go full screen, or create a Split View.

Magnified pointer

If you lose the pointer on a crowded desktop, wiggle the mouse or wiggle your finger on the trackpad, and the pointer grows momentarily to draw your eye.

Spotlight (page 103)

Move or resize the Spotlight window. Spotlight draws on more sources of information and can deliver results for weather, sports, stocks, web video, and transit information. It responds more intelligently to searches phrased in natural language ("pictures that I took in Yellowstone National Park in June 2015"). Natural-language queries also work in Mail ("emails from July") and Finder ("files that I worked on yesterday").

Mail (page 131)

Point to a message in the message list and then flick two fingers left or right on the trackpad to delete that message or mark it as read/unread (the same way that Mail behaves in iOS). In full-screen view, the New Message window uses tabs, letting you work on several messages at once, and shrinks to the bottom of the screen when you click outside it. You can drag images and other attachments down to a shrunken message. Search in Mail responds to natural-language queries like "unread mail from Diane in July" or "emails with attachments from last week". Mail can update your calendar and contacts by recognizing meeting suggestions, events, locations, and contact information in your messages.

Notes (page 134)

Notes gets a major overhaul. Store notes locally or in iCloud. Export notes as PDF files. Format notes with text styles. Create checklists (to-do lists). Recover notes from the Recently Deleted folder. Share notes from other apps: Notes now appears in share sheets in Safari, Photos, Photo Booth, Maps, Contacts, Finder, and more. Paste, drag, or share to attach photos, videos, digital sketches, map locations, websites, audio, and documents to notes. Attachments appear as clickable boxes in notes—use the Attachments Browser to see everything in one place.

Photos (page 135)

The Photos app replaces iPhoto and Aperture. Photos' features should satisfy IPhoto users, but it's less capable than Aperture. Photos accepts third-party editing extensions that appear alongside the built-in editing tools, but if they don't satisfy your needs, then look into competing products such as Adobe Lightroom.

Safari (page 138)

Pin your favorite websites to the left side of the tab bar. Quickly mute tabs that play audio. Stream video from a webpage (YouTube or Vimeo, for example) to your HDTV via Apple TV and AirPlay without showing everything else on your desktop. The status bar (the narrow strip at the bottom of the window) is now translucent and vanishes when you're not pointing to a link. In Reader mode, you can change the font.

Maps (page 132)

Get public-transit directions (train or bus) for certain major cities around the world. Transit view displays color-coded train lines and stations. Click a station to see its train lines, schedule, nearest train, and more.

Calendar (page 123)

Add events such as flights and restaurant reservations found in Mail messages. Learn when to leave for an appointment based on locations and traffic conditions in Apple Maps.

Disk Utility (page 126)

Disk Utility has been redesigned. The new version sports a modern interface, provides more-detailed information about drives, and displays color-coded content maps of drives and partitions. The Disk Utility app loses a few features, such as the ability to repair permissions, but you can still use the `diskutil` command in Terminal to invoke those features. (macOS now fixes permissions every night automatically, and every time that you install a program.) The `diskutil` command is unchanged and will continue to work in any scripts that use it.

Desktop and Finder

Autohide the menu bar when you're not using it (System Preferences > General). Choose whether double-clicking a window's title bar minimizes or zooms the window (System Preferences > Dock). When you right-click a file or folder icon, the Rename command is now in the shortcut menu (right-click and hold down the Option key to see the new Copy as Pathname command as well). If you're copying files but have to shut down your Mac or put it to sleep, macOS resumes copying later where it left off. The Finder sidebar displays an iCloud Drive sync progress indicator. Settings for spring-loaded folders are now in System Preferences > Accessibility > Mouse & Trackpad (moved from Finder > Preferences).

Force click

A Force Touch trackpad (on 2015 and newer MacBooks) lets you Force click by pressing on the trackpad and then applying more pressure. Force clicking offers new ways to interact with many apps and system features. For details, read the Apple support article "Using a Force Touch trackpad" at *support.apple.com/ HT204352*.

New system font

The system font is now San Francisco (replacing Helvetica Neue). The San Francisco typeface, designed by Apple, is also the system font for iOS 9 devices and the Apple Watch. The change is subtle, but typography fans will notice that individual characters are generally narrower and taller than Helvetica Neue characters, resulting in tiny increases in the spacing between letters. San Francisco is optimized for high-resolution (Retina) displays, but the character spacing and reduced blurring can improve readability on standard screens as well.

System Integrity Protection (page 183)

System Integrity Protection, also called "rootless", prevents users (including administrators) and processes from modifying the contents of system-protected folders, including /System, /bin, /usr, and /sbin.

Performance

Everyday actions such as opening and switching apps, opening email, and opening PDFs are noticeably faster (on newer Macs, at least). Apple's Metal technology lets developers improve the look and performance of graphics-intensive apps (games, video editors, and 3D-rendering programs, in particular).

Features for China and Japan

New system fonts, enhanced keyboard input, and improved trackpad handwriting make Chinese and Japanese text easier to read and write.

Odds & ends

Set a password policy for additional downloads from the Mac App Store (System Preferences > App Store). Notification Center has a new Find My Friends widget. Choose whether display color accuracy self-adjusts in different lighting environments (System Preferences > Displays > Ambient light compensation). Parental Controls and the Color Picker dialog box get modest updates. Dictionary gets new languages. New extensions are available (System Preferences > Extensions). The three-finger drag option is now in System Preferences > Accessibility > Mouse & Trackpad > Trackpad Options (moved from System Preferences > Trackpad). The spinning beachball (wait cursor) is now flat 🔵.

New Features from Yosemite

Sierra inherits the following new features from Yosemite (OS X 10.10):

Design

> macOS gets an iOS-style makeover. The redesigned user interface includes new icons, blurred translucency effects, subtle animations, clean lines, and flat colors. Traditional title bars have disappeared from Maps, Safari, Contacts, and other apps. The dock is now a 2D translucent rectangle (instead of a 3D shelf). You can darken the menu bar and dock (sometimes handy for working with photos and videos).

Family Sharing (page 78)

> Family Sharing lets up to six people in a family share each other's iTunes, iBooks, and App Store purchases without sharing Apple ID accounts. All family purchases are made with the same credit card, and adults can remotely approve childrens' spending. Families also share photo albums, calendars, reminders, and location information.

iCloud Drive (page 78)

> Store any file in iCloud and access it from your Mac, Windows PC, iPhone, iPad, or iPod touch. Your files are synchronized across all devices. Any changes that you make to a file while offline are synced automatically as soon as your Mac is back online. iCloud Drive appears in the Finder sidebar and Go menu like any other system folder.

Continuity (page 169)

> Continuity lets you move seamlessly between your Mac, iPhone, iPad, and iPod touch, or use them together. You can start an email or document on your iPhone, for example, and then pick up where you left off on your Mac. You can use your Mac to make and receive phone calls through your iPhone.

Extensions (page 76)

> Extensions are small, functional add-ons that enhance and customize macOS. You can choose which extensions appear in Action menus, Share menus, Finder, and Notification Center's Today view. Third-party developers can also provide extensions that add functionality to macOS.

Notification Center (page 52)

> Notification Center now mimics its iPad counterpart with Notifications view and Today view. You can customize Today view with widgets.

Spotlight (page 103)

> Spotlight search results and previews now appear in a desktop window. Search results now include Wikipedia articles, map locations, Bing.com search results, unit conversions, local movie showtimes, digital media from the iTunes and iBooks stores, and software from the Mac App Store.

Full-screen apps (page 48)

> The green button ⬤ now takes an app full screen. The dedicated full-screen button in the toolbar is gone. (To use the old zoom behavior, Option-click the green button.)

Apple menu (page 27)

> The Software Update menu item is gone, and the App Store item has assumed its duties. The Dock menu item is gone.

Game Center (page 127)

> Game Center now looks and acts like its iPad counterpart. Abstract colored spheres have replaced wood grain and green felt textures.

FaceTime (page 126)

> Answer FaceTime calls on the lock screen without having to enter your password. Put your current conversation on hold to answer another incoming call (call waiting). Set custom ringtones to identify callers.

Script Editor (page 139)

AppleScript Editor is now called Script Editor, and supports JavaScript for Automation.

Dictation Commands (page 63)

Dictation Commands (formerly called Speakable Items) has been updated and merged with Dictation (page 68).

Batch-rename files (page 96)

You can quickly rename a set of selected files or folders in Finder, and add custom text and numbers to each filename.

Tags (page 99)

Drag a tag from the Finder sidebar to the dock for quick access to all the files with that tag.

Default web browser (page 77)

Set the default browser in the General panel in System Preferences.

Preview panel

The preview panel in Finder (View > Show Preview) lets you preview a file or folder without opening it or using Quick Look.

New Features from Mavericks

Sierra inherits the following new features from Mavericks (OS X 10.9):

Free

Upgrading to the current version of macOS from OS X Lion or later costs nothing.

Finder tabs (page 88)

Finder tabs let you declutter your desktop by consolidating multiple Finder windows into a single, tabbed window (similar in concept to a tabbed web browser). Each tab behaves like its own Finder window, so you can change the view of each one independently. You can open folders in new tabs, switch among them, move them, close them, drag files between them, and more.

Tags (page 99)

Assign meaningful words and phrases to files to make them easy to sort and find—tag a batch of photos with *san francisco* and *2015*, for example. macOS comes with some sample tags, and you can create your own to describe and organize your files. You can tag files in apps or in Finder, and use the Finder sidebar to quickly show all files with specific tags.

Multiple displays (page 73)

Each display has its own menu bar. The dock is available on all screens. Each display can independently show the desktop or a full-screen app. Use Mission Control to get an overview of what's running on each display. With AirPlay and an Apple TV, you can use an HDTV as a full-fledged display, complete with dock and menu bar.

iBooks (page 129)

macOS gets Apple's ebook reader from iOS. Shop for books in Apple's iBooks Store and read them in iBooks. Store purchases are downloaded to all your Macs and iDevices automatically. Open multiple books in separate windows. Read books in one-page or two-page view. Go full screen to focus on the words without distraction. Turn pages by clicking, flicking, or using keyboard shortcuts. Bookmarks, highlights, notes, and reading progress are synced across all your devices.

Maps (page 132)

Apple's iOS mapping and navigation app comes to macOS. Open multiple maps in separate windows. Find a business or other point of interest and get its address, phone number, and other info. Mark spots on a map. Find your current location. Get travel directions (walking or driving). Plan a trip on your Mac and then send the map to your iPhone. Show real-time traffic conditions. Show 3D views and photo-realistic Flyover views. Zoom, pan, tilt, or rotate the map. Bookmark your favorite places. Switch to satellite view. Share locations with friends. Print a map or export it as a PDF file.

iCloud Keychain (page 78)

iCloud Keychain encrypts and stores your website user names and passwords on the devices that you've approved (Macs or iDevices), and syncs them wirelessly and automatically across those devices. When you need to create a new password for a website, Password Generator suggests a strong password and saves it to your iCloud Keychain. Passwords and user names are filled in automatically when you need them, so you don't have to remember or type them. iCloud Keychain can also store and sync encrypted credit-card details for online shopping.

Notification Center (page 52)

Respond to email, message, or FaceTime notifications without leaving the app you're in. Sign up with websites to receive news headlines, sports scores, auction (eBay) alerts, and more as notifications, even when Safari isn't running. View notifications when your Mac is locked. Silence notifications with Do Not Disturb.

Redesigned apps

Calendar, Contacts, and Notes all get an iOS-style makeover (clean lines, flat colors, lightweight fonts, and no fake leather or textures) and now resemble their iPad counterparts. Activity Monitor has been redesigned and has a new Energy tab that lists power-hogging apps (now also listed in the battery status menu).

Safari (page 138)

Redesigned Top Sites. New sidebar. Shared Links shows you links from people you follow on Twitter and LinkedIn.

Preferences

Bigger icons. Software Update is now App Store. Mail, Contacts & Calendars is now Internet Accounts. Print & Scan is now Printers & Scanners. Language & Text is now Language & Region. The Text and Input Sources panes have moved from Language & Region to Keyboard. Accessibility lets you set the fonts and formatting of video language tracks, subtitles, and closed captions. Dictation lets you dictate offline. App Store permits automatic updates.

Removed or replaced in Mavericks

Tags replace colored labels in Finder. iTunes DJ is gone.

New Features from Mountain Lion

Sierra inherits the following new features from Mountain Lion (OS X 10.8):

Notification Center (page 52)
Collate alerts and reminders from various apps and display them on your desktop.

Dictation (page 68)
Talk anywhere that you can type, and Dictation converts your words into text (internet connection required).

Gatekeeper (page 112)
Restrict which downloaded apps can be installed, protecting your Mac from viruses, spyware, and other malware.

Game Center (page 127)
Play games on Apple's online multiplayer social gaming network.

Messages (page 132)
Send iMessages and SMS/MMS messages, chat with video or audio, and exchange files.

Notes (page 134)
Type notes on a virtual pad of scratch paper.

Reminders (page 137)
Create and manage to-do lists.

Share sheets (page 168)
Share text, documents, links, photos, contacts, locations, videos, and more from apps that have a Share button Share button or Share menu.

Twitter integration (page 167)
Tweet text, links, and photos directly from Safari, Photo Booth, Photos, and other apps.

Facebook integration (page 167)
Post photos, links, comments, or locations via share sheets; add Facebook friends to Contacts; get Facebook notifications in Notification Center; or update your status.

AirPlay mirroring (page 168)
Wirelessly mirror (duplicate) whatever is on your Mac's screen to a high-definition TV (HDTV) via Apple TV.

Power Nap (page 187)
When your Mac is sleeping, silently and automatically download updates, make backups, and more.

Widget browser (page 46)
Dashboard now has a full-screen widget browser instead of a widget bar.

Screen-saver slideshows (page 67)
Screen Saver now offers slideshows as well as traditional screen savers.

Launchpad search box (page 115)
Launchpad now has a search box that helps you find and launch apps quickly.

Deeper iCloud integration (page 78)
Pages, Numbers, and Keynote let you save or open online documents in iCloud for synced access across Macs and iOS devices. Preview and TextEdit let you move documents to the cloud. Third-party developers can also tap into iCloud.

Software updates via App Store (page 186)
Updates for macOS and other Apple software are now released through the Mac App Store rather than through the dedicated Software Update app (which has been dropped from macOS).

Features for China
New features for Chinese speakers include a Chinese dictionary; Baidu search in Safari; QQ Mail, 163, and 126 services in Internet Accounts; new Chinese fonts; Sina Weibo, Youku, and Tudou share sheets; and improved Chinese keyboards and text input.

Apps renamed or replaced
iChat is now Messages. Address Book is now Contacts. iCal is now Calendar. Universal Access is now Accessibility. Speech is now Dictation & Speech.

Removed from Mountain Lion
iCloud replaces MobileMe. App Store replaces Software Update. RSS support has been removed from Safari and Mail. Notes has been removed from Mail (Notes is now a separate app). Java and X11 are now on-demand downloads.

New Features from Lion

Sierra inherits the following new features from Lion (OS X 10.7):

Multitouch gestures (page 25)
Tap, drag, flick, pinch, spread, and rotate your fingers on a trackpad to control what's on your screen.

Full-Screen Apps (page 48)
Expand certain applications to fill your screen edge to edge, hiding the dock and other windows.

Mission Control (page 50)
Display a bird's-eye view of what's open on your computer.

iCloud (page 78)
iCloud stores your content online and syncs it wirelessly and automatically across your Mac, Windows PC, iPhone, iPad, and iPod touch.

Launchpad (page 115)
Show a full-screen grid of application icons to open, switch, or delete apps.

Resume (page 116)
When you open an app, it starts where you left off the last time you ran it, with the same windows open in the same positions. When you log in or restart, all the apps that you were using automatically relaunch with the same open windows.

Auto Save and Versions (page 117)
Certain applications save your documents automatically in the background as you work (you don't even have to save before you quit the app). You can create, browse, and revert to past versions of documents by using a Time Machine-like interface.

Mac App Store (page 64)
Buy, download, install, and update macOS applications directly from Apple's online store.

AirDrop (page 158)
Quickly and wirelessly send files to other nearby AirDrop users, without any setup, passwords, special settings, or base stations.

Removed from Lion
Front Row. iSync. iDisk. Native faxing. FTP services. To-do lists in Mail. PowerPC app support. People Finder, Business, and iTunes dashboard widgets. Boot Camp support for Windows Vista and XP (Boot Camp supports Windows 7 and later).

Installing Sierra

Unlike early (pre-Lion) versions of macOS, you can't get a copy of Sierra on a DVD. Instead, you download Sierra from the Mac App Store (> App Store > Updates pane). Sierra is a large download (~5 GB); if you don't have a fast or reliable network connection, you can take your Mac to an Apple retail store to get help installing Sierra. You can install it on any Mac that meets Apple's system requirements. The general requirements are:

- OS X 10.7.5 or later (that is, Lion or later)

- 2 GB of memory

- 8.8 GB of available space

- MacBook (Late 2009 or newer)

- MacBook Pro (Mid 2010 or newer)

- MacBook Air (Late 2010 or newer)

- Mac mini (Mid 2010 or newer)

- iMac (Late 2009 or newer)

- Mac Pro (Mid 2010 or newer)

Tip: If you're running OS X 10.6 (Snow Leopard), you must upgrade to OS X 10.11 (El Capitan) and *then* upgrade to Sierra. If you're running OS X 10.5 (Leopard) or earlier, you must upgrade to Snow Leopard before proceeding; you can buy Snow Leopard from the online Apple Store.

Some features, such as Handoff (page 169) and AirDrop (page 158), require recent (2012 or newer) models. For details, read the Apple support article "Upgrade to macOS Sierra" at *apple.com/macos/ how-to-upgrade*. To determine whether your Mac qualifies, choose > About This Mac. The Overview pane shows your model, release date, and memory (click Storage to check free space). You can install Sierra on all your Macs, without serial numbers or copy protection.

Tip: In Terminal, you can use the command **uname -a** to print technical details about your hardware and operating system.

Reinstalling Sierra

Should the need arise, you can reinstall Sierra without using a DVD or disk image. When you first install Sierra, the installer silently creates a new partition on your hard drive that you can use to reinstall Sierra. (Your existing data are safely preserved during repartition.) This stealth partition, named Recovery HD (or Recovery-10.12), is invisible in Finder and Disk Utility, but you can see it by using the `diskutil list` command in Terminal. To recover Sierra, hold down the Option key during startup and then choose Recovery HD when the list of startup partitions appears. Alternatively, hold down Command+R during startup to boot directly to Recovery HD. For details, read the Apple support article "About OS X Recovery" at *support.apple.com/ HT201314*. To create a bootable macOS installer on a USB flash drive, read "Create a bootable installer for OS X" at *support.apple.com/HT201372*. You can also boot to Recovery HD from a locally connected Time Machine backup drive.

Tip: If FileVault (page 179) is turned on, Recovery HD won't appear when you hold down the Option key during startup, but you can still hold down Command+R to boot directly to it.

Startup

Pressing the Power button ⏻ starts (**boots**) the Mac normally. macOS also offers startup options for special situations. See also "Drives" on page 109.

To start normally: Press ⏻.

To start from a bootable CD/DVD: Hold down C when you press ⏻.

To start from the first drive/partition: Hold down D when you press ⏻.

To reset the laptop display: Hold down R when you press ⏻.

To start from a network (NetBoot) server: Hold down N when you press ⏻.

To start in target disk mode: Hold down T when you press ⏻. Target disk mode (page 190) lets one FireWire/Thunderbolt-equipped Mac act as an external hard drive on another Mac.

To start from an external drive/disc: Hold down Shift+Option+Command+Delete when you press ⏻.

To start in 64-bit mode: Hold down 6 and 4 when you press ⏻.

To prevent automatic login: Press ⏻ and then hold down the left Shift key when the spinning progress indicator appears. See also "Logging In" on page 16.

To suppress Login Items and Finder windows at login: Hold down Shift after clicking the Log In button in the login window.

To select a startup drive/partition: Hold down Option when you press ⏻. Boot Camp (page 122) users can use this feature to start Windows.

To force-boot macOS even if another OS is the default: Hold down Command+X when you press ⏻.

To eject a CD/DVD at startup: Hold down the left mouse button when you press ⏻.

To start in safe mode (safe boot): Hold down Shift when you press ⏻ and then release Shift when the login screen indicates a safe boot. For details about safe mode, read the Apple support article "Try safe mode if your Mac doesn't finish starting up" at *support.apple.com/HT201262*.

To troubleshoot at startup: When you press ⏻, hold down Command+S (single-user, Unix command-line mode), Command+V (verbose mode showing Unix console messages), or Option+Command+P+R (resets NVRAM/Parameter RAM—wait for the second chime).

To reinstall (recover) macOS: Hold down Command+R when you press ⏻.

To start, wake, sleep, or shut down automatically at a specified time: Choose > System Preferences > Energy Saver > Schedule.

To designate the startup drive for future startups: Choose > System Preferences > Startup Disk (click 🔒 if the settings are dimmed).

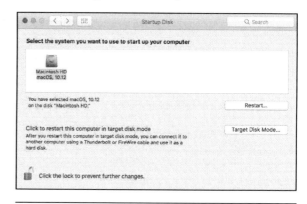

Tip: To select the current startup drive, in Finder, hold down the Shift key and then choose Go > Select Startup Disk on Desktop.

User Accounts

macOS lets many people use the same computer without being able to see or change each other's files and settings. **User accounts** identify who has permission to log in to a particular computer (or network).

To start an macOS session, you log in to your user account, which gives you personalized access to the system. You, like each user, have your own files and settings, including:

- Login items
- Application preferences
- Desktop setup
- System preferences
- Email and internet accounts
- Screen saver
- Apple ID
- iCloud account
- System language
- Files and folders
- Documents
- Internet settings (including bookmarks, home page, history, cookies, and cached webpages)
- User (personal) fonts
- Sharing permissions
- Network connections

Your private files, folders, and preferences generally are stored on the macOS drive in /Users/*user_name*—your home folder (page 86)—which lets macOS personalize your desktop each time that you log in.

On a new computer or during a clean installation, you create the first user account when you set up macOS. If you upgraded from an earlier version of macOS, your existing accounts migrated to the new installation and appear in the login window. If you're on a large network, ask your network administrator how to log in.

To create an account: Choose > System Preferences > Users & Groups > Add button (+) (click if the settings are dimmed).

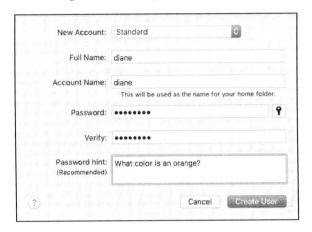

Complete the following account settings:

New Account

Select one of the following account types from the New Account pop-up menu:

Administrator. An administrator has sweeping systemwide rights to create, edit, and delete user accounts and passwords; open, edit, move, and delete everyone's files and folders; install programs, fonts, and hardware; change preferences; use Disk Utility; and bypass FileVault.

Standard. This account has access only to its own home folder and to shared folders. Standard users can change settings related to only their own accounts (picture, password, and desktop preferences, for example) and install programs for only their own use.

Managed with Parental Controls. This account is the same as a standard user but with additional usage limits set by an administrator using Parental Controls (page 182).

Sharing Only. This account can access the computer only remotely (over a network) to share files. It has no home folder and can't change settings or log in via the login window.

Group. A group contains the names of one or more other accounts and is used to set sharing privileges for multiple users at the same time. In the Membership box that appears, select the accounts of the group members.

Full Name

The full name typically is the name of a person (first, last, or both names) but can be any word(s). You can change the full name after creating the account.

Account Name

macOS proposes a **short name** but you can change it to any word without spaces or punctuation. The login window lets you use your full or short name, but network and dial-up connections require a short name. The user's home folder is labeled with the short name. You can't (easily) change this name after creating the account.

Password, Verify

Type and then retype the user's password, or leave both fields empty for a passwordless account. To get password advice, click 🔑 .

Password hint

Type an (optional) memory-jogging hint for the password. (All users can see this hint.) The login window shows hints only if they're enabled in Login Options (page 16).

Click the "Create User" button and then complete the following options in the Password pane. The available options depend on your account type (administrator, standard, and so on) and whether you're changing your own account or someone else's.

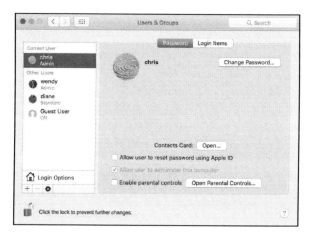

Picture

Accept the sample picture or click it to choose another or take a snapshot by using a built-in camera. You can also drag a picture from a folder onto the sample picture.

Change Password/Reset Password

Change the user's login password and password hint.

Contacts Card

View or edit the user's Contacts entry.

Allow user to reset password using Apple ID

Lets the user reset a forgotten password after entering an Apple ID.

Tip: An **Apple ID** (*appleid.apple.com*) identifies you uniquely for Apple.com store transactions, iTunes Store, App Store, iBooks Store, Messages, AirDrop, iCloud, Apple retail store reservations, and Apple.com support. An Apple ID requires a valid email address to register. Use a personal address that you anticipate having for a long time (such as a Gmail or Yahoo email address); don't use your work or school email address. See also "iCloud" on page 78.

Allow user to administer this computer
Gives a standard or managed user administrative rights.

Enable parental controls
Adds Parental Controls restrictions to Standard accounts.

Login Items
Click Login Items to specify any programs, documents, drives, network servers, files, or folders to open automatically at log in. To add a program to this list quickly, right-click (or click-and-hold) its dock icon and then choose Options > Open at Login.

To edit an account: Choose > System Preferences > Users & Groups > select the account (click if the settings are dimmed). Nonadministrators can change only some settings. You can't edit another user who's logged in via fast user switching (page 17).

To delete an account: Choose > System Preferences > Users & Groups > select the account (click if the settings are dimmed) > Delete button (–). You can archive the former user's home folder, leave it undisturbed, or delete it. You can't delete another user who's logged in via fast user switching.

To enable the Guest account for temporary, passwordless logins: Choose > System Preferences > Users & Groups > select Guest User (click if the settings are dimmed) > select "Allow guests to log in to this computer". You can also apply parental controls and prevent guests from using shared folders. When the guest logs out, the account is reset and all its files, email, browser history, and settings are erased.

To set an administrative master password (to access encrypted home folders): Choose > System Preferences > Users & Groups > Gear button (click if the settings are dimmed) > Set Master Password.

Logins & Logouts

Logging in starts your session in macOS. **Logging out** ends the session and prevents others from accessing your files and settings. **Fast user switching** maintains your session in the background when others are logged in. When you're finished using your computer, you can put it to sleep or shut it down.

Logging In

After startup, you'll see the **login window**. Logging in identifies you uniquely so that macOS can load your personal settings, grant you certain permissions, and take you to the desktop.

To log in: In the login window, click your name (or type it if there's no list), type your password if prompted, and then press Return or click the arrow icon in the password box. In a long list, use the arrow keys to scroll to your name or type its first few letters.

To suppress Login Items and Finder windows at login: Hold down Shift while logging in.

To correct a mistyped password: The password box shakes when you type the wrong password: correct it or click the question mark in the password box to show your password hint (if you've set one in Users & Groups). Passwords are case-sensitive; ⇧ appears in the password box if Caps Lock is on. By default, you can mistype your password an unlimited number of times.

To log in automatically at startup: Choose > System Preferences > Users & Groups > Login Options (click if the settings are dimmed) > "Automatic login" pop-up menu. Other users still can use their accounts via fast user switching or when you log out. This option is convenient but insecure because anyone can log in just by turning on the computer.

To prevent automatic login at startup: Press ⏻ and then hold down the left Shift key when the progress indicator appears.

To require logins for all users: Choose > System Preferences > Security & Privacy > General pane >

select "Disable automatic login" (click if the settings are dimmed).

To set up the login process: Choose > System Preferences > Users & Groups > Login Options (click if the settings are dimmed).

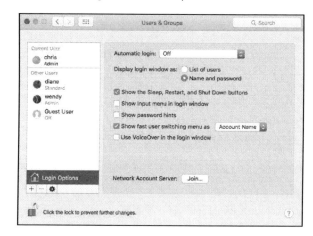

Set the following options:

Automatic login

Enable automatic login for a specific user (more convenient) or force all users to log in (more secure). Automatic login works best if only one person uses the Mac, or uses it most of the time. When auto-login is turned on, startup bypasses the login window and shows the specified user's desktop automatically. Other users still can use their accounts via fast user switching or when the user logs out (> Log Out). This option is convenient but insecure because anyone can log in just by turning on the computer.

Display login window as

The "List of users" option (more convenient) shows a list of user names and pictures in the login window. The "Name and password" option (more secure) hides the pictures and makes every user type a name and password.

Show the Sleep, Restart, and Shut Down buttons

Choose whether to show these buttons in the login window (more convenient) or hide them (more secure). A technically savvy enemy can circumvent macOS security by bypassing the login window during a restart (restarting at the Unix Terminal or in target disk mode, for example). Turning off this option adds a modest layer of security, but for strong security, use FileVault (page 179).

Show Input menu in login window
Choose whether to let users select a keyboard language in the login window. Turn on this option if the Mac's various account holders speak different languages or use different keyboard layouts and alphabets.

Show password hints
Choose whether to let users see their password hints set in Users & Groups. macOS displays a password hint on the login window at the user's request. If this option is turned off, then hints don't appear (which adds a layer of security, depending on how obvious the hints are).

Show fast user switching menu as
Choose whether simultaneous logins are allowed.

Use VoiceOver in the login window
Choose whether to have VoiceOver speak the parts of the login window (for blind users).

Network Account Server
If you're on a large network, your network administrator will tell you how to connect to an open directory server, active directory domain, or macOS Server.

Tip: For more login options, choose > System Preferences > Security & Privacy > General pane.

Forgotten Passwords

You forgot your login password.

If you're not an administrator (or if you are one but there's another administrator account), then the administrator can choose > System Preferences > Users & Groups, click your account name, and then click Reset Password.

If you're the only administrator, you have several options, provided you turned them on in advance:

- **Password hint.** Show the password hint that you set in > Preferences > Users & Groups. The login window shows hints only if they're enabled in Login Options.

- **Apple ID.** If "Allow user to reset password using Apple ID" was previously turned on in > System Preferences > Users & Groups, then you can click the question mark in the password box when you're logging in. A message appears: "If you forgot your password, you can reset it using your Apple ID". Click → to open the Reset Password dialog box. Enter your Apple ID and password and then click Reset Password. A message appears telling you that changing your account password creates a new keychain (page 180). (The old keychain remains and can be unlocked if you remember your old password.) Click OK. Enter a new password (twice) and password hint, and then click Reset Password. Click Continue Log In to log in with your new password.

- **FileVault recovery key.** If FileVault (page 179) is turned on, then you can use your recovery key (an emergency master password) to log in. (If you opted to store the recovery key with Apple, then call Apple tech support; they'll give it to you.) Restart the Mac. On the login window, click your name, click the question mark, and then click "Reset it using your Recovery Key", and then type your recovery key.

Switching Users

Fast user switching lets multiple users stay logged in at the same time. You can leave your programs running and documents open securely and invisibly in the background while someone else logs in. When you switch back to your account, macOS resumes your session where you left off. Fast user switching is handy when you're logged in, and someone else wants to use the computer for a moment to check email or a calendar. Depending on how many programs are open and how much memory your Mac has, switching accounts may cause small delays and increased drive activity.

To enable fast user switching: Choose > System Preferences > Users & Groups > Login Options (click if the settings are dimmed) > select "Show fast user switching menu as". Use the pop-up menu to show the accounts menu as a user name or a compact icon .

To switch users: Choose another user name from the accounts menu on the right side of the menu bar. This menu appears only when fast user switching is turned on and shows a check mark next to the name of each logged-in user. To be safe, save all work before switching (in case another logged-in user shuts down or restarts the computer).

If you try to shut the Mac down or restart it while other people are logged in, a dialog box tells you, "There are currently logged in users who may lose unsaved changes if you shut down this computer". You can click Cancel or you can type an administrator password and then click Shut Down (shutting down all accounts open in the background and their open documents, possibly making enemies of the other users).

Tip: You can't make changes to accounts (in System Preferences) that are still logged in. You also can't turn off fast user switching or turn on FileVault (page 179) while other people are logged in.

Logging Out

When you log out, macOS disconnects your online connections and prevents others from using your user account to access your files or network. Programs that don't use Auto Save (page 117) prompt you to save any unsaved work. Your computer remains turned on and macOS shows the login window to let the next person log in.

To log out after a cancelable delay: Choose > Log Out *user_name* (Shift+Command+Q) > Log Out (Return).

To log out immediately: Hold down the Option key and then choose > Log Out *user_name* (Shift+Option+Command+Q).

To log out automatically after an idle period: Choose > System Preferences > Security & Privacy > Advanced button (click if the settings are dimmed) > select "Log out after _ minutes of inactivity".

Sleeping, Locking, Restarting, and Shutting Down

When you're not using your computer, you can put it to sleep, lock its screen, or shut it down. **Sleep** blanks the screen but maintains your session; your computer stays on but draws little power and awakens quickly. **Locking** keeps you logged in but hides and password-locks your screen, though administrators can unlock it and any user can shut down and restart. You can **restart** your computer to troubleshoot or complete a software update. **Shutting down** powers off the computer (if you have a laptop, wait for it to shut down completely before closing the lid). If you restart or shut down, macOS prompts you to save any unsaved work.

Tip: You can create an "If found, contact…" message that always appears in the login window: choose > System Preferences > Security & Privacy > General (click if the settings are dimmed). Turn on "Show a message when the screen is locked", click Set Lock Message, and then type your message (press Option+Return to create a new paragraph).

To sleep: Do any of the following:

- Choose > Sleep.
- Press Option+Command+Eject ⏏.
- Close the laptop lid.
- Press Ctrl+Eject ⏏ > Sleep (S).
- On an Apple Remote, press-and-hold the Play button.

To sleep automatically after an idle period: Choose > System Preferences > Energy Saver > Computer Sleep slider.

To sleep by moving the pointer to a screen corner: Choose > System Preferences > Mission Control > Hot Corners > Active Screen Corners menus > Put Display to Sleep (holding modifier key(s), if desired).

To wake a sleeping computer: Press a key, click the mouse, tap the trackpad, or open the laptop lid.

To disable sleep: Choose > System Preferences > Energy Saver > Computer Sleep slider > Never.

To disable sleep for a fixed time period: In Terminal, type the command `caffeinate -t timeout`, where *timeout* is the number of seconds to prevent your Mac from sleeping. To prevent sleep for an hour, for example, type `caffeinate -t 3600`.

To configure sleep: Choose > System Preferences > Energy Saver and > System Preferences > Bluetooth > Advanced > "Allow Bluetooth devices to wake this computer".

To lock (password-protect) the screen: Choose > System Preferences > Security & Privacy > General pane > select "Require password after sleep or screen saver begins". If fast user switching is enabled, the password dialog box lets you choose a user when you unlock.

To restart after a cancelable delay: Choose > Restart.

To restart immediately: Do any of the following:

- Hold down the Option key and then choose > Restart.
- Press Ctrl+Command+Eject ⏏.
- Press Ctrl+Eject ⏏ > Restart (R).
- Press ⏻ > Restart (R).

To force restart (last resort): Press Ctrl+Command+⏻.

To shut down after a cancelable delay: Choose > Shut Down.

To shut down immediately: Do any of the following:

- Hold down the Option key and then choose > Shut Down.
- Press Ctrl+Option+Command+Eject ⏏.
- Press Ctrl+Eject ⏏ > Shut Down (Return).
- Press ⏻ > Shut Down (Return).

To force shut down (last resort): Press-and-hold ⏻.

To shut down/sleep/wake/restart automatically at a specified time: Choose > System Preferences > Energy Saver > Schedule.

The Keyboard

Apple has changed its keyboards and keyboard layouts over the years. This book covers the thin aluminum keyboards and newer laptop keyboards.

Keyboard Shortcuts

Keyboard shortcuts save you from moving your hand from keyboard to mouse repeatedly. These shortcuts involve the **modifier keys** that sit in the bottom corners of the keyboard's main section. Press these keys—**Shift** ⇧, **Control** ⌃ (Ctrl), **Option** ⌥ (equivalent to the Alt key in Windows), **Command** ⌘, and **Fn**—together with other keys to change the action. The C key pressed by itself types a lowercase c; pressed along with the Shift key, it types an uppercase C; and pressed along with the Command key, it issues the Copy command.

In this book, modifier keys are joined to other keys with a plus sign. Command+C, for example, means "Press the Command key, hold it down while you press the C key, and then release both keys". A three-key combination such as Shift+Command+N means "Hold down the first two keys while you press the third one and then release all three keys". The modifiers are always listed first.

Shortcuts change over time. This book gives the current ones. The F3 key, for example, invokes Mission Control and is labeled ▤ on newer keyboards (F3 used to invoke the Copy command).

Special Keys

Function and Fn

The **function keys** (F1, F2, F3, and so on) invoke Mac-specific features. F1 ☀ and F2 ☀, for example, change screen brightness; F4 ⠿ displays Launchpad; and F10 ◂, F11 ◂), and F12 ◂)) change the speaker volume. To invoke program-specific functions, hold down the **Fn key** and press a function key. Fn+F1 undoes the last action in Microsoft Word, for example. You can configure the keyboard to reverse Fn-key behavior.

Navigation

The **navigation keys** move things around and scroll windows. The four **arrow keys** ←→↑↓ scroll in that direction, move the insertion point or selected item(s), or select the adjacent item. **Home** (Fn+←) and **End** (Fn+→) jump to the start or end of whatever is active: a webpage or document, a list of files in Finder, the frames of a movie, a series of photos, a line of text, the cells of a table row, and so on. **Page Up** (Fn+↑) and **Page Down** (Fn+↓) scroll up or down one page or windowful.

Return and Enter

The **Return key** and the **Enter key** usually do the same thing (typically, insert a paragraph break, complete an entry, or confirm a dialog box).

Delete

The **Delete key** (or **backspace key**), labeled "delete" or ⌫, deletes the character or selection *before* the insertion point. The **Forward Delete key**, labeled "del" or "delete" or ⌦, deletes *after* the insertion point; if your keyboard lacks this key, Fn+Delete mimics it.

Eject

Press-and-hold the **Eject key** ⏏ to eject a CD or DVD.

Tab

The **Tab key** advances to the next tab stop in a line of text, cycles through dialog-box and webpage fields, jumps to the next cell in a spreadsheet, or moves to the next item in a series. Shift+Tab jumps backward. Its behavior depends on the context and active program.

Escape

The **Escape key**, in the keyboard's upper-left corner, means "Never mind" or "Stop". Press it to close dialog boxes, cancel commands, interrupt long processes, close menus, change modes, or dismiss message boxes. Sometimes Escape does nothing. Its behavior depends on the context and active program.

Configuring the Keyboard

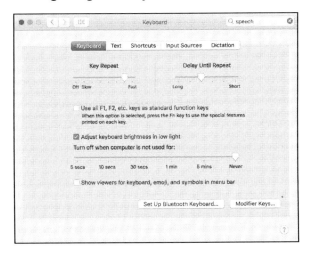

To change how fast characters repeat when you hold down a key: Choose > System Preferences > Keyboard > Keyboard pane. Drag "Delay Until Repeat" to set the wait before a character starts to repeat and then drag "Key Repeat" to set how fast it repeats.

To change Fn+Function Key behavior: Choose > System Preferences > Keyboard > Keyboard pane. To use unmodified function keys for Mac-specific functions (volume, brightness, Mission Control, and so on) and Fn+function keys for program-specific functions, select "Use all F1, F2, etc. keys as standard function keys". To reverse this behavior, clear this checkbox.

To get a list of keyboard shortcuts: In Finder, choose Help > Mac Help and then search for *keyboard shortcuts* by using the Search box. See also Chapter 12.

To change keyboard shortcuts: Choose > System Preferences > Keyboard > Shortcuts pane. Click a category in the list on the left. In the list on the right, use the checkboxes to toggle shortcuts. To assign or change keyboard shortcuts, click a shortcut's name and then press Return (or click to the right of a shortcut's name), and then type the new keystroke. To return the shortcuts to their original settings, click Restore Defaults.

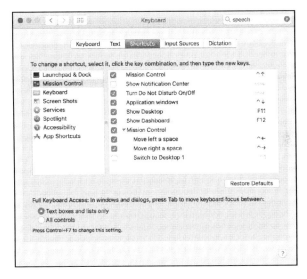

To change the modifier and Caps Lock keys: Choose > System Preferences > Keyboard > Keyboard pane > Modifier Keys. You may find it convenient to remap Caps Lock as either Control or Command.

To set up a Bluetooth keyboard: Turn on the keyboard. Choose > System Preferences > Keyboard > Keyboard pane > Set Up Bluetooth Keyboard.

To toggle keyboard backlighting: Choose > System Preferences > Keyboard > Keyboard pane. Select "Adjust keyboard brightness in low light". To save power by dimming an idle keyboard, drag the slider away from "Never".

To make the keyboard easier to use if you're disabled: Choose > System Preferences > Accessibility > Keyboard.

Spelling, Text Substitutions, and Smart Quotes

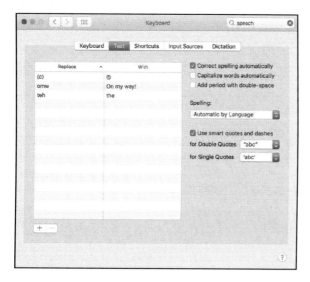

The settings in the Text pane in the Keyboard panel work systemwide in Apple programs (TextEdit, Messages, Mail, Calendar, Safari, Stickies, and so on).

Replace/With (text substitutions)
Automatically replaces text with other text (like AutoCorrect in Microsoft Word). Autoreplace *jqp* with *John Q. Public*, for example. To add or remove substitutions, click (+) or (–). To use this feature, choose Edit > Substitutions > Text Replacement in each target application (such as TextEdit).

Correct spelling automatically
Autocorrect spelling errors in applications that support it.

Capitalize words automatically
Capitalize the first letter after a period, question mark, or exclamation point in applications that support it.

Add period with double-space
Double-tap the spacebar at the end of a sentence to end it with a period, move one space to the right, and start the next sentence with an uppercase letter, in applications that support it.

Spelling
Choose the language(s) that you want to use to check your spelling as you type.

Use smart quotes and dashes
Determines the type of quotes—"curly" or "straight", for example—inserted automatically when you type single or double quotation marks. To use this feature, choose Edit > Substitutions > Smart Quotes in each target application. Smart dashes turns double hyphens (--) into em dashes (—).

International Keyboards

If you communicate in more than one language, the Input Sources pane in the Keyboard panel lets you add keyboards for other languages. You can switch keyboards at any time.

To type in a different language: Choose > System Preferences > Keyboard > Input Sources pane.

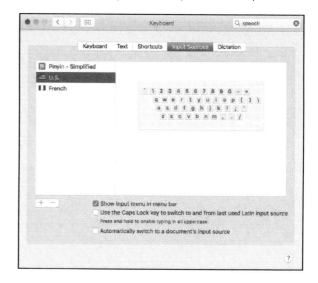

Click (+) and then select the desired language(s). Select "Show Input menu in menu bar". On the right side of the menu bar, choose a keyboard from the Input menu (a flag icon or similar symbol) and then start typing in the selected language. To show the

Input menu in the login window, see "Logging In" on page 16. To remove a language, select it and then click (–). See also "Language & Region" on page 82.

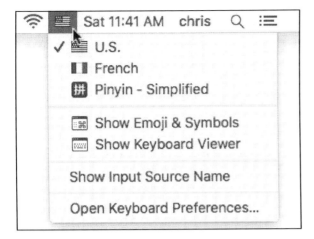

To view the onscreen keyboard or type special characters: Choose > System Preferences > Keyboard > Input Sources pane > select "Show Input menu in menu bar". Click the Keyboard pane and then select "Show viewers for keyboard, emoji, and symbols in menu bar". On the right side of the menu bar, choose Show Keyboard Viewer from the Input menu. To see or type special characters, hold down modifier keys in Keyboard Viewer or choose Input menu > Show Emoji & Symbols. To change the Input-menu keyboard shortcuts, choose > System Preferences > Keyboard > Shortcuts pane > Keyboard. To resize Keyboard Viewer, click its zoom button or drag its corner.

The Mouse

Most mice have a left and a right button; the left button is used for most actions but frequent use of the right button, which opens a shortcut menu, is a key to working quickly.

Mouse Gestures

Clicking and dragging

To **point**, move the tip of the **pointer** over the target item to which you want to point. To **click**, point to an item and then press and release the left mouse button without moving the mouse. To **double-click**, point to an item and then click the left mouse button twice quickly without moving the mouse (if you click too slowly, macOS interprets it as two single clicks). To **right-click**, point to an item and then click the right mouse button without moving the mouse. (To "right-click" with a one-button mouse, hold down the Ctrl key and then click normally.) To **drag**, point to an item, press-and-hold the left mouse button while you move the pointer to a new location, and then release the button (press Esc during a drag to cancel the drag). The normal pointer ▸ may change depending on what you're dragging or pointing to.

Tip: If you lose the pointer on a crowded desktop, wiggle the mouse or wiggle your finger on the trackpad, and the pointer grows momentarily to draw your eye (> System Preferences > Accessibility > Display > "Shake mouse pointer to locate").

Scrolling

If your mouse has a wheel, ball, or multitouch surface, you can use it to scroll documents, webpages, and more. By default, content moves in a direction *opposite* that of scrolled content in Windows and older (pre-Lion) macOS versions. This default behavior mimics that of touchscreen devices (such as the iPad and iPhone); if you find this to be disorienting, you can revert to the traditional scrolling behavior by using Mouse preferences.

Modifiers

Modifier keys work with the mouse gestures. To **Command-click**, hold down Command and then click before releasing the key. To **Command-drag**, hold down Command and then drag and drop before releasing the key. To **Command-scroll**, hold down Command while spinning the mouse wheel. Clicks, drags, and scrolls can be similarly modified with the Shift, Control, and Option keys.

Insertion point

In text documents, don't confuse the **insertion point** (also called the **cursor**), a steadily blinking vertical bar I, with the pointer, a nonblinking I-beam I. The insertion point indicates where text or graphics will be inserted when you type or paste.

Configuring the Mouse

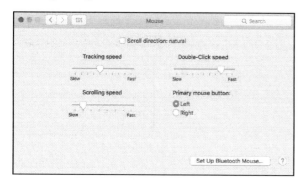

To reverse the scrolling direction: Choose > System Preferences > Mouse > "Scroll direction: natural". To use the traditional (Windows and pre-Lion) scrolling behavior, clear this checkbox.

To change mouse sensitivity: Choose > System Preferences > Mouse. "Tracking Speed" sets the pointer's acceleration (which moves the pointer farther onscreen than you move the mouse on your desk). Fast settings are useful if you have multiple monitors. "Double-Click Speed" sets the tiny time interval that distinguishes a double-click from two single clicks. "Scrolling Speed" affects the response

to the scroll wheel or ball. "Primary mouse button" swaps the functions of the left and right buttons. For an Apple Magic Mouse, more options appear. Settings for non-Apple mice may appear elsewhere in Preferences.

To zoom by using the mouse (if available): Choose > System Preferences > Mouse. Select "Zoom using scroll wheel while holding". Select a modifier key from the pop-up menu or press multiple modifier keys. To set how the zoomed image moves with the pointer, click Options. This feature is useful for examining photos closely and reading small type; it's not available if your mouse lacks a ball, wheel, or multitouch surface. See also "Accessibility" on page 63.

To set up a Bluetooth mouse: Turn on the mouse. Choose > System Preferences > Mouse > Set Up Bluetooth Mouse.

To resize the pointer: Choose > System Preferences > Accessibility > Display > Cursor Size.

To make the mouse easier to use if you're disabled: Choose > System Preferences > Accessibility > Mouse & Trackpad.

The Trackpad & Multitouch Gestures

If you have a built-in laptop trackpad, an Apple Magic Trackpad, or an Apple Magic Mouse, then you can interact with macOS by using your fingertips to do multitouch gestures. *Multitouch* refers to a touch-sensing surface's ability to recognize the presence of two or more points of contact (fingertips) with the surface.

Multitouch Gestures

macOS's multitouch gestures are the same as those for iPad and iPhone.

- To **tap**, gently tap the trackpad with one finger.

- To **double-tap**, tap twice quickly (if you tap too slowly, macOS interprets it as two single taps).

- To **touch and hold**, touch the trackpad with your finger and maintain contact with the surface.

- To **drag**, touch and hold a point on the trackpad and then slide your finger across the surface.

- To **flick** (or **swipe**), fluidly whip your finger across the trackpad.

- To **pinch**, touch your thumb and index finger to the trackpad and then pinch them together or spread them apart.

- To **rotate**, spread your thumb and index finger, touch them to the trackpad, and then rotate them clockwise or counterclockwise.

- A Force Touch trackpad (on 2015 and newer MacBooks) lets you **Force click** by pressing on the trackpad and then applying more pressure. Force clicking offers new ways to interact with many apps and system features. For details, read the Apple support article "Using a Force Touch trackpad" at *support.apple.com/ HT204352*.

Tip: Modifier keys work with the trackpad; you can hold down Shift, Control, Option, or Command during a gesture.

Common Multitouch Tasks

The effect of a multitouch gesture depends on which application you're using. Gestures are usually accompanied by animations that clarify the effect. Common gestures include:

Click
> Tap one finger to simulate a mouse click.

Right-click
> Tap two fingers to right-click.

Define a word
> Tap a word with three fingers to look it up in the built-in dictionary.

Scroll
> Drag two fingers to scroll documents, webpages, and more. You can choose whether scrolled content moves in the same or opposite direction in which you move your fingers.

Zoom
> Spread two fingers apart or pinch them together to zoom in or out of documents, webpages, photos, and more.

Smart zoom
> Double-tap two fingers to magnify a particular image or block of text.

Navigate pages
> Drag two fingers left or right to flip through documents, webpages, and more.

Move among screens
> Flick three fingers left or right to move among spaces, full-screen apps, and the dashboard.

Show Mission Control
> Flick three fingers up to see a miniature image of every open window.

Exposé view
> Flick three fingers down to see a miniature image of every open window for the current application.

Preview in Quick Look
> Select one or more files in Finder and then tap three fingers to see a pop-up thumbnail image of the files.

Show Launchpad
> Pinch three fingers and your thumb to show Launchpad.

Show the desktop
> Spread three fingers and your thumb to move all open windows off the screen, revealing the desktop.

Open Notification Center
> Flick two fingers leftward from the right edge of the trackpad.

Configuring the Trackpad

To reverse the scrolling direction: Choose > System Preferences > Trackpad > Scroll & Zoom pane > "Scroll direction: natural". To use the traditional (Windows and pre-Lion) scrolling behavior, clear this checkbox.

To change trackpad sensitivity and toggle gestures: Choose > System Preferences > Trackpad > Point & Click pane. The "Tracking speed" slider sets the pointer's acceleration (which moves the pointer farther onscreen than you drag your fingers on the trackpad). In the different panes, use the checkboxes and drop-down menus to toggle or fine-tune individual gestures. Hover the pointer over a particular gesture to trigger a tutorial video.

To make the trackpad easier to use if you're disabled: Choose > System Preferences > Accessibility > Mouse & Trackpad.

Menus

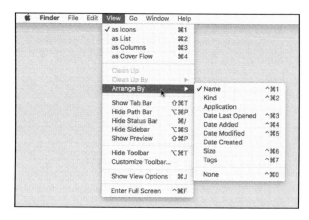

macOS has one **menu bar** that runs along the top of the screen (unlike Microsoft Windows, where each window has its own menu bar). The **pull-down** menus in the bar list commands in groups. A command with a ▶ next to it has additional choices listed in a **submenu**. A **checked command** √ represents an on/off option or mutually exclusive choice. An **inactive command** is dimmed if it's unavailable in the current context (the Copy command is unavailable if nothing is selected, for example) or you lack the administrative privileges to invoke that command.

Tip: To autohide the menu bar when you're not using it, choose > System Preferences > General > Automatically hide and show the menu bar.

Most commands take effect as soon as you choose them. A command followed by an ellipsis (Ellipsis) opens a dialog box because it needs more information to complete. The Find command, for example, has an ellipsis because it needs to know what to find.

Menus show keyboard shortcuts for commonly used commands. The modifier keys and their symbols are:

- Shift ⇧
- Control ⌃
- Option ⌥
- Command ⌘
- Arrow keys ←→↑↓

- Home ↖
- End ↘
- Page Up ⇞
- Page Down ⇟
- Return ↩
- Enter ⌤
- Delete (Backspace) ⌫
- Forward Delete ⌦
- Eject ⏏
- Tab ⇥
- Escape ⎋
- Power ⏻

Apple Menu

The leftmost menu is the **Apple menu** , which contains common macOS-specific commands that are always available regardless of which application is active. You can't customize the Apple menu, but you can press and hold the Option key or the Shift key to use command variants. To choose which items appear in the Recent Items submenu, choose > System Preferences > General > "Recent items".

Application Menus

Next to the menu are the **application menus**, which change depending on the active window. The name of the active application (Finder, iTunes, or Photoshop, for example) appears first, in bold, followed by other application-specific menus. The File, Edit, Window, and Help menus are fairly consistent across programs. The File menu usually has the commands New, Open, Save, Save As, and Print. Edit has Undo, Cut, Copy, and Paste.

Menu Extras

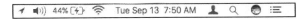

The right side of the menu bar holds status menus, represented by icons, for various macOS system preferences and programs. (Menu extras are the equivalent of the icons found in the Windows taskbar system tray.)

To add or remove a menu, look in a program's preferences. The ◀) menu, for example, shows the speaker-volume slider and is toggled with > System Preferences > Sound > "Show volume in menu bar". Option-clicking a status menu usually reveals extra commands or information.

Shortcut Menus

A **shortcut menu** is a context-sensitive menu that appears when you right-click (or two-finger tap) an item. Shortcut menus offer common commands quickly and macOS provides them for almost everything: icons, files, folders, drives, desktop, dock, and so on. Commands apply only to the item (or group of items) to which you point. Applications have custom shortcut menus: right-click a link in Safari, selected text in TextEdit, or a picture in Photos, for example.

Tip: If a program adds its own commands to shortcut menus with or without your permission, you can usually remove those commands via the program's Preferences dialog box (Command+,) or by turning off the program's Services keyboard shortcuts (> System Preferences > Keyboard > Shortcuts pane > Services).

Menu Tasks

To choose a menu command by using the keyboard: Press Ctrl+F2 (or Fn+Ctrl+F2) to highlight the menu or Ctrl+F8 (or Fn+Ctrl+F8) to highlight menu extras. Use the arrow keys ←→↑↓ to navigate to a menu command (or type a command name in the selected menu), and then press Return. To close a menu without choosing a command, press Esc or click outside the menu.

To change the color of selected menu items: Choose > System Preferences > General > Appearance pop-up menu.

To rearrange menu-extras icons: Hold down the Command key and then drag the icons left or right. To remove an icon, Command-drag it out of the menu bar. (You can't rearrange or remove the or application menus.)

To change the menu language: See "Configuring the Keyboard" on page 21.

To darken the menu bar (and dock): Choose > System Preferences > General > select "Use dark menu bar and Dock". If the menu bar is not dark, then the desktop wallpaper colors will show blurrily under the menu bar.

To autohide the menu bar when you're not using it: Choose > System Preferences > General > "Automatically hide and show the menu bar". When this option is turned on, the menu bar disappears when the pointer moves away from the menu bar and reappears when it moves toward it.

Toolbars

A **toolbar** is a block of buttons and controls that runs along the top of windows in Finder, Preview, Mail, Safari, and many other programs. Hover the pointer over a control for a pop-up tip. Toolbars provide quick access to common menu commands. Toolbar commands vary by application; some of the following commands apply to only Finder toolbars.

To show or hide a toolbar: Choose View > Hide/Show Toolbar (Option+Command+T).

To rearrange toolbar icons: Hold down the Command key and then drag the icons. To remove an icon, Command-drag it off the toolbar. You can also Command-drag the spacers between icons.

To customize a toolbar: Choose View > Customize Toolbar, or right-click the toolbar and then choose a command. If a window is too narrow to show all its toolbar icons, click Chevron right on the right edge of the toolbar.

To use a toolbar via the keyboard: Press Ctrl+F5 (or Fn+Ctrl+F5) to move to the toolbar; press ←, →, or Tab to select an icon; press Return to "click" the selected icon.

Icons

An **icon** is a small picture that represents an item you can manipulate. macOS uses icons on the desktop and in folders to represent folders, files, drives, documents, programs, the Trash, and hardware devices.

You select (highlight) an icon or group of icons to perform an action. Left-click to select; right-click to open the shortcut menu; or drag to move.

What happens when you open (double-click) an icon depends on the icon's type. A folder, drive, removable-storage, or portable-device icon opens in a Finder window. A document, picture, video, or music icon opens in its associated program, launching that program if it's not already open. An application icon launches the program. A smart-folder icon searches your computer and lists all files that match what you're looking for. The Trash icon shows the items to be deleted when you empty it.

To select an icon: Do any of the following:

- Click it.
- Press the arrow keys until the icon is selected.
- Press the first letter of the icon's name. If the correct icon isn't selected, press Tab, Shift+Tab, or the arrow keys to select it.

To select multiple icons: Do any of the following:

- Command-click each icon to select it.
- Drag a selection rectangle diagonally around the icons.
- In a list or column view, click the first icon that you want to select, and then Shift-click the last icon (all icons in between are selected automatically).
- In a list or column view, click an empty area in a row and then drag up or down.

To extend a previous selection: Normally, selecting icons deselects any previously selected icons. To keep these icons selected, press Command or Shift when you make a new selection.

To select all icons: Choose Edit > Select All (Command+A). To select *almost* all icons, select them all, and then Command-click each icon that you *don't* want.

To deselect icons: To deselect all icons, click anywhere in the window or desktop other than a selected icon (or press Option+Command+A). To deselect a specific icon in a multiple selection, Command-click it.

To change an icon's picture: Copy the new picture to the clipboard, typically by opening it in Preview and then choosing Edit > Copy (Command+C). Select the file or folder whose icon you want to replace, choose File > Get Info (Command+I), and then, at the top of the Info window, click the icon picture and then choose Edit > Paste (Command+V).

To change the color of a selected icon's name: Choose > System Preferences > General > "Highlight color" pop-up menu.

Windows

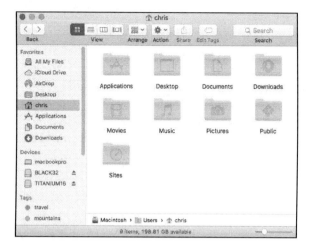

macOS lets you work with multiple overlapping windows. You identify the window by its **title bar**, which runs along the top of the window and gives the title of the window's folder, application, document, or device. Each window has its own boundaries and can present different views of its contents. Some applications—including Maps, Safari, Notes, Reminders, and Contacts—lack a traditional title bar.

When multiple windows are open, only one is active at any time. The **active window**, identified by its darker title bar, is the one that receives your keystrokes (text entry, navigational movements, or commands). An inactive window can be hidden behind other windows and remains inactive until you bring it to the foreground.

The buttons ⊗ ⊖ ⊕ in the window's top-left corner let you **close** a window, **minimize** it to an icon in the dock, or expand it to **full screen**. You can also resize a window freely. To manage multiple windows, see Chapter 2.

To activate a window: Do any of the following:

- Click anywhere in the window.

- Click its icon in the dock.

- Right-click (or click-and-hold) the application icon in the dock and then choose the window when the menu appears.

- Command+Tab to the desired application or window.

- Press F3 (or Fn+F3) to open Mission Control and then click the desired window.

To move a window: Drag its title bar or, if present, the status bar running along the bottom edge of the window. If the window lacks a traditional title bar, drag an empty area in the space at the top of the window where the title bar would normally appear (be careful not to click a button or other control when you're hunting for valid draggable area).

To move a window without activating it: Command-drag its title bar or status bar.

To close a window: Click the red button ⊗ or choose File > Close (Command+W). In some applications, a centered dot • instead of × in the red button denotes a document with unsaved work. In Finder, Safari, Terminal, and other applications that use tabbed windows, choose File > Close Window (Shift+Command+W) or File > Close Tab (Command+W).

Tip: In macOS (unlike Windows), closing an application's only open window doesn't usually quit the application. To quit, choose File > Quit (Command+Q).

To minimize a window to the dock: Click the yellow button ⊖. In Finder, Command+M works too. You can also double-click the window's title bar if you choose > System Preferences > Dock > "Double-click a window's title bar to minimize".

To expand a window to full screen: Click the green button ⊕. To restore the window to its previous size, move the pointer to the top edge of the screen and then, when the menu bar appears, click the green button ⊕; alternatively, press Ctrl+Command+F or (for some programs) press Esc once or twice. If the application doesn't support full-screen view, then the window will enlarge (zoom) but not to full screen. For details, see "Full-Screen Apps" on page 48.

To enlarge (zoom) a window without making it full screen: Hold down the Option key and then click the green button ⬤. You can also double-click the title bar if you choose > System Preferences > Dock > "Double-click a window's title bar to zoom". To restore the window to its previous size, hold down the Option key and then click the green button again ⬤. Some applications also have a Window > Zoom command.

To apply the same action to all a program's windows: Hold down Option during the action. To minimize all Finder windows, for example, Option-double-click a folder's title bar, or press Option+Command+W to close them all.

To resize a window: Drag any window edge or corner. The pointer becomes a double-headed arrow near a window's border.

Scrolling

A window that's too small to show all its contents displays scrollbars. A **scrollbar** is a vertical or horizontal bar at the side or bottom of a window used to slide that window's contents around. Drag the **scroll box** to move to an arbitrary location, or click an empty area in the scrollbar **shaft** (the long, narrow background in which the scroll box travels) to jump by one windowful at a time. Old-style scrollbars have **scroll arrows** at the ends for moving contents incrementally.

The size of a scroll box is proportional to the fraction of the window contents displayed, so the scroll box indicates visually how much you *can't* see, as well as showing you where you are.

Many programs scroll automatically in common situations. Dragging or extending a selection of text or graphics near a window's edge autoscrolls in the direction of the drag, often at a speed proportional to how far past the edge you drag. Tabbing to a text box or typing in a partially hidden text box autoscrolls a form to reveal the whole box. Using Find, Go To, or a similar command autoscrolls to show the matching selection or new cursor location.

You can replicate most scroll-bar actions by using the mouse wheel, navigation keys, or multitouch gestures.

To configure scrollbars: Choose > System Preferences > General. The "Show scroll bars" options determine whether scrollbars fade away when not in use. The "Jump to the spot that's clicked" option scrolls to the spot where you click on the scroll-bar shaft instead of scrolling by one windowful ("Jump to the next page"). Option-clicking in the shaft swaps between the two methods temporarily. To reverse the scrolling direction, use Mouse and Trackpad preferences.

To toggle smooth scrolling: macOS uses **smooth scrolling**, which slides content rapidly when you press Page Up or Page Down (rather than changing the view instantaneously). Older (pre-Mountain Lion) versions of macOS let you turn off smooth scrolling easily, but you can still disable it if it draws your eye too much. In Terminal, type the commands:

```
defaults write -g \
NSScrollAnimationEnabled -bool NO
killall Dock
```

To return to smooth scrolling, retype the commands, but change **NO** to **YES**.

Dialog Boxes & Controls

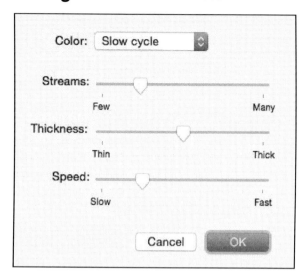

A **dialog box** is a small temporary window that a program opens to respond to a command or event. **Controls** let you enter new content or view or change existing settings. The common controls in dialog boxes and other parts of the user interface include:

- *Radio buttons* ⦿◯ choose one of several mutually exclusive options.

- *Checkboxes* ☑☐ turn options on or off.

- *Pop-up menus* [Small ⇕] select one option from a list.

- *Sliders* ▭◇▭ set a value in a restricted range.

- *Buttons* [OK] are labeled by actions (pressing Return "clicks" the darker, pulsing button).

- Clicking a menu item or button with an *ellipsis* (...) [Options...] makes a dialog box appear.

- *Text boxes* [15] contain typed or pasted (input) text.

- *Tabs* [Desktop][Screen Saver] show individual panes within a dialog box.

When a control is dimmed, it's unavailable in the current context or you lack the administrative privileges to use it.

To use the keyboard to navigate in a dialog box: Choose > System Preferences > Keyboard > Shortcuts pane > "All controls" (at the bottom). With this option turned on, Tab and Shift+Tab move forward and backward through controls; the arrow keys and letter keys choose items in lists and open pop-up menus; and Spacebar "clicks" the active control. Keyboard shortcut to toggle this setting: Ctrl+F7 (or Fn+Ctrl+F7).

Get Info

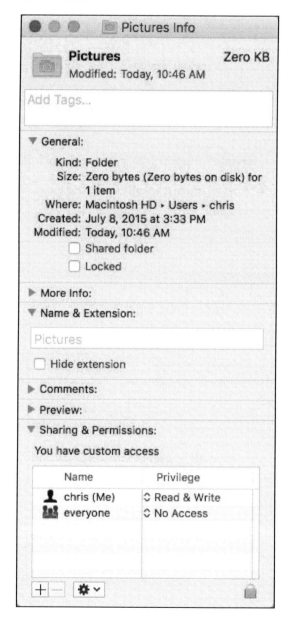

Almost every item (icon) has an Info window full of information, called **metadata**, about its contents and settings. The attributes shown are appropriate for the item selected. The Info window for a drive shows capacity statistics, for example; for a file or folder, it shows creation and modification dates. You can summon separate Info windows for each selected item or a single summary window, called an Inspector window, for multiple items.

To open separate Info windows for each item: Select an item, or group of items, and then choose File > Get Info (Command+I), or right-click any selected item and then choose Get Info.

To open a summary Info window for multiple items: Select the items, hold down the Ctrl key, and then choose File > Get Summary Info (Ctrl+Command+I), or Ctrl-click any selected item and then choose Get Summary Info.

To open a window that shows information about the current selection: Select any item, hold down the Option key, and then choose File > Show Inspector (Option+Command+I), or Option-click any item and then choose Show Inspector. The contents of the Inspector window change to reflect whatever is selected.

To show or hide a panel in an Info window: Click ▶ or ▼ in the panel.

Tip: The Info window also lets you add tags (page 99) to files and folders.

Transferring Content

macOS gives you a few ways to move data around: copy webpage text to an email message, embed charts and graphics in reports and slides, move paragraphs around in a document, and so on.

Cut, Copy, and Paste

Cut, copy, and paste are used to organize documents, folders, and drives. **Cut-and-paste** removes (cuts) content and places it on the clipboard so that it can be moved (pasted) elsewhere. Cutting deletes the content from its original location. **Copy-and-paste** copies content to the clipboard so that it can be duplicated (pasted) elsewhere. Copying leaves the original content intact (nothing visible happens when you copy).

The **clipboard** (in Finder, choose Edit > Show Clipboard) is the invisible area of memory where macOS stores cut or copied content, where it remains until it's overwritten when you cut or copy something else. This scheme lets you paste the same thing multiple times in different places. You can transfer content from one program to another provided that the second program can read content generated by the first. A little experimenting shows that you often can combine dissimilar content; you can paste text from TextEdit into Photoshop, for example. You can't paste something that you've **deleted** or **cleared** (as opposed to cut), because macOS doesn't place the deleted item on the clipboard.

The Cut, Copy, and Paste commands are in a program's Edit menu, but each program may handle these operations differently. In Finder, for example, you can copy files and folders from one drive or folder to another. In Mail, you can copy or move text or graphics to another part of a message or to a different message. In Safari, you can only copy material from webpages, not cut it.

To cut: Select (highlight) the content to remove, and then choose Edit > Cut (Command+X), or right-click the selection and then choose Cut.

To copy: Select (highlight) the content to copy, and then choose Edit > Copy (Command+C), or right-click the selection and then choose Copy.

To paste: Click the mouse (or move the cursor to) where you want the content to appear, and then choose Edit > Paste (Command+V), or right-click and then choose Paste.

To undo a cut or paste: Immediately choose Edit > Undo (Command+Z).

Tip: You can also copy and paste text to the clipboard by using the **pbcopy** and **pbpaste** commands in Terminal.

Universal Clipboard

Use the **universal clipboard** to copy text, pictures, video, or other content from an app on your Mac and then paste it into another app on your nearby iPhone or iPad—or vice versa. The universal clipboard works between any combination of Macs and iOS devices (between two Macs, for example, or between an iPhone and an iPad) that are logged in to the same iCloud account. All communication is local; your data never appear on Apple's servers. When you copy content on your Mac, the Mac then advertises over Bluetooth that it has something on the clipboard, the same as it would do if it had content available via Handoff (page 169). Unlike Handoff, however, no visual indicator appears on nearby Macs and iDevices showing that there's content ready to paste. If a large amount of content is pasted, then a small, pop-up progress bar accompanies the action. The universal clipboard is part of Continuity (page 169) and works only when two devices are near each other. To toggle the universal clipboard on your Mac, choose > System Preferences > General > Allow Handoff. There's no way to keep Handoff but not the universal clipboard.

Drag-and-Drop

TextEdit, Mail, iWork, Microsoft Office, and many other programs let you drag-and-drop as a faster alternative to cut-and-paste: click in the middle of some highlighted content and then drag it elsewhere within the same document or to a different window or program. (This technique doesn't involve the clipboard and won't change its contents.) You can often press a modifier key, such as Ctrl or Option, as you drag to copy, rather than move, the content. Dragging text to the desktop creates a "scrap" or "clipping" file for later reuse.

Intermediate Formats

Another way to exchange data between programs is to save it in a format that both the source and target programs can read and write. To read a list of addresses into a mailing-list program from a spreadsheet or database, for example, save the addresses in a CSV-format file (a text file of comma-separated values), and then open it in the mailing-list program. The source program's Save As dialog box lists the format types that you can save. The target program usually autoconverts the CSV file when you open it with File > Open, but you may have to step through an "interview" to organize the incoming data. Image-editing programs such as Photoshop can exchange files in JPEG, GIF, TIFF, PNG and other popular graphic formats.

Import/Export

Use import and export tools to transfer large amounts of data or data in incompatible formats. Most address-book, browser, email, office-suite, and database programs have Import and Export commands, typically in the File menu. The commands vary by program (they're not part of macOS), so read the documentation for both the source and target programs. Import/export operations can be routine—most database and accounting programs can skip the CSV step and export to the native Excel format directly, for example—but they're superlative when no standard exchange-format exists. If you want to try new email and browser programs, then import/export is the only practical way to transfer all your addresses, messages, bookmarks, cookies, and other content. Choosing File > Import Bookmarks in Safari, for example, lets you import browser bookmarks from Mozilla Firefox.

Getting Help

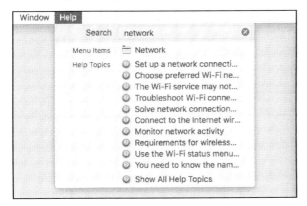

macOS's Help system lets you use web-style links and searches to access standard documentation, animated tutorials, and troubleshooting guides. Each program has its own set of help files, accessed from its Help menu. macOS-specific help is available when Finder is active. The Mac Help window floats atop other windows; minimize or resize it if it's in the way.

Tip: macOS help files are stored in /Library/Documentation/Help.

To get help by searching: Choose Help (Shift+Command+?) and then type or paste a search phrase (one or more keywords) in the Search box. Help shows relevant topics as you type. Click any link in the results list or click Show All Help Topics for a complete list. Pointing to a Menu Items link opens the relevant menu.

To get help by browsing: Choose Help > Mac Help (if this command isn't visible, click × in the Search box). Use the Search box or click a linked topic to open it. Use the toolbar buttons to revisit help topics, show or hide the table of contents, or save, share, or print help topics.

To find text within a help topic: Press Command+F.

System Information

System information is useful when diagnosing problems, getting technical support, or installing new hardware.

To get general system information: Choose > About This Mac.

To get detailed system information: Click the System Report button in the About This Mac window or choose Applications > Utilities (Shift+Command+U) > System Information.

Preferences

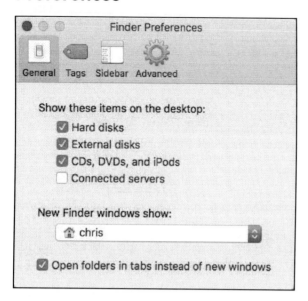

Most applications have a Preferences dialog box that sets programwide options. Preferences is one of the first places to look at when you're new to a program. In general, any changes that you make to preferences apply to only your user account.

To open Preferences: Open or activate the desired program and then choose Preferences from the application menu or press Command+, (comma). Some programs have a similar dialog box, named Options, available in the program's application menu or Tools menu.

CHAPTER 2

The Desktop

After you log in, macOS shows the **desktop**, which is the backdrop of your working environment and lets you organize your computer's resources. This chapter covers the main desktop-management tools:

- The dock lets you access often-used files, folders, and programs.

- Stacks expands the contents of docked folders and drives.

- Exposé declutters a screenful of windows.

- Spaces organizes windows into groups.

- Dashboard gives you instant access to specialized miniprograms called widgets.

- Full-screen apps fill your screen edge to edge, hiding the dock and other windows.

- Split View places two full-screen apps side by side.

- Mission Control unites macOS's window-management features to give you a bird's-eye view of all your open spaces, widgets, programs, documents, and folders.

- Notification Center collates alerts from various apps and displays them on the desktop.

- Siri is a voice-controlled personal assistant that can answer questions, make recommendations, and complete common tasks.

The other parts of the desktop, covered elsewhere, are the menu bar, Finder, and the Trash. You can also use various System Preferences (Chapter 3) panels to personalize your desktop.

The Dock

The **dock** comes with (removable) Apple-installed icons, and you can add shortcuts to your own files, folders, drives, programs, documents, and internet bookmarks. An icon in the dock is only a pointer; removing it doesn't delete the file to which it's linked, nor does dragging an icon to the dock move the original file, though you can drag icons (or Command-drag them freeze the dock icons for better accuracy) directly into docked folders and their spring-loaded (page 98) subfolders.

Each dock icon has its own shortcut menu, available via right-clicking.

The dock itself has its own shortcut menu for customizing the dock (right-click the dock divider).

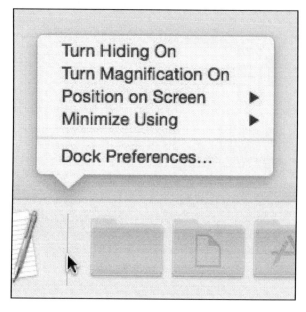

Hovering the pointer over an icon shows its name. Clicking an application or document icon opens it, or activates it if it's already open. Clicking a folder or drive icon shows its contents in a stack. To make a small dot appear next to the dock icon of every open application, choose > System Preferences > Dock > select "Show indicators for open applications". All open applications appear in the dock. All minimized windows appear in the dock as thumbnails or are accessed by right-clicking the dock icons of their parent programs.

Some apps try to get your attention by displaying an **alert badge**—a number in a little red circle superimposed on the app's dock icon. The number is the count of new, unread, or unattended items for that app. Mail shows the number of incoming mail messages, for example; App Store shows the number of updates available.

A divider separates application icons from all other types of icons. Application icons sit to the left of the divider. Everything else (documents, folders, the Trash, and so on) sits to the right.

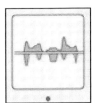

Some application icons show "live" information. The icon for Mail, for example, shows the number of un-read messages; the icon for Activity Monitor can show a real-time graph of CPU usage and other statistics.

To open or activate a dock item: Click its dock icon.

To open a document by using the dock: Drag the document from the desktop or a folder window onto a compatible dock application. To force-open, Option-Command-drag (some apps can't be forced).

To see an item's shortcut menu: Right-click (or click-and-hold) its icon in the dock.

To see the dock's shortcut menu: Right-click the dock divider.

To add items to the dock: Drag an icon (or group of icons) from the desktop or a folder window to the dock, or drag a proxy icon (page 91) from a window's title bar to the dock. Drag applications to the left of the dock divider, and files, folders, and drives to the right.

To add an open program to the dock: Right-click (or click-and-hold) its icon in the dock and then choose Options > Keep in Dock.

To reorder items: Drag dock icons to reorder them.

To remove an item: Drag it out of the dock, or right-click it and then choose Options > Remove from Dock. You can't remove icons for Finder, the Trash, and minimized documents. If you remove the icon of an open program, it vanishes from the dock after you quit that program.

To see an item in Finder: Command-click its dock icon, or right-click its dock icon and then choose Options > Show in Finder.

To switch to another program and hide the active one: Option-click the dock icon of the program that you want to activate.

To hide all programs but one: Option-Command-click the dock icon of the program that you want to activate.

To quit an open program: Right-click (or click-and-hold) its dock icon and then choose Quit.

To force-quit a frozen program: Hold down Option, right-click (or click-and-hold) its dock icon, and then choose Force Quit.

To navigate the dock by using the keyboard: Press Control+F3 (or Fn+Control+F3) to activate the dock. Press ← or → to select an icon; press Return to open an icon; or press ↑ or ↓ to open or close an icon's shortcut menu. To cancel without choosing a command, press Esc.

To view or change dock-related keyboard short-cuts: Choose > System Preferences > Keyboard > Shortcuts pane > Launchpad & Dock.

To configure the dock: Choose > System Preferences > Dock. For quick access to a subset of dock preferences, right-click the dock divider and then use the dock's shortcut menu.

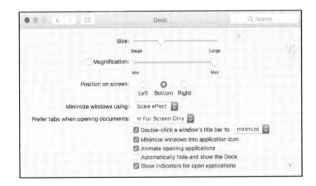

To choose when to open documents as tabs rather than as new windows: Choose > System Preferences > Dock > "Prefer tabs when opening documents". Choose always, only when you're working with full-screen apps (page 48), or manually (only when you deliberately open a document as a tab). To consolidate all open app windows in a single tabbed window, choose Window > Merge All Windows. This setting applies only to applications that support tabbed documents (Finder, Safari, Maps, and Pages, for example).

To minimize or enlarge (zoom) windows easily: Choose > System Preferences > Dock > select "Double-click a window's title bar to". Choose whether to minimize a window to an icon in the dock when you double-click its title bar, or to enlarge (zoom) the window (without making it full screen). To restore a zoomed window to its previous size, double-click its title bar again. You can also zoom windows by holding down the Option key and then clicking the green button .

To determine how windows behave when you minimize them: Choose > System Preferences > Dock > "Minimize windows into application icon". When this option is turned off, windows minimize to thumbnails in the dock (often leading to a crowded dock). When this option is turned on, windows minimize invisibly into the dock icons of their parent applications. To open a minimized window, right-click (or click-and-hold) its parent application's dock icon and then click the document name in the shortcut menu (a check next to the name denotes the active document; a diamond denotes a minimized document).

To autohide the dock when you're not using it: Choose > System Preferences > Dock > "Automatically hide and show the Dock". When this option is turned on, the dock disappears when the pointer moves away from the dock and reappears when it moves toward it. To toggle this feature on and off quickly, press Option+Command+D.

To show small indicators (dots) next to the dock icons of open applications: Choose > System Preferences > Dock > "Show indicators for open applications". Older (pre-Lion) versions of macOS showed these indicators by default. Keeping too many applications open at the same time makes macOS juggle memory (RAM), possibly draining battery power quickly.

To magnify the dock by using the keyboard: Hold down Shift+Control as the pointer approaches the dock.

To reposition the dock by using the mouse: Shift-drag the dock's divider to an edge of the screen.

To reset the dock: In /Users/*user_name*/Library/Preferences, delete the file com.apple.dock.plist, and then relogin. (If you don't see the Library folder in Finder, hold down Option and then choose Go > Library.) Resetting the dock reverts it to its factory settings. A reset is useful if you accidentally drag a large number of files *onto* the dock instead of *into* a folder in the dock (deleting many dock icons one at a time would take ages).

To add a folder of recently used or favorite items to the dock: In Terminal, type the commands:

```
defaults write com.apple.dock \
persistent-others -array-add \
'{ "tile-data" = \
{ "list-type" = 1; }; \
"tile-type" = "recents-tile"; }'
killall Dock
```

When the stack appears in the dock, right-click it to choose which items to show.

To increase the dock's maximum size: In Terminal, type the commands:

```
defaults write com.apple.dock \
tilesize -int 256
killall Dock
```

Don't exceed 256. To change the dock's size, choose > System Preferences > Dock > Size slider.

To increase the dock's maximum magnification: In Terminal, type the commands:

```
defaults write com.apple.dock \
largesize -int 512
killall Dock
```

Don't exceed 512. To change the dock's magnification, choose > System Preferences > Dock > Magnification slider.

Stacks

A **stack** is a folder or drive shortcut in the dock. Clicking a stack springs open its contents in an arced fan of icons (for few items), a grid of icons (for many items), or a list of names (for a compact view). The dock comes with (removable) Apple-installed stacks, and you can add your own. It's common practice to create a stack folder named, say, Favorites and fill it with aliases (page 98) of often-used programs, files, and folders. Clicking an item in a stack opens that item, or activates it if it's already open, and then closes the stack.

To add a stack to the dock: Drag a folder or drive icon from the desktop or a folder window to the dock (to the right of the dock divider).

To remove a stack from the dock: Drag it out of the dock, or right-click it and then choose Options > Remove from Dock.

To open a stack: Click a folder or drive icon in the dock. To open it in slow motion, Shift-click.

To open an item in a stack: Open the stack and then do any of the following:

- Click the item.

- Use the arrow keys to highlight it and then press Return.

- Type the first few letters of the item's name to highlight it and then press Return.

- Scroll the mouse wheel to highlight the item and then click.

- Drag on the trackpad to highlight the item and then tap.

Tip: In grid and list views, scrollbars appear in crowded stacks. In grid view, clicking a subfolder opens it within the stack. To return to the parent folder, click ⟨ in the stack's top-left corner.

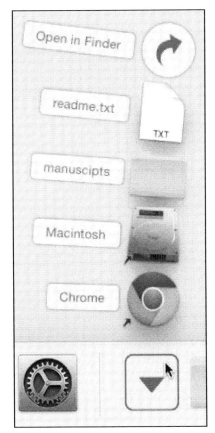

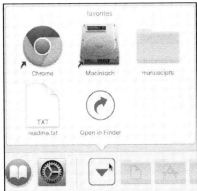

To show a stack item in a Finder window: Open the stack and then Command-click the item.

To move an item by using a stack: Open the stack and then drag the item out of the stack to the desktop or a folder window.

To copy an item by using a stack: Open the stack and then Option-drag the item out of the stack to the desktop or a folder window.

To alias an item by using a stack: Open the stack and then Option-Command-drag the item out of the stack to the desktop or a folder window.

To open multiple items without closing a stack (fan and grid views): Open the stack and then hold down Option while you click items.

To close a stack without opening an item: Press Esc, click off the stack, or click the stack's dock icon (which changes to ▼ when the stack is open).

To open a stack's shortcut menu: Right-click the stack's dock icon.

To change a stack's sort order: Right-click the stack icon and then choose an option under "Sort by".

To change a stack's dock icon: Right-click the stack icon and then choose an option under "Display as". The option Stack shows a pile of the icons contained in the stack. The option Folder shows an ordinary folder or drive icon.

To force a particular stack view: Right-click the stack icon and then choose an option under "View content as". The option Automatic lets macOS determine the view based on your screen size. The option Fan isn't available if the dock is positioned on the screen's left or right edge.

To bypass a stack view: Right-click the stack icon and then choose Open "*item_name*".

Exposé

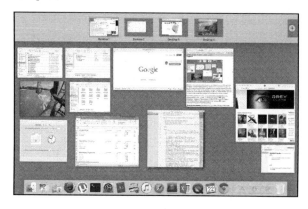

Exposé shrinks and tiles all open windows on your screen so you can find a particular window on a crowded desktop. By using keyboard shortcuts or multitouch gestures, you can tile all windows, tile only a certain program's windows, or hide all windows (revealing the desktop). If you press-and-hold an Exposé keyboard shortcut, the windows return to their original size when you release the keys. If you tap the keys quickly, Exposé stays activated until you dismiss it or choose a window.

The need to press the Fn modifier key for keyboard shortcuts depends on your keyboard type (standard, portable, or old) and your setting for > System Preferences > Keyboard > Keyboard pane > "Use all F1, F2, etc. keys as standard function keys". Multitouch gestures depend on your settings in > System Preferences > Trackpad > More Gestures pane.

To see all open windows: Press the Mission Control key F3 ▦ (or Fn+F3) or press Control+↑ or flick three fingers up. To activate a window, click it, tap it, or point to it and press the keyboard shortcut again. To dismiss Exposé without activating a window, press the keyboard shortcut again (without pointing to a window), repeat (or reverse) the multitouch gesture, or press Esc.

To see all open windows for the current program: Press Control+↓ or flick three fingers down. Alternatively, right-click (or click-and-hold) a program's icon in the dock and then choose Show All Windows. The window-activation commands described above also apply here.

To hide all windows and show the desktop: Press F11 (or Fn+F11) or spread three fingers and your thumb. The dock, Finder, menu bar, icons, Eject, and other parts of desktop operate normally in this desktop view. To dismiss desktop view, press the keyboard shortcut again, repeat (or reverse) the multitouch gesture, click a screen edge or window edge, or double-click an icon. See also "Hiding Programs" on page 51.

Tip: Press Spacebar to Quick Look (magnify) a highlighted thumbnail preview.

To switch among Exposé's views: Use the keyboard shortcut or multitouch gesture for the desired view (twice), even when in another view.

To run Exposé in slow motion: Hold down Shift when you press an Exposé keyboard shortcut.

To activate Exposé by moving the pointer to a screen corner: Choose > System Preferences > Mission Control > Hot Corners > Active Screen Corners pop-up menus (holding down modifier key(s), if desired).

To change how windows are grouped in Exposé view: Choose > System Preferences > Mission Control > "Group windows by application". When this option is turned on, windows are grouped in piles, one pile per application. When this option is turned off, windows maintain their relative desktop positions (the resulting arrangement is a bit haphazard, but shows more of each window's content).

To change the Exposé keyboard shortcuts: Choose > System Preferences > Mission Control and then use the pop-up menus in the Keyboard and Mouse Shortcuts section. Alternatively, choose > System Preferences > Keyboard > Shortcuts pane > Mission Control (this pane lets you restore the default shortcuts).

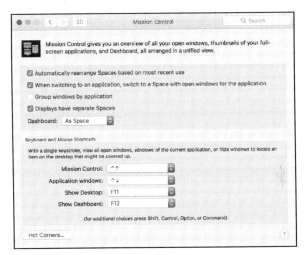

To attach a file to an email message by using Exposé: Start dragging the file and then trigger Exposé to show all windows (F3 or Control+↑). Drag the file over the target email window, press F3 or Control+↑ again and then drop the file in the message. You can use the same technique, but pressing Control+↓, to copy or drag text or graphics between only a particular program's windows.

To move or copy an item to the desktop by using Exposé: Start dragging the item and then trigger Exposé to show the desktop (F11). To move the item, drop it on the desktop. To copy it, hold down Option before dropping. To make an alias, hold down Option+Command before dropping. You can also drag an item onto a program's dock icon and hover until Exposé displays the program's windows; hover again over the target window until it activates and then drop the item.

Spaces

Spaces organizes windows into user-defined groups called **spaces**. Each space is a virtual screen containing only the windows assigned to that space. You typically define a space by logically related tasks (an "internet" space for browsing, email, and chat, for example) or by specific projects or events (a "travel" space with itinerary, photos, and emergency numbers). The same application can run in multiple spaces but with different documents open in each one, or you can assign applications to particular spaces. You can see only one space at a time and switch among them by using keyboard shortcuts or multitouch gestures. Spaces pays off nicely after some initial fine tuning, memorization, and disorientation.

To create a new space: Press the Mission Control key F3 ⌨ (or Fn+F3) or press Control+↑ or flick three fingers up. Move the pointer (or drag a window) to the top-right corner of the screen and then click the Add button (+). You can create up to 16 spaces. When you're done`, press the keyboard shortcut again (without pointing to a window), repeat (or reverse) the multitouch gesture, or press Esc.

To set Spaces keyboard shortcuts and multitouch gestures: For keystrokes, choose > System Preferences > Keyboard > Shortcuts pane > Mission Control. For gestures, choose > System Preferences > Trackpad > More Gestures pane. The default Control+arrow-key shortcuts scroll left or right through spaces. The default Control+1 shortcut jumps directly to Desktop 1. You can press any combination of modifier keys (Shift, Control, Option, or Command) when you assign a custom keyboard shortcut.

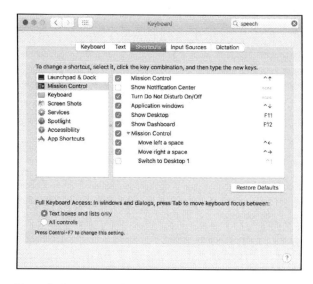

To switch spaces: Do any of the following:

- Open Mission Control (F3 or Control+↑) and then click the target space at the top of the screen. The text labels at the top of the screen turn into thumbnail previews when you point to them.

- Press a Spaces keyboard shortcut (Control+→ or Control+1, for example).

- Flick three fingers left or right.

To move a window from one space to another: Do any of the following:

- Drag the window to a screen edge, pause until the adjacent space slides into view, and then drop the window in the new space.

- Click-and-hold anywhere in the window and then press the arrow-key or number-key keyboard shortcut of the target space.

- Switch to the space that contains the window that you want to move, open Mission Control (F3 or Control+↑), and then drag the window up to the target space at the top of the screen.

Tip: Drag a window to the top edge of the screen and then hold the pointer there for a moment to open Mission Control. Now, drop the window on the Add button (+) to create a new space or drop it on an existing space (Desktop) to move the window to that space.

To assign an application to particular spaces: If the application's icon isn't visible in the dock, then open the application. Right-click (or click-and-hold) the application's icon in the dock, point to Options, and then choose This Desktop (to make the app open in only the current space), All Desktops (to make the app open in every space), or None (to make the app open in whatever space you're currently using).

To reorder spaces: Open Mission Control (F3 or Control+↑) and then, at the top of the screen, drag the thumbnails for the spaces (or full-screen apps) left or right.

To delete a space: Open Mission Control (F3 or Control+↑), point to the target space, and then click the Delete button ⊗ that appears (after a slight delay) on the space. If the deleted space contains windows, the windows are moved to another space.

To configure Spaces: Choose > System Preferences > Mission Control.

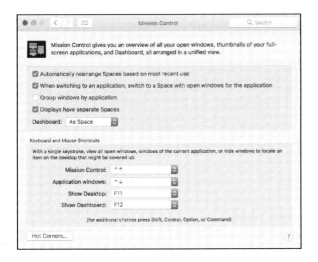

Set the following options:

Automatically rearrange Spaces based on most recent use
> Determines whether spaces are sorted dynamically so that you can access recently used ones quickly. Turning on this option makes Mission Control keep the desktops that you're using most often next to each other, making back-and-forth switching easier.

When switching to an application, switch to a Space with open windows for the application
> Determines whether the desktop autoscrolls to the space containing the open windows of an application that you open or switch to. For example, if you have Safari open in Desktop 3 while you're working in TextEdit in Desktop 1, and you then switch to Safari by pressing Command+Tab, you'll jump to Desktop 3. Turning off this option prevents the jump (you'll activate Safari but stay in Desktop 1).

Displays have separate Spaces
> Determines whether you can set up separate spaces for each display, if you're using multiple displays.

Dashboard
> Choose "As Space" to make the dashboard appear when you open Mission Control (F3 or Control+↑) or switch spaces. Choose "As Overlay" to make the dashboard appear as a semi-transparent overlay over the desktop or any space. Choose "Off" to disable the dashboard and widgets.

Dashboard & Widgets

 Dashboard displays a host of widgets in a separate screen or space. **Widgets** are single-purpose mini-programs grouped on a dark or semi-transparent background that can be summoned or dismissed at any time. macOS comes with starter widgets (weather, stock ticker, and so on) stored in the widget browser, and you can get more online.

To show or hide the dashboard and widgets: Do any of the following:

- Click the Dashboard icon in the dock or in the Applications folder.

- Press F12 (or Fn+F12). On older Macs, press F4 ⊙ (or Fn+F4).

- Open Mission Control (F3 or Control+↑) and then click the dashboard thumbnail image at the top of the screen. (This method works if the dashboard is configured to appear as a space.)

- Move the pointer into one of the screen's four corners (> System Preferences > Mission Control > Hot Corners > Dashboard).

  To hide the dashboard, press the keyboard shortcut again, press Esc, use a Spaces keystroke or gesture (page 44), click the arrow in the dashboard's bottom-right corner, or click an empty area on the dashboard overlay.

To configure the dashboard: Choose > System Preferences > Mission Control. Select the dashboard type from the "Dashboard" pop-up menu, set the Show Dashboard keyboard shortcut, or click Hot Corners to show the dashboard by moving the pointer to a screen corner. For shortcuts to common dashboard tasks, right-click (or click-and-hold) the Dashboard icon in the dock.

To open or close the widget browser: To open the widget browser, show the dashboard and then click ⊕ in the dashboard's lower-left corner. To find specific widgets, type in the search box at the top of the widget browser. To close the widget browser, press Esc or click an empty area on the screen.

To add a widget to the dashboard: Click it in the widget browser. You can add multiple copies of the same widget. For example, add multiple World Clock or Weather widgets for different cities.

To move a widget: Drag it around the dashboard or the widget browser.

To close a widget: In the dashboard, hold down Option or click ⊖, move the pointer over the target widget, and then click ⊗.

To customize a widget: In the dashboard, move the pointer over the widget and then click the small Info button *i* that appears in one corner. Features vary by widget (widgets that can't be customized don't have an *i* button).

To update a widget's data from the internet: Click the widget and then press Command+R (for "refresh" or "reload").

To download and install widgets: Open the widget browser and then click More Widgets in the lower-left corner. The Dashboard Widgets website opens in your default browser (on the desktop, not in the dashboard). Locate a widget and then click its Download button. When the Widget Installer opens, click Install. If the installer doesn't open automatically, go to the downloaded file and open it; if the filename has the extension .zip, double-click it to unzip it and then open the .wdgt file. The new widget is added to the widget browser.

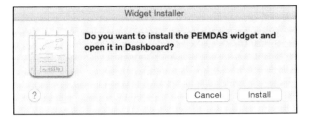

To group widgets into folders in the widget browser: To create a folder, drag one widget's icon over another, and then drag other widgets to add to the folder. To change a folder's name, click the folder to open it, click the current name, and then type the new name. To move a widget out of a folder, click the folder to open it, and then drag the widget out of the folder.

To delete a widget: Open the widget browser, hold down Option or click ⊖, and then click ⊗ on the target widget. (A widget with no ⊗ is an Apple-installed widget.) Your personal widgets are stored in /Users/*user_name*/Library/Widgets.

To delete an Apple-installed widget: In Finder or Terminal, go to /Library/Widgets and then delete the widget's .wdgt file. (Apple-installed widgets can't be easily reinstalled after they're deleted.)

To show an auto-updating portion of a webpage (Web Clip) on the dashboard: Open Safari and then go to the desired webpage. In the Safari toolbar, click ✂, point to highlight the desired portion of the page, and then click. If necessary, drag the highlight box to reposition it or drag its edge handles to resize it. Click Add. To customize the widget, move the pointer over it and then click its Info button *i*. If ✂ isn't visible on the toolbar, choose View > Customize Toolbar.

Full-Screen Apps

You can expand certain applications to fill your screen edge to edge, hiding the dock, the menu bar, and other windows. Apps that can go full screen include Finder, Maps, iBooks, iTunes, Mail, Messages, Calendar, Safari, Notes, Photo Booth, FaceTime, Preview, Photos, iMovie, GarageBand, QuickTime Player, Game Center, Chess, Keynote, Pages, Numbers, and Microsoft Office apps. Not all apps can expand to full screen (full-screen Calculator, for example, makes little sense). You can have multiple full-screen apps open at the same time and move among them easily. Full-screen apps stay full screen even when you switch to another app or to the desktop. If you're using multiple displays, you can run an app full screen on each display.

To expand an application to full screen: Do any of the following:

- Click the green button ● in the top-left corner of the window. (If the app can't go full screen, then the window will enlarge, but not to full screen.)

- Choose View > Enter Full Screen.

- Press Ctrl+Command+F.

- Drag the window to the top edge of the screen and then hold the pointer there for a moment to open Mission Control. Drop the window in an empty area at the top of the screen. A placeholder graphic shows where the full-screen window will appear when dropped. Existing thumbnail previews slide out of the way when you drag between them.

Tip: To enlarge (zoom) a window without making it full screen, hold down the Option key and then click the green button ●. To restore the window to its previous size, hold down the Option key and then click the green button again ●. This type of window zooming was the normal behavior for the green button in older (pre-Yosemite) versions of macOS.

To see the menu bar of a full screen app: Move the pointer to the top edge of the screen.

To move from window to window in full-screen view: Do any of the following:

- Flick three fingers left or right.

- Press a Spaces keyboard shortcut (page 44).

- Open Mission Control (F3 or Control+↑) and then click the target window at the top of the screen. The text labels at the top of the screen turn into thumbnail previews when you point to them.

Tip: To open documents as tabs, choose > System Preferences > Dock > "Prefer tabs when opening documents".

To reorder full-screen apps: Open Mission Control (F3 or Control+↑) and then, at the top of the screen, drag the thumbnails for the full-screen apps (or spaces) left or right.

To exit full-screen view: Do any of the following:

- Move the pointer to the top edge of the screen. When the menu bar appears, click the green button ● in the top-left corner of the application window or choose View > Exit Full Screen.

- Press Ctrl+Command+F.

- Press Esc once or twice (for some programs).

- Open Mission Control (F3 or Control+↑) and then drag the thumbnail preview of the target window down to the desktop, or point to the preview and then click the button ⊛ that appears (after a slight delay).

To set the full-screen multitouch gesture: Choose > System Preferences > Trackpad > More Gestures pane.

Split View

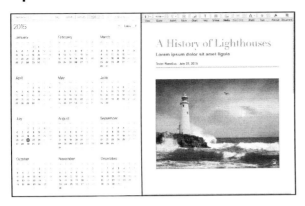

Split View places two full-screen apps side by side, divided by a vertical line that can be dragged to resize the windows. This feature is useful for reducing clutter and avoiding distractions. You can create a Split View with TextEdit (for writing) and Safari (for research), for example, or with Mail and Calendar. You can also split two different windows of the same app: two Finder windows, for example, or two Safari windows.

To create a Split View, click-and-hold the green button ● of an application window that supports Split View and then drag and drop it on the left or right half of the screen. The window expands to fill half the screen and Exposé-style thumbnail previews of other open windows fill the other half. Click a preview to create the Split View (previews for apps that don't support Split View are dimmed).

Tip: Third-party (non-Apple) apps that support full-screen view don't necessarily also support Split View.

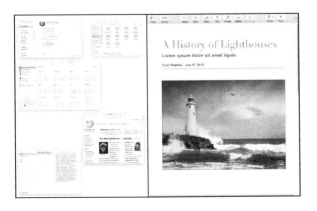

Alternatively, open the first window in full-screen view and then open Mission Control (F3 or Control+↑). Drag the thumbnail preview of the second window to the top of the screen, and then drop it on the preview of the first window to create the Split View.

Calendar & Pages

A vertical divider line separates the two windows in Split View. You can drag the divider to change how much real estate each window occupies. The default view is 50/50, but many apps support a 25/75 split (though some, such as Calendar, won't shrink that far).

Exit Split View in the same way that you exit full-screen view (page 48).

Mission Control

Mission Control unites Exposé, Spaces, Dashboard, Full-Screen Apps, Split View, and multiple displays into a comprehensive view of what's open on your computer. All open windows are tiled as thumbnail previews in Exposé view. Spaces, full-screen windows, Split Views, and the dashboard are shown as separate thumbnails at the top of the screen.

To open Mission Control: Press the Mission Control key F3 ▦ (or Fn+F3) or press Control+↑ or flick three fingers up. To activate a window (or space), click it, tap it, or point to it and press the keyboard shortcut again. To dismiss Mission Control without activating a window, press the keyboard shortcut again (without pointing to a window), repeat (or reverse) the multitouch gesture, or press Esc.

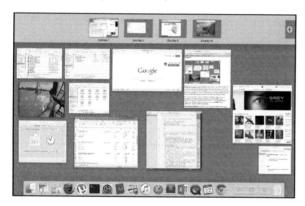

To configure Mission Control: Do any of the following:

- To set general preferences, choose > System Preferences > Mission Control.

- To set keyboard shortcuts, choose > System Preferences > Keyboard > Shortcuts pane > Mission Control.

- To set multitouch gestures, choose > System Preferences > Trackpad > More Gestures pane.

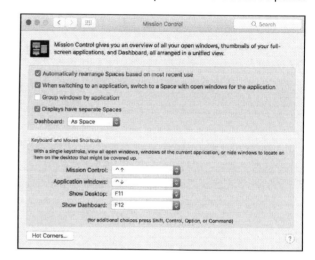

Hiding Programs

Program-hiding is a quick alternative to Exposé for getting programs out of your way. Hiding a program causes all its windows and panels to vanish. They return when you unhide it. The bold application menu (next to the menu) has the Hide commands.

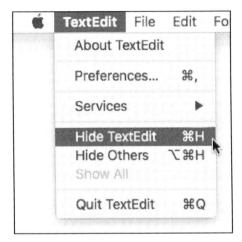

To hide the current program: Choose the Hide command (Command+H) from the program's application menu, or Option-click any visible spot on the desktop.

To hide the current program and open another: Option-click the other program's icon in the dock or any visible part of the other program's windows.

To hide any open program: Command+Tab to the program's icon, release the Tab key, and then press H. (If the program is already hidden, it unhides.)

To hide all programs but the current one: Choose Hide Others (Option+Command+H) from the program's application menu.

To open a program and hide all others: Option-Command-click the program's icon in the dock.

To unhide a program: Command+Tab to it, click its dock icon, or choose Show All from any application menu.

Organizing Desktop Icons

macOS provides clean-up tools for desktop icons.

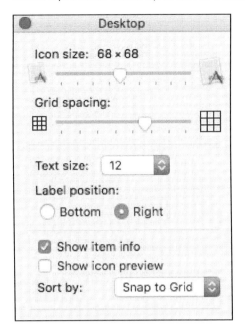

To set the size, spacing, labels, and arrangement of desktop icons: Right-click an empty area on the desktop and then choose Show View Options.

To choose which items appear on the desktop: Click an empty area on the desktop to activate Finder, choose Finder > Preferences > General pane, and then select the desired desktop items.

To snap desktop icons to an invisible grid: Right-click an empty area on the desktop and then choose Clean Up or Clean Up By.

To change the sort order of desktop icons: Right-click an empty area on the desktop and then choose Sort By.

Notification Center

Notifications Center provides you with timely alerts and reminders from applications (Notifications view) and an overview of your day's events (Today view). Notification Center for macOS works like its counterpart feature on iOS devices (iPad, iPhone, and iPod touch).

Notifications View

Certain applications can push notifications to your Mac, even when you're not actively using the program. Notification Center is the central list of all the apps that are trying to get your attention. Apps that can send notifications include:

- Calendar for events and invitations.

- Reminders for reminders coming due.

- Game Center for friend requests and game invitations.

- Mac App Store for software updates.

- Mail for incoming email from all senders, only contacts, or only VIP senders.

- Messages for new messages.

- Safari for website alerts. You can sign up with websites to receive news headlines, sports scores, auction (eBay) alerts, and more as notifications, even when Safari isn't running.

- FaceTime for missed calls.

- Twitter for direct messages and mentions (you can also tweet right to Twitter from Notification Center).

- Facebook for Facebook notifications (you can also post right to Facebook from Notification Center).

- Third-party apps whose developers tap into Notification Center.

When you receive a notification, a small floating window appears in the top-right corner of the screen, containing the notification. Notifications come in two forms: banners and alerts. A **banner** slides into

view and then disappears after 5 seconds. An **alert** remains visible until you acknowledge it by clicking Close, OK, Dismiss, Options, Read, Snooze, or whatever. Clicking a banner opens the corresponding application to show the related item. Some notifications are interactive—if you receive an email, message, or FaceTime call, for example, you can respond without leaving the app you're in.

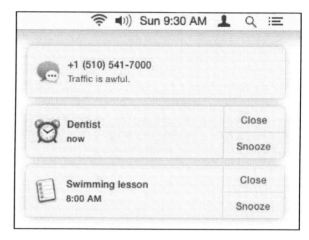

If a banner notification disappears before you can get to it, you can open Notification Center at any time (even from a full-screen app) to see a list of recent notifications.

When you open Notification Center, an overlay shifts leftward to reveal all current notifications in a sorted list along the right edge of your screen.

Tip: Some notifications will appear even if the associated application is closed, whereas others will appear only if the underlying application is open (whether it's active or in the background). Notifications for new messages, for example, appear even if the Messages app is closed, whereas new-mail notifications appear only if the Mail app is open. An open program will have a small dot next to its icon in the dock.

To open Notification Center: Do any of the following:

- Click the Notification Center icon near the right edge of the menu bar. (You can't hide this icon.)

- Flick two fingers from the right edge of the trackpad into the center (as if you were pulling something away from the right side of the screen). Accuracy counts: you must start to flick from the right edge. To toggle this gesture, choose > System Preferences > Trackpad > More Gestures.

- Press the Notification Center keyboard shortcut. To assign this shortcut, choose > System Preferences > Keyboard > Shortcuts pane, click Mission Control (on the left), select Show Notification Center (or double-click it if it's already selected), and then hold down the new keys for the shortcut.

- Move the pointer into one of the screen's four corners (> System Preferences > Mission Control > Hot Corners > Notification Center).

To read notifications: Click the Notifications button at the top of Notification Center.

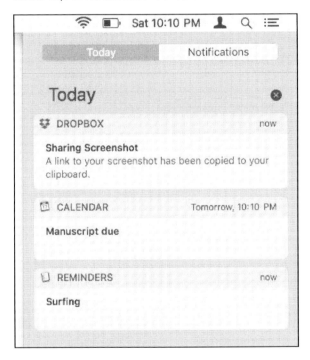

To close Notification Center without responding to a notification: Do any of the following:

- Click ☰ in the menu bar.
- Flick two fingers to the right.
- Click anywhere off Notification Center.

To hide alerts and banners temporarily (Do Not Disturb): Do any of the following:

- Hold down the Option key and then click ☰ in the menu bar.

- Open Notification Center, scroll to the top of the pane, and then turn on "Do Not Disturb".

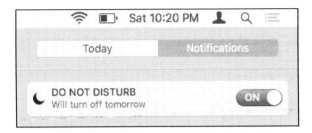

Only pop-up alerts and banners are hidden. Notifications still appear when you open Notification Center. To fine-tune Do Not Disturb to fit your schedule, choose > System Preferences > Notifications > Do Not Disturb.

Tip: Alerts and banners are hidden automatically when you're presenting in Keynote, when your Mac is connected to a projector, or (optionally) when your display is sleeping or mirrored on an external display.

To configure Notification Center: Choose > System Preferences > Notifications, or open Notification Center and then click the gear icon in the bottom-right corner.

Apps that can send notifications are listed on the left. Click an app to change its settings.

For each app, you can set:

- Whether an app sends notifications.

- Whether you receive banner or alert notifications (or none at all).

- The order in which notifications are listed (for manual sorting, drag apps up or down to reorder the list).

- How many recent notifications appear in Notification Center.

- Whether to display an alert badge (a number in a little red circle) on the notifying app's dock icon.

- Whether the notification appears when your Mac is locked.

- Whether to play a sound as part of the notification.

- Whether to display a short preview of a message or email.

Some applications let you set additional notification and alert options within the app itself (typically in the Preferences dialog box). In Mail, for example, choose Mail > Preferences > General pane > "New message notifications". In Safari, choose Safari > Preferences > Notifications pane.

Today View

Today view summarizes the day's events, reminders, upcoming birthdays, weather, and so on, and previews tomorrow's schedule. The current day and date always appear at the top of Today view, and you can customize the rest of the view by adding, removing, or reordering **widgets**—small, single-purpose panels that display up-to-date information. macOS comes with a handful of widgets (Calendar, Weather, Reminders, and so on), and you can find more from third-party developers in the Mac App Store (page 121).

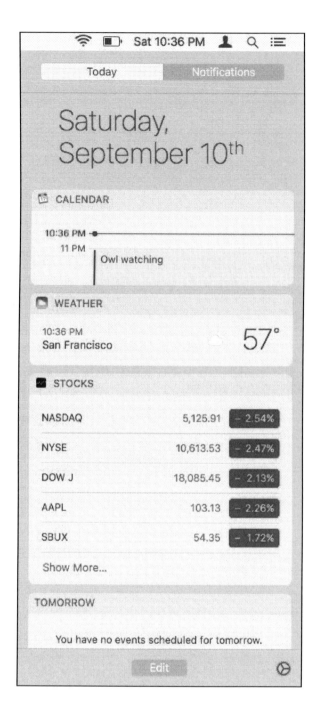

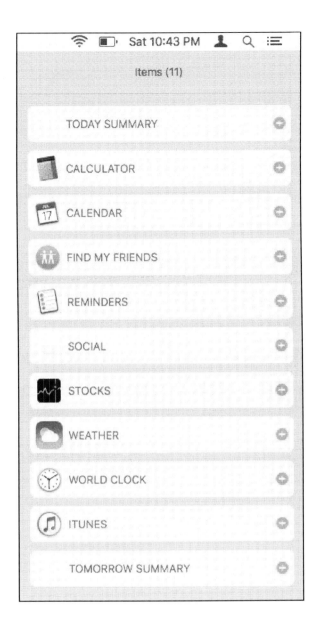

To add or remove widgets: Click the Today button at the top of Notification Center and then click Edit at the bottom of the view. The widget drawer opens. To add or remove widgets, click the green (+) or red (−) buttons, or drag widgets to or from the view or widget drawer. When you're finished, click Done.

Tip: You can add the responses of Siri (page 56) requests as widgets that update automatically.

To reorder widgets: In Today view, drag widgets up or down. The Today Summary and Tomorrow Summary widgets are anchored at the top and bottom of the view, respectively—they can be added or removed, but not reordered.

To configure an individual widget: In Today view, point to the widget and then click the circled i that appears in the widget's upper-right corner. Not all widgets can be configured individually—you can configure Stocks and Weather, for example, but not Calendar and Reminders.

Tip: You can also select and reorder widgets by using the Extensions panel (page 76) in System Preferences.

Siri

Siri is a voice-controlled personal assistant that requires no voice training or special syntax. You query Siri in natural language (casual speech) and it answers questions, makes recommendations, and completes common tasks. You can speak to Siri to open apps, find files, report the weather, make restaurant reservations, get travel directions, set reminders, and much more. Over time, Siri adapts to your individual preferences and personalizes results. Siri understands variations of the same request; you can say, "What's the weather like in Miami this weekend?" or "Will I need an umbrella in Miami?" or "Give me the Miami weather for this weekend." It's quickest, however, to omit filler words in your requests and say, "Miami weekend weather" or "Weekend weather Miami".

To use Siri, you must be connected to the internet (Chapter 8). What you say is sent to Apple to be interpreted. Some personal information (such as contact names) is sent too. For details, choose > System Preferences > Siri > About Siri and Privacy. Siri supports parental controls (page 182).

Setting Up Siri

To set up Siri, choose > System Preferences > Siri, and then set the following options:

- **Enable Siri.** You can turn off Siri if transmitting your personal information to Apple gives you the creeps. Apple's servers collect everything that you say to Siri, including the names of your files and songs, your personal info in Contacts (page 124), and all the other names in Contacts (so that Siri can recognize them when you refer to them).

- **Language.** Choose your speaking language. Language variants are listed by country, region, or dialect.

Tip: Over time, Siri learns your accent and other characteristics of your voice. If you like, you can reset what Siri has learned about your voice by turning Siri off and then back on.

- **Siri Voice.** Choose an accented male or female voice for the specified language.

- **Voice Feedback.** Siri generally responds to your requests with both text and a synthesized voice. This option lets you mute the voice response.

- **Mic Input.** You can use any of your connected microphones, and you can set Siri's mic independently of the mic used by the rest of the system.

- **Keyboard Shortcut.** Choose one of the suggested Siri keyboard shortcuts, or choose Customize to define your own shortcut. Note that the Hold Command Space shortcut is similar to the default shortcut for Spotlight (Press Command Space), making it easy to invoke either Spotlight or Siri by using the same keys.

- **Show Siri in menu bar.** The Siri menu ⬤ appears on the right side of the menu bar.

- **About Siri and Privacy.** Read Apple's privacy policy regarding Siri.

Using Siri

To use Siri:

1 To open the Siri window, do any of the following:

   ▶ Click the Siri icon  in the menu bar.

   ▶ Click the Siri icon in the dock or in the Applications folder.

   ▶ Press the Siri keyboard shortcut (⌘ > System Preferences > Siri > Keyboard Shortcut).

   ▶ Press Command+Spacebar to open the Spotlight search window, type *siri*, select the Siri application, and then press Return.

   Siri double-beeps and the Siri window appears near the top-right corner of your screen.

2 Ask your question or say your command.

   Speak calmly at a normal pace. The animated audio wave shows your speaking volume. Siri hears you through the specified microphone (⌘ > System Preferences > Siri > Mic Input) and echoes your request in the Siri window.

Tip: Siri may understand you better if you exaggerate slightly the ending consonants of words.

---

3 When you're finished speaking, click the audio wave, or just be quiet.

   After a moment, Siri processes your request and then presents (and speaks) its response.

Tip: If Siri recognizes what you said but can't answer the question, it responds with the results of a web search or a Search the Web button.

---

4 To save a continually updated result of a Siri query as a Today View widget in Notification Center (page 52), click the (+) button in the top-right corner of the Siri response. For example, you can save news, weather, sports scores, and Finder searches as auto-updating widgets.

5 To keep using Siri, click the microphone icon at the bottom of the Siri window. Siri double-beeps to signal that it's ready for your next question or command.

Tip: To scroll through Siri's earlier responses in the current session, press the arrow keys, spin the mouse wheel, or flick or drag up or down with two fingers in the Siri window.

---

6 To dismiss Siri, press Esc once or twice, click the (×) button in the top-left corner of the Siri window, or say "Goodbye" or "Bye, Siri".

What You Can Say

If you've used Siri on an iPhone or iPad, then you have a head start for using Siri on your Mac. Sending email, making appointments, and performing many other tasks work similarly for the iOS and macOS versions of Siri. Siri can also do most of what Spotlight (page 103) can do.

For examples of what you can say to Siri, click the (?) button in the bottom-left corner of the Siri window, or say, "What can I say?" or "What can you do?" or "Help me." Siri responds with a list of examples of things that it can do, along with ways you can ask for things. Click any item in the list for specific examples.

If you open the Siri window and wait silently, then Siri will eventually respond with a list of sample questions that you can ask.

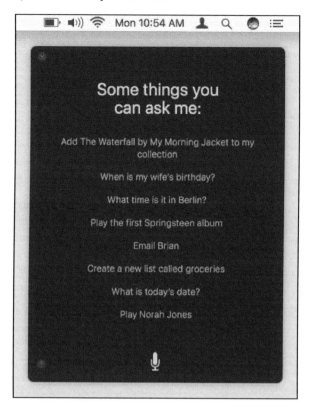

Siri works with most of the Mac's built-in apps, and can figure out which apps to use to provide you with answers. Siri also uses information from your contacts, music library, calendars, and reminders to respond accurately when you ask to make a FaceTime call, send a message, play music, or create an appointment or reminder. Siri also draws on various online services, including Twitter, Rotten Tomatoes, Wikipedia, Bing, and Wolfram Alpha.

Apple continually expands Siri's sphere of knowledge. Numerous books, articles, and webpages catalog the things Siri understands and the ways it can help you. Try searching the web for *siri tips*, *siri commands*, or *use siri*.

If you're feeling bored or whimsical, you can say things like, "What is the meaning of life?" or "Will you marry me?" or "Tell me a joke." For other oddball requests, search the web for *siri funny*, *siri fun*, or *siri easter eggs*.

Location-Based Reminders

Siri uses Location Services (page 184) to know your current location ("here"), and uses Contacts (page 124) to understand other locations like "home" and "work". You can set location-based reminders that alert you when you leave or arrive at a certain place. You can say, "Remind me to call my wife when I leave the office" or "Remind me to check in with Tom when I leave here" or "Remind me to shower when I get home".

If you don't want Siri to use your location, choose > System Preferences > Security & Privacy > Privacy pane > Location Services and then turn off Siri & Dictation (click 🔒 if the settings are dimmed). Regardless of how you set Location Services for Siri, information about your location isn't tracked or stored outside your Mac.

Tip: Siri understands "home" and "office" and "work"—both yours and other people's—only if you've entered those addresses in the corresponding people's cards in Contacts.

Specifying Your Relationships

The My Card entry in Contacts (page 124) contains your information and lists your relationships. Siri uses this information to respond to requests like "Email my mom" or "Give me directions to my sister's house" or "Remind me to buy spinach". (To designate your card in Contacts, open your card and then choose Card > Make This My Card.)

If you want to tell Siri, "Email my mom" or "Text my sister" or "Remind me to bring wine to my friend's party", then you must let Siri know about your relationships to the people in your Contacts list. You have several ways to do so:

- **Tell Siri.** Tell Siri something like, "Diane Reckis is my girlfriend" or "My manager is Montgomery Burns". When Siri asks for confirmation, say "Yes" or click Yes. The available relationships include mother (mom), father (dad), parent, brother (bro), sister (sis), child (kid), son, daughter, grandmother (grandma), grandfather (grandpa),

spouse, wife, husband (hubby), partner, assistant, manager, boss, girlfriend, boyfriend, and friend.

- **Let Siri ask.** If you say, "Text my wife", Siri asks, "What is your wife's name?" Just say her name.

- **Edit the contact.** Siri remembers your relationships by silently editing the entries in your Contacts card. To update your relationships manually, open Contacts, choose Card > Go to My Card, click Edit, click (+), and then choose More Fields > Related Name. You can also edit or delete any existing fields labeled Mother, Father, Manager, and so on.

Tip: In typed responses (and some spoken ones), Siri addresses you by your first name in Contacts. To make Siri call you by a different name say, "Call me Al" or "Call me Johnson" or "Call me master" or whatever.

Phonetic Spellings of Names

If a contact has a foreign or unusual name that Siri can't understand, you can add a **phonetic** spelling to that person's Contacts card. A phonetic spelling is an alteration of ordinary spelling that better represents the spoken language. To add a phonetic spelling, open Contacts, open the person's card, click Edit, click (+), and then choose More Fields > Phonetic First/Last Name. Type a phonetic spelling of the name. For the last name Leszczynska, for example, you can type "LESH-chin-ska". You may have to experiment with different phonetic spellings to get Siri to understand the name when you speak it. (Using Phonetic fields affects how Siri sorts contact names in responses.)

CHAPTER 3

System Preferences

You can change macOS's factory settings to suit your own preferences and abilities. The hundreds of customizable settings range from superficial to meaningful. Changes to graphics, colors, and animation are usually cosmetic, whereas some other settings—the language used or features for disabled users—change the way that you work with macOS.

System Preferences

 Use **System Preferences** panels to change personal and systemwide settings. Changes that affect everyone who uses the computer, rather than only your user account, require administrator access. The controls for administrator settings are dimmed and locked, click 🔒 (in the panel's lower-left corner) to unlock them with an administrator password.

You can list panel icons in functional categories (hardware, internet, and so on) or alphabetically (preferred by experienced users who have memorized the icon names). You can open System Preferences showing icon shortcuts to all panels or jump straight to a specific panel.

To open System Preferences: Do any of the following:

- Click the System Preferences icon in the dock.

- Choose > System Preferences.

- Press Command+Spacebar to open Spotlight search, type *sys*, and then press Return when System Preferences is highlighted.

To show or hide specific icons: In System Preferences, choose View > Customize, toggle the checkboxes next to each icon, and then click Done.

To view all icons (return to the main Preferences panel): In System Preferences, choose View > Show All Preferences (Command+L) or click the ⊞ button. (The Show All command doesn't unhide hidden icons.)

To change how icons are organized: In System Preferences, choose View > Organize by Categories or View > Organize Alphabetically.

To open a specific panel: With System Preferences open, do any of the following:

- Click the panel's icon.

- Choose the panel from the View menu.

- Click-and-hold the ⠿ button and then choose the panel from the pop-up menu.

- Right-click (or click-and-hold) the System Preferences icon in the dock and then choose the panel from the pop-up menu (you may have to hold down the Control key when you click the dock icon).

- In the search box (Command+F), start typing the panel name or setting name (*brightness*, for example) and then click the relevant highlighted icon.

To open System Preferences in a specific panel: Do any of the following:

- Click a menu-extras icon on the right side of the menu bar and look for a Preferences command (the Wi-Fi menu 🛜, for example, has the command Open Network Preferences).

- Hold down Option and press a Function key (press Option+F3, for example, to open the Mission Control panel). You may have to hold down the Fn key too.

- Press Command+Spacebar to open Spotlight search, start typing the panel name or setting name (*network*, for example) and then choose the relevant panel when it appears in the results list under System Preferences.

To require an administrator to unlock each System Preferences panel individually: Normally, only administrators can change System Preferences that affect the entire computer and everyone who uses it (Date & Time, Users & Groups, Network, and Security & Privacy, for example). A nonadministrator can change these secure preferences only if an administrator clicks 🔒 and enters a name and password to approve the changes. Unlocking any *one* System Preferences panel, however, unlocks them *all*, and the user can keep making changes without the administrator's knowledge. To require an administrator to unlock each System Preferences panel individually, choose > System Preferences > Security & Privacy > Advanced button (click 🔒 if the settings are dimmed) > select "Require an administrator password to access system-wide preferences".

Accessibility

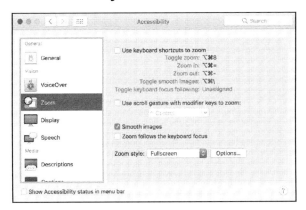

Use the Accessibility panel to toggle and configure features for disabled users with poor eyesight, hearing, or mobility. Keyboard shortcut: Option+Command+F5.

VoiceOver

VoiceOver describes aloud what appears onscreen and speaks the text in documents and windows. To read and listen to a VoiceOver tutorial, click Open VoiceOver Training. To set up VoiceOver, click Open VoiceOver Utility. VoiceOver also supports braille displays. On/off keyboard shortcut: Command+F5 (or Fn+Command+F5).

Zoom

Enlarge all or part of the onscreen image. Keyboard shortcuts: Option+Command+8 (on/off), Option+Command+= (zoom in), and Option+Command+- (zoom out).

Display

Use high-contrast or grayscale color schemes, or enlarge the pointer. Keyboard shortcuts: Ctrl+Option+Command+8 (white-on-black), Ctrl+Option+Command+comma (reduce contrast), and Ctrl+Option+Command+dot (increase contrast). See also "Displays" on page 72.

Speech

Use a synthesized voice to read aloud alert messages (including text in dialog boxes) or text that you highlight. (You can also convert text to speech by using the **say** command in Terminal.)

Descriptions

Listen to a description of the visual content in movies, TV episodes, and other video, if available.

Captions

Set the fonts and formatting of video language tracks, subtitles, and closed captions.

Audio

Add a widescreen flash to alerts or convert multichannel sound to single-channel sound (useful if you have hearing loss in one ear). See also "Sound" on page 83.

Dictation

Control macOS by speaking commands that edit or format text, quit or switch applications, open or save documents, and so on. macOS comes with basic dictation commands, and you can create more. See also "Dictation" on page 68.

Keyboard

Set additional options for the keyboard. Sticky Keys lets you press keyboard combinations, such as Ctrl+Option+Command, one key at a time, or show pressed keys onscreen (on/off keyboard shortcut: tap Shift five times). Slow Keys lets you increase the amount of time that macOS takes to recognize that a key is being pressed.

Mouse & Trackpad

Set additional options for the mouse, trackpad, and spring-loaded folders. Mouse Keys lets you move the pointer around the screen by using the numeric keypad. On/off keyboard shortcut: tap Option five times.

Switch Control

Enable access for assistive devices.

Dwell Control

Control the mouse by using head- or eye-tracking devices.

App Store

Updates macOS software (page 186).

Bluetooth

Use the Bluetooth panel to set up Bluetooth devices. This panel appears only on Macs with a built-in or USB Bluetooth transmitter. **Bluetooth** is a wireless technology that provides short-range (about 30 feet/10 meters) radio links among computers, phones, mice, keyboards, earpieces, iPads, and other Bluetooth-equipped devices. It doesn't need a line-of-sight connection and eliminates cable clutter while simplifying communications, sharing, and data synchronization between computers and devices. For two Bluetooth gadgets to talk to each other, they must both be made **discoverable** and then be **paired**. Bluetooth is turned off by default to save battery power. See also "Bluetooth File Exchange" (page 122) and "Bluetooth Sharing" (page 166).

To set up a Bluetooth device: Choose > System Preferences > Bluetooth. Click Turn Bluetooth On. If macOS doesn't detect your Bluetooth device automatically, click Advanced, launch the Bluetooth Setup Assistant, and then follow the onscreen instructions. When the list of discoverable, in-range Bluetooth devices appears, choose the one that you want to pair. If you're pairing a secure device such as a keyboard or mobile phone, then note or set the passcode used for pairing. You may be prompted for other settings, such as syncing. After setup, the device is listed on the Bluetooth panel.

To delete a Bluetooth device: In the Bluetooth panel, select the device and then click ×.

To quickly view Bluetooth connection information: Hold down the Option key and then click the Bluetooth menu ✳ in the menu bar. (To show the Bluetooth menu, choose > System Preferences > Bluetooth > select "Show Bluetooth in menu bar".)

To configure Bluetooth: In the Bluetooth panel, click Advanced and then set the following options:

Open Bluetooth Setup Assistant at startup if no keyboard/mouse/trackpad is detected
Determines whether the Bluetooth Setup Assistant opens automatically when your Mac can't find a particular input device at startup.

Allow Bluetooth devices to wake this computer
Determines whether a sleeping Mac wakes when you press a key or click a button on a paired Bluetooth device.

CDs & DVDs

Use the CDs & DVDs panel to set the Mac's default action when you insert a blank, music, photo, or movie CD or DVD. (See also "Burning CDs & DVDs" on page 108.)

Ask what to do
Asks you what to do with the disc.

Open [application]
Opens the specified program automatically. Choose "Open other application" to specify an unlisted program.

Run script
Runs the specified script (page 139).

Ignore
Shows the disc icon on the desktop and does nothing.

Date & Time

Use the Date & Time panel to set system date, time, and time zone, and configure the menu-bar clock (click 🔒 if the settings are dimmed). macOS uses the system time to time-stamp files and email, schedule tasks, and record events.

Date & Time Pane

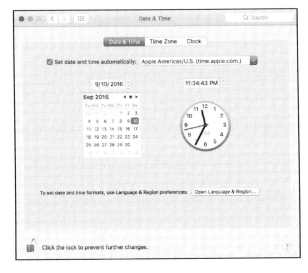

Set date and time automatically
>Determines whether you set the time manually or macOS sets it automatically off an internet time server, accounting for daylight savings time where applicable. Turn on this option if you have an always-on internet connection. If you connect via dial-up modem, turn it off to suppress autodialing.

Calendar and clock
>Sets the date and time manually if automatic updating is turned off. To change a number, click it, and then type a new number, press the up and down arrow keys, or click the arrow buttons. Press Tab to highlight the next number. You can also click a date in the calendar or drag the hands of the clock.

Open Language & Region
>Opens the Language & Region panel (page 82). Use this panel's Formats pane to format the date and time.

Time Zone Pane

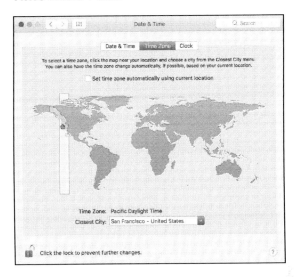

Set time zone automatically using current location
>Sets the time zone automatically and drops a pin on the map to show your current location. A wireless or internet connection is required to locate you. To disable autolocation, choose > System Preferences > Security & Privacy > Privacy pane > Location Services > clear Enable Location Services (click 🔒 if the settings are dimmed).

Map
>To set the time zone manually, click the point on the map closest to you, and then select or type the name of the closest town or city in your time zone.

Clock Pane

Show date and time in menu bar
>Determines whether the current date and time appear on the right side of the menu bar. Choose a digital (5:58 PM) or analog ① clock face and set the other options. "Use a 24-hour clock" (19:18 instead of 7:18 PM) affects only the menu-bar clock. You can click the clock on the menu bar to show the day and date, toggle analog/digital display, or open the Date & Time panel.

Announce the time
>Makes the Mac speak the current time at specified intervals ("It's seven forty-five").

Desktop & Screen Saver

Use the Desktop & Screen Saver panel to set the background of your screen and the (optional) screen saver. Shortcut to this panel: right-click the desktop and then choose Change Desktop Background.

Desktop Pane

You can change the image (**wallpaper**) that appears under the icons on your desktop to a solid color, pattern, or photo (your own or the ones that come with macOS).

To set up the desktop background: Click an image category in the list on the left, and then click a specific image in the sample box on the right. "Photos" show photos that you've imported to the Photos application. "Folders" shows any JPEG, PICT, and TIFF images in your Pictures folder. When you choose an imported image, a pop-up menu appears above the sample box to help you fit the image on your desktop. High-resolution (≥1024 × 768 pixels) photos look best.

To use images from a folder other than Pictures, click (+) to add it to the list. To remove an added folder, select it and then click (−). To autochange images at a specified interval, select "Change picture". To view the images in random order rather than alphabetically by file name, select "Random order".

Tip: To make the menu bar, dock, and other screen elements opaque, choose > System Preferences > Accessibility > Display > "Reduce transparency".

Screen Saver Pane

A screen saver blanks the screen or shows images after a specified time passes without keyboard, mouse, or trackpad activity. Pressing a key, moving the mouse, or tapping the trackpad deactivates the screen saver. macOS offers two type of screen savers: slideshows and traditional screen savers. An animated slideshow cycles through a collection of pictures (either a built-in collection or a folder containing your own pictures). A traditional screen saver shows dancing patterns of light, artwork, or text.

To set up the screen saver: Click a slideshow or a screen saver in the list on the left (scroll the list to see all the choices). If you choose a slideshow, click the Source pop-up menu under the sample box and then choose a built-in picture collection or a folder containing your own pictures. High-resolution ($\geq 1024 \times 768$ pixels) photos look best. If you choose a screen saver, click the Screen Saver Options button (if available) under the sample box to fine-tune the display.

To change the screen saver every time that it activates, select the "Random" screen saver. To show the time on the screen saver, select "Show with clock". To see a full-screen preview, hover the pointer over the image in the sample box and then click Preview. To set the idle time before the screen saver starts, click the "Start after" pop-up menu ("Never" disables the screen saver). To start or disable the screen saver by moving the pointer to a specified corner of the screen, click Hot Corners and then choose "Start Screen Saver" or "Disable Screen Saver" from any of the pop-up menus. To password-lock a screen saver, choose > System Preferences > Security & Privacy > General pane > select "Require password after sleep or screen saver begins". See also "Energy Saver" on page 74.

Tip: You can use a Terminal command to specify any time interval (not only the preset menu choices) that must pass before the screen-saver password requirement kicks in: `defaults -currentHost write com.apple.screensaver askForPasswordDelay -int` *interval*, where *interval* specifies the number of seconds to wait before a password is required.

Dictation

Use the Dictation pane to make macOS type spoken words.

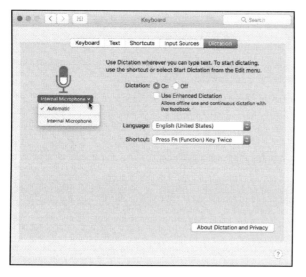

You can dictate text instead of typing on the keyboard. Dictation works with text areas in any macOS app, without special setup or voice training (for third-party apps, no additional third-party developer support is required). To dictate, you must be connected to the internet (unless you select Use Enhanced Dictation). When you dictate text, what you say is sent to Apple to convert it to text. Other personal information (such as contact names) may be sent too. For details, click About Dictation and Privacy in the Dictation pane. Dictation supports parental controls.

To set up dictation:

1   Choose > System Preferences > Keyboard > Dictation pane.

2   Turn on Dictation.

3   To enable dictation when your Mac isn't connected to the internet, select Use Enhanced Dictation.

4   Choose your language and dialect from the Language pop-up menu.

5   If you like, use the Shortcut pop-up menu to change the keyboard shortcut that triggers dictation.

    To create a shortcut that's not in the list, choose Customize and then press two or more keys you want to use.

6   To dictate by using a specific microphone, click the pop-up menu under the microphone icon.

To dictate text:

1   Place the insertion point where you want the dictated text to appear.

    You can dictate text anywhere that you can type it.

2   Press the Fn key twice or choose Edit > Start Dictation.

3   When the microphone icon appears, speak your text calmly at a normal pace.

    The icon glows to show your speaking volume.

4   When you're done, press the Fn key or click the Done button.

    Your spoken text appears.

To practice, try dictating a note in Notes (page 134).

To enter punctuation, say the punctuation mark. Suppose that you want to dictate "Let's eat, grandma." Say this:

Let's eat comma grandma period

The more you use Dictation, the better it understands you. Unclear text is underlined in blue. If the text is wrong, click it and then select an alternate, or type or dictate the correct text. Make sure that the mic is unobstructed by hands, clothing, or other objects. If you dictate in a noisy or echo-prone place, it may help to use a headset microphone. If you use an external mic, set its input volume high enough to respond to your voice (choose > System Preferences > Sound > Input pane).

Tip: Dictation is integrated with Contacts. Say a contact's name, and Dictation knows who you mean and spells it correctly.

Line break
> To insert a line break (like pressing the Return key once), say "new line".

New paragraph
> To start a new paragraph (like press the Return key twice), say "new paragraph".

Punctuation
> "period" or "full stop" types . (followed by a space and an uppercase letter)
>
> "dot" or "point" types . (without a trailing space)
>
> "comma" types ,
>
> "semicolon" types ;
>
> "colon" types :

"question mark" types ?

"exclamation point" types !

"inverted question mark" types ¿

"inverted exclamation point" types ¡

"hyphen" types - (without surrounding spaces)

"dash" types – (with surrounding spaces)

"em dash" types — (with surrounding spaces)

"quote" types "

"unquote" or "end quote" or "close quote" types " (with a trailing space)

"open single quote" types ' (without a trailing space)

"close single quote" types ' (with a trailing space)

"backquote" types ´ (with a trailing space)

"ampersand" types &

"slash" types /

"asterisk" types *

"at sign" types @

"underscore" types _

"ellipsis" or "dot dot dot" types ...

"section sign" types §

"tilde" types ~

"vertical bar" types |

"pound sign" types #

"open parenthesis" or "open paren" types (

"close parenthesis" or "close paren" types)

"open bracket" types [

"close bracket" types]

"open brace" types {

"close brace" types }

Capitalization

"cap" or "capital" capitalizes the next word

"caps on" or "caps off" toggles capitalization for the first letter of every word

"all caps" makes the next word all uppercase

"all caps on" or "all caps off" toggles all uppercase

"no caps" makes the next word all lowercase

"no caps on" or "no caps off" toggles all lowercase

Tip: The first new word after a period, question mark, or exclamation point is capitalized automatically (you don't need to say "cap").

Spacing

"spacebar" inserts a space instead of a hyphen in a normally hyphenated word; for example, "first spacebar class hotel" types *first class hotel*

"no space" prevents a space between words

"no space on" or "no space off" toggles spaces between words

Tip: Speak each of the capitalization and spacing on/off commands as a separate utterance, with a small pause before and after.

Numbers

To type *5* rather than *five*, say "numeral five". Saying more than one digit in a row also produces numerals: saying "four five" types *45*, not

four five. Say "point" or "dot" to insert a decimal point: "six point five" types *6.5*.

Mathematical symbols and operators

"plus sign" types +

"minus sign" types -

"asterisk" types *

"slash" types /

"caret" types ^

"percent sign" types %

"greater-than sign" types >

"less-than sign" types <

"degree sign" types °

"equals sign" types =

Currency

"dollar sign" types $

"cent sign" types ¢

"euro sign" types €

"yen sign" types ¥

"pounds sterling sign" types £

Tip: Currency amounts are recognized automatically. "fourteen dollars and twenty five cents" types *$14.25*. "five hundred yen" types *¥500*. "six point five euros" types *€6.5*.

Dates

Dates are recognized automatically. "july twenty seventh twenty twelve at six thirty AM" types *July 27, 2012 at 6:30 AM*.

Emoticons (smileys)

"smiley" or "smiley face" or "smile face" types :-)

"frowny" or "frowny face" or "frown face" types :-(

"winky" or "winky face" or "wink face" types ;-)

Web and email addresses

You can say "dub dub dub" to type the "www" part of a web address (URL). Say "dub dub dub dot apple dot com", for example, to type *www.apple.com*.

Dictation recognizes email addresses by listening for the central "at sign". Say "john underscore smith at sign gmail dot com", for example, to type *john_smith@gmail.com*.

Trademarks and copyrights

"copyright sign" types ©

"registered sign" types ®

"trademark sign" types ™

Alphabet letters

To type *A B C D* and so on, say "a bee cee dee" and so on. (This method typically isn't very accurate.)

Tip: You can say letters to voice-type words rather than inserting punctuation or symbols. For example, to voice-type the word "dot" (rather than insert a dot or period symbol), say "no space on, no caps on, dee, oh, tee, no space off, no caps off". Typing with your fingers is usually easier in cases like these.

Displays

Use the Displays panel to adjust your monitor(s). Shortcut to this panel: Option+F1/F2 (or Fn+Option+F1/F2). The panes and options that appear in this panel depend on your monitor setup.

Display Pane

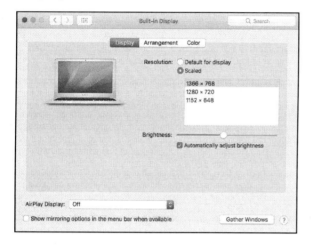

Resolution

Sets the fineness of detail of your screen's image, expressed in pixels wide by pixels high. (A **pixel** is the smallest building block—"dot"—of the display.) Higher resolutions make screen text and objects smaller but show a greater area. For LED, LCD, laptop, and Retina displays, choose "Default for display" to use **native resolution**. To use a different resolution, choose Scaled. A non-native resolution may blur your screen image.

Brightness

Adjusts the screen luminosity. Keyboard shortcuts: F1 and F2 (or Fn+F1/F2).

Rotation (swivel displays only)

Rotates the screen image in 90-degree increments.

AirPlay Display

Choose an Apple TV to use an HDTV as a display via AirPlay (page 168).

Show mirroring options in the menu bar when available

When multiple displays are being used, this option shows or hides the mirroring menu on the right side of the menu bar.

Gather Windows (multiple displays only)

Moves all open Displays preferences windows (one per display) to the same screen.

Automatically adjust brightness

Determines whether the light sensor dims the screen and backlit keyboard automatically in dark rooms.

Ambient light compensation (some displays)

Determines whether display color accuracy self-adjusts in different lighting environments.

Colors (CRT displays only)

Sets the number of colors (typically, Millions) that the screen can show simultaneously.

Refresh Rate (CRT displays only)

Sets the frequency at which the screen is redrawn to maintain a steady image. Higher refresh rates yield less flicker and eyestrain.

Using Multiple Displays

If your Mac is connected to multiple displays:

- You can set up the displays as an extended, continuous desktop, or show the same image on all screens (**mirroring**). To mirror displays, choose > System Preferences > Displays > Arrangement pane > Mirror Displays.

- Each display has its own menu bar.

- The dock is available on all screens (there's no primary or secondary display). If the dock isn't visible on a display, move the pointer to the screen edge where the dock normally appears (typically the bottom edge) to make the dock slide into view.

- Each display can independently show the desktop (with multiple open windows) or show a full-screen app.

- Open Mission Control (F3 or Control+↑) to get an overview of what's running on each display. You can drag app thumbnails between displays to customize the view.

- With AirPlay and an Apple TV (page 168), you can use an HDTV as a full-fledged display, complete with dock and menu bar.

Tip: To allow a single window to span multiple displays, choose > System Preferences > Mission Control, and then clear "Displays have separate Spaces".

Color Pane

Use this pane to create a ColorSync profile (page 124) when you calibrate your display to show colors accurately. You can switch among multiple color profiles or, if you have multiple displays, assign a different profile to each display. To create a profile, click Calibrate, and then follow the onscreen instructions.

Dock

Configures the dock (page 38).

Energy Saver

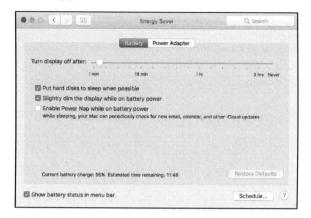

Use the Energy Saver panel to configure hardware features that reduce power consumption and extend the life of computer parts by switching them to a low-power state. This panel's options vary by Mac model (laptop, desktop, old, new, and so on). See also "Activity Monitor" on page 121.

Graphics
> Adjusts the tradeoff between better battery life (for writers and shoppers) and higher graphics performance (for gamers and film editors). Relogin to effect the change.

Battery/Power Adapter panes
> A desktop has only one set of sliders and options. A laptop has two sets: Battery applies when running on battery power and Power Adapter applies when plugged into a power source.

Computer/Display sleep sliders
> Sets the computer, or only the display, to sleep automatically after it's idle for the specified time period ("Never" disables sleep). Put only the display to sleep if your computer is in the middle of a task that you want to finish.

Prevent computer from sleeping automatically when display is off
> Let the display sleep but not the computer. Turn on this setting if your computer is in the middle of a task that you want to finish.

Put the hard disks to sleep when possible
> Determines whether to stop an idle hard drive's disks from spinning.

Wake for Wi-Fi network access
> Determines whether you can access a sleeping Mac's shared resources (printers or iTunes, for example) over a wireless network.

Start up automatically after a power failure
> Determines whether the Mac restarts automatically after a power interruption.

Slightly dim the display while on battery power
> Determines whether laptop screen brightness is dimmed when on battery power.

Enable Power Nap
> Toggles Power Nap (page 187), which lets App Store updates, iCloud synchronization, and other updates and backups occur while your Mac sleeps, draining little power.

Allow power button to put the computer to sleep
> On desktop Macs, determines whether pressing ⏻ shuts down or sleeps the Mac.

Automatically reduce brightness before display goes to sleep
> Determines whether the screen brightness dims (typically as a warning to move the mouse) before the display fully sleeps.

Restore Defaults
> Restore the default Energy Saver settings for the current pane (battery or power adapter).

Show battery status in the menu bar

Shows the battery menu on the right side of the menu bar. The battery's icon indicates its status: draining (shrinking progress bar), charging (lightning bolt), fully charged (full battery), or something's wrong (×). This menu also lists power-hogging apps and shows the estimated time remaining until the battery dies or, if plugged in, is fully charged. Choose Show Percentage to display the remaining battery charge on the menu bar. Option-click this menu to see the battery condition.

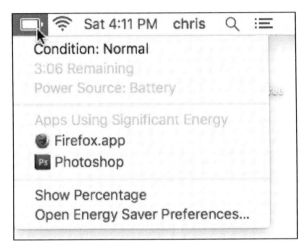

Schedule

Sets a daily schedule for putting your computer to sleep or turning it off and on.

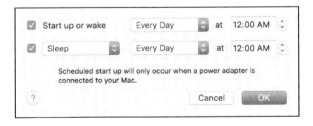

Extensions

Extensions are small, functional add-ons that enhance and customize macOS. You can use the Extensions panel to choose which extensions appear in Action menus ⚙, Share menus ⬆, and Notification Center's Today view (page 54).

Third-party developers can also provide extensions that add functionality to macOS. Extensions come bundled with applications; they can't be purchased or installed separately. A single application can provide multiple extensions.

You can't launch extensions directly. Instead, macOS finds extensions automatically and launches them in response to your actions. macOS can launch an extension even when its containing application isn't running. Extension processes are short lived—macOS kills them quickly when they're no longer needed.

The same privacy settings that apply to an application also apply to its extensions. If you let an application access your Contacts data, for example, then all that app's extensions can also access Contacts data.

The Extensions panel lists the types of extensions, including:

- **All** extensions are provided by third-party applications (that is, extensions other than macOS's Apple-provided native extensions).

- **Actions** extensions alter content within an application. The Markup feature in Mail, for example, is an action extension.

- **Finder** file-management and cloud-storage extensions appear in Finder.

- **Photos** editing extensions appear in Photos.

- **Share Menu** extensions appear in macOS's ubiquitous Share menus ⬆.

- **Today** extensions, called widgets, appear in Notification Center's Today view.

General

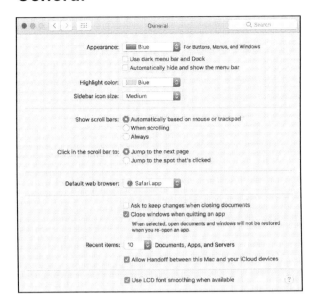

Use the General panel to make minor alterations to the look of windows, menus, buttons, scrollbars, and fonts.

Appearance
Blue is the standard macOS color for default buttons, menu highlighting, progress bars, window-sizing buttons, and other odds and ends. Graphite mutes the color scheme to grayscale.

Use dark menu bar and Dock
Use dark backgrounds and light text for the menu bar and dock (sometimes handy for working with photos and videos). Darkened elements are still translucent, not opaque.

Automatically hide and show the menu bar
Autohides the menu bar when you're not using it. When this option is turned on, the menu bar disappears when the pointer moves away from the menu bar and reappears when it moves toward it.

Tip: To make the menu bar, dock, and other screen elements opaque, choose ⌘ > System Preferences > Accessibility > Display > "Reduce transparency".

Highlight color
Choose the highlight color of selected text. This color also outlines windows that you drag icons into.

Sidebar icon size
Changes the size of icons in the sidebar of Finder windows.

Show scroll bars/Click in the scroll bar to
Changes the appearance and behavior of scrollbars.

Default web browser
Choose the web browser that opens when you click a link in email, messages, documents, and so on.

Ask to keep changes when closing documents
Determines whether unsaved changes are saved automatically when you close documents. To be prompted to save changes, turn on this option. See also "Auto Save and Versions" on page 117.

Close windows when quitting an app
Determines whether document windows open to their previous size and position when you relaunch an app. If you want to launch apps with a clean slate, turn on this option. See also "Resume" on page 116.

Recent items
Sets how many of your recently opened programs, documents, and servers appear in the Recent Items submenu in the Apple menu ⌘.

Allow Handoff between this Mac and your iCloud devices
Toggles Handoff (page 169) and the universal clipboard (page 34).

Use LCD font smoothing when available
Determines whether onscreen (but not printed) text is smoothed (**antialiased**). The smoothing effect may be subtle, so experiment with various small and large type sizes to see which setting you prefer. After you change this setting, close then reopen a program to see the change; for Finder, you must log out and then log in again.

iCloud

iCloud is an online storage and computing service that uploads (copies) your content to Apple's remote data center and pushes it wirelessly to your Mac, Windows PC, and iOS devices (iPhone, iPad, and iPod touch). Your music, photos, documents, and more are available on-demand across all your computers and iDevices. iCloud is integrated with your programs and works in the background silently and automatically (without manual syncing or sending). You can also view and manage your content and settings at *icloud.com* in a modern browser. Some iCloud features work across macOS, Windows, and iOS, whereas others are iOS-only.

A few iCloud tips:

- The minimal system requirements for iCloud are at "System requirements for iCloud" at *support. apple.com/HT204230*.

- iCloud provides unlimited free storage for purchased music, TV shows, iOS apps, and books. It also includes 5 GB of free storage for mail, documents, and backups. Higher storage capacities are available for an annual fee (*support. apple.com/HT201318*). You can manage your storage by controlling backups and choosing which documents to store in the cloud (*support. apple.com/HT204247*).

- iCloud identifies you by your Apple ID (*support. apple.com/HT204053*).

- iCloud stores your data securely. For details, read "iCloud security and privacy overview" at *support.apple.com/HT202303*.

To set up iCloud (macOS): Choose > System Preferences > iCloud, enter your Apple ID and password (if prompted), and then select the services that you'd like to enable. The following services are available:

Family Sharing

Family Sharing (also available on iOS 8 and later) lets purchases be shared among members of a single household while still allowing everyone to have their own Apple ID. Each family has one organizer who can invite up to five additional members. Invitees receive an email, and once they accept, become members of the family group.

All purchases by family members use a single payment method controlled by the organizer. Family members get immediate access to each other's purchased music, movies, TV shows, books, and apps on their Mac. The family organizer and (optionally) other adult family members can remotely approve purchases made by children in the iTunes Store, iBooks Store, and App Store. Being part of a family also includes shared photo albums, calendars, reminders, and location information.

To set up Family Sharing, choose > System Preferences > iCloud > Set Up Family, and then follow the onscreen instructions. For details and restrictions, read the Apple support article "Family Sharing" at *support.apple.com/ HT201060*.

iCloud Drive

iCloud Drive lets you securely store all your files (including the entire contents of your Desktop and Documents folders) in iCloud and access them from your iPhone, iPad, iPod touch, Mac, or Windows PC. To upload files to iCloud, drag them into the iCloud Drive folder on your Mac or Windows PC. Or start a new document by using an iCloud-enabled app on your iOS device. Then you can access the latest version of these files from all your devices. You can start creating a presentation on your Mac at home, for example, and then make final edits and present it at work by using your iPad. All the changes that you make along the way appear automatically on all your devices.

iCloud Drive requires OS X Yosemite (OS X 10.10) or later on a Mac, Windows 7 or later on a PC, and iOS 8 or later on an iPhone, iPad, or iPod touch. iCloud Drive completely replaces "Documents & Data" storage (see below) found in older (pre-Yosemite) versions of OS X. Upgrading to iCloud Drive is an optional, irreversible, one-time process. You'll be prompted to upgrade during the account setup process. If you decline, you can upgrade later by turning on iCloud Drive in the iCloud panel in System Preferences.

In macOS, iCloud Drive appears in the Finder sidebar and Go menu like any other system folder (its specific location is /Users/*user_name*/Library/Mobile Documents). Deleting or moving a file stored in iCloud Drive is accompanied by a warning to remind you that such an operation has far-reaching effects and isn't just a normal file manipulation. Progress bars in Finder indicate the synchronization status of files in iCloud Drive. Files in iCloud Drive are available on your Mac even when you're not connected to the internet. Any changes that you make to a file while offline are synced automatically as soon as your Mac is back online. For details, read "iCloud Drive FAQ" at *support.apple.com/HT201104*.

Documents & Data

Transfer Pages, Keynote, and Numbers documents between your computer and your iOS devices. Sign in to *icloud.com* in a modern browser, and all your iWork for iOS and iWork for iCloud documents will be there, complete with your most recent edits. You can also drag an iWork for Mac or Microsoft Office document (Word, PowerPoint, or Excel) from your computer to one of the iWork apps on *icloud.com*; it will appear automatically on all your iOS devices for viewing and editing. Third-party developers can make their apps work with iCloud, too. If you

can't update or upload documents to iCloud, read "iCloud: Troubleshooting Documents in the Cloud" at *support.apple.com/HT203517*. You can also move documents to the cloud from Preview (page 135) and TextEdit (page 140).

Tip: Documents & Data storage has been superseded by iCloud Drive (see above) in OS X Yosemite (OS X 10.10) and later.

Photos

When **My Photo Stream** is turned on (click Options), photos imported to your Mac or Windows PC are pushed to iCloud automatically, as are photos taken on iOS devices. On your Mac, you can view the photos in the Photos application (page 135). For details, read the Apple support article "My Photo Stream FAQ" at *support.apple.com/HT201317*. You can also use My Photo Stream photos as a screen saver. iCloud Photo Library and iCloud Photo Sharing work with the Photos app (page 135).

Mail

iCloud includes an *icloud.com* (formerly *me.com*) email account that keeps your mail and folders up-to-date across all your devices. For details, read "iCloud: Set up iCloud Mail on your devices" at *support.apple.com/kb/PH2621*.

Contacts

Changes to your contacts in Contacts, iOS Contacts, and Microsoft Outlook 2007 or later are pushed automatically to iCloud across all your devices.

Calendars

Changes to your calendars in Calendar, iOS Calendar, and Microsoft Outlook 2007 or later are pushed automatically to iCloud across all your devices. You can share your calendars with other iCloud users.

Reminders

Changes to your reminders in Reminders, iOS Reminders, and Microsoft Outlook 2007 or later are pushed automatically to iCloud across all your devices.

Safari

Your Safari bookmarks, Reading List, and open tabs are pushed automatically to iCloud. In Windows, Safari and Internet Explorer bookmarks are pushed. To view synced tabs in Safari, click the iCloud button ☁ in the Safari toolbar.

Notes

Changes to your notes in Notes and iOS Notes are pushed automatically to iCloud across all your devices.

Keychain

iCloud Keychain encrypts and stores your website user names and passwords on the devices that you've approved (Macs or iDevices), and syncs them wirelessly and automatically across those devices. When you need to create a new password for a website, Password Generator suggests a strong password and saves it to your iCloud Keychain. Passwords and user names are filled in automatically when you need them, so you don't have to remember or type them. iCloud Keychain can also store and sync encrypted credit-card details for online shopping. See also "Keychain Access" on page 180.

Back to My Mac

Provides remote access to your Mac from another Mac anywhere on the internet. For details, read "Set up and use Back to My Mac" at *support.apple.com/HT204618*.

Find My Mac

Helps locate a missing Mac. Sign in at *icloud.com* to see your missing Mac on a map. You can send a message, lock the Mac, or securely erase all its data.

To set up iCloud (Windows): Download and install the iCloud Control Panel from Apple at *icloud.com/icloudcontrolpanel*. On the Windows desktop, choose Start > Control Panel > Network and Internet > iCloud, enter your Apple ID and password (if prompted), and then select the desired services.

To set up iCloud (iOS): On the Home screen of your iPad, iPhone, or iPod touch, tap Settings > iCloud, enter your Apple ID and password (if prompted), and then turn on the desired services.

Other iCloud Services

Other iCloud services, not specific to macOS, include:

iTunes in the Cloud (Automatic Downloads)

Automatically downloads newly purchased iTunes music, movies, TV shows, iOS apps, and books to all your iOS devices wirelessly over a wi-fi or cellular signal (previous purchases are downloaded at no charge). To enable automatic downloads, open iTunes on your Mac, and then choose iTunes > Preferences > Store pane > Automatic Downloads. In iTunes for Windows, choose Edit > Preferences (Control+,) > Store pane > Automatic Downloads. In iOS, on the Home screen, tap Settings > iTunes & App Store > Automatic Downloads.

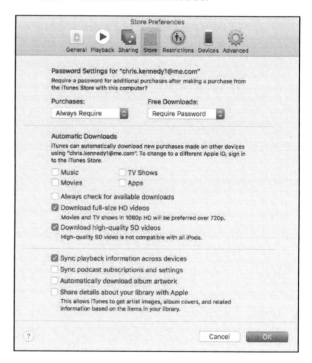

iTunes Match

A fee-based service that gives the benefits of iTunes in the Cloud for music that you didn't buy from iTunes, including pirated music and music ripped from CDs. iTunes Match is built into iTunes on your Mac or Windows PC and the Music app on your iOS devices. You can download your entire music library from iCloud at any time.

Backup

iCloud automatically backs up important data on your iOS devices daily over wi-fi. Backups include purchased music, TV shows, apps, and books; photos and video in the Camera Roll; device settings; app data; home screen and app organization; messages (iMessage, SMS, and MMS); and ringtones. To restore a backup on your device (or set up a new device), connect the device to wi-fi, and then enter your Apple ID and password. Your backed-up data will appear on your device. For details, read "Archive or make copies of your iCloud data" at *support. apple.com/HT204055.*

Find My iPhone/iPad

Works like Find My Mac, but for iOS devices. To see your missing device on a map, sign in at *icloud.com* or use the Find My iPhone app (available from the iOS App Store) on another iOS device.

Find My Friends

Use the Find My Friends app (available from the iOS App Store) to locate people. iOS users who share their location with you appear on a map. Privacy controls let you turn off location-sharing or share temporarily with a specific group of people. Parental restrictions let you manage how your children use Find My Friends.

Internet Accounts

Use the Internet Accounts panel to enter and edit your internet accounts with iCloud, Microsoft Exchange, Google, Twitter, Facebook, LinkedIn, Yahoo, and other service providers so that you can quickly access them in Mail, Calendar, Reminders, Messages, Notes, and other account-based apps. You can sync account information to iCloud.

To add an account: Click a service provider on the right (if your provider isn't listed, click Add Other Account), enter your account information, click Set Up, and then select the apps with which to associate the account. The account list on the left shows accounts created within this panel, as well as accounts created within other account-based apps and services (such as Mail or iCloud).

To edit an account: Select the account in the list and then toggle the app checkboxes on the right or click Details or Manage.

To delete an account: Select the account in the list and then click (-).

Keyboard

Configures the keyboard (page 20).

Language & Region

Use the Language & Region panel to set the display language; country-specific ("localization") settings; and date, time, number, and currency formats.

Preferred languages

> Set the language used on menus, dialog boxes, and buttons. Drag the desired language to the top of the list. To add or remove languages, click (+) or (−). If a program can't show the first language in the list, it shows the second, and so on. To effect the change in a particular program, quit and then reopen the program. To effect the change systemwide, log out and then log back in.

Region

> Choose a geographic region for date, time, number, and other formats.

First day of week

> Designate the first day of the week for displaying calendars and doing date arithmetic.

Calendar

> Choose the civil calendar for your country or region.

Time format

> Show the time as a 24-hour or 12-hour clock.

Temperature

> Choose Celsius or Fahrenheit.

List sort order

> Determines the order of icons when they are sorted by name in Finder.

Keyboard Preferences

> Add international keyboards (page 22).

Advanced

> Fine-tune the formats for dates, times, numbers, currencies, and measurement units displayed in programs and Finder.

Mission Control

Configures Mission Control (page 50).

Mouse

Configures the mouse (page 23).

Network

Configures online connections (Chapter 8).

Notifications

Configures Notification Center (page 52).

Parental Controls

Configures Parental Controls (page 182).

Printers & Scanners

Configures printing, scanning, and faxing (Chapter 6).

Security & Privacy

Configures security and privacy settings (Chapter 9).

Sharing

Configures sharing settings (Chapter 7).

Siri

Configures Siri (page 56).

Sound

Use the Sound panel to configure your Mac's sound system, including volume, alert sounds, playback, and recording. Shortcut: Option-click the Sound menu ◀) to view or set input/output audio devices.

To adjust the master volume: Do any of the following:

- Drag the "Output volume" slider at the bottom of the Sound panel (or select the Mute checkbox).

- Drag the volume slider ◀) in the menu bar (if necessary, select "Show volume in menu bar" in the Sound panel).

- Press and F10 ◀, F11 ◀), or F12 ◀) to mute, decrease, or increase the volume, respectively (you may have to hold down the Fn key too). To adjust by fine increments, hold down Shift+Option as you press these keys.

- On an Apple Remote, press the Volume Up and Volume Down buttons.

Sound Effects Pane

Use this pane to set the alert sound and volume.

Select an alert sound
> Sets the sound that macOS makes to get your attention or when you click or type somewhere that you shouldn't.

Play sound effects through
> Sets the output speakers or headset for sound effects.

Alert volume slider
> Adjusts the alert volume relative to the master volume (never exceeding the master volume). You can also adjust this setting by Option-dragging the volume slider ◀) in the menu bar. Dragging this slider all the way to the left mutes the alert sound but plays music, games, and movies at the volume set by the master "Output volume" slider.

Play user interface sound effects
> Determines whether sound effects play during some Finder operations such as dragging an item into the Trash, off the dock, or into a folder.

Play feedback when volume is changed
> Determines whether the volume is muted when you adjust the volume. To temporarily reverse this setting, hold down Shift as you adjust the volume.

Output Pane

Use this pane to select speakers, an Apple TV, or a headset for audio output and adjust the left–right balance.

Input Pane

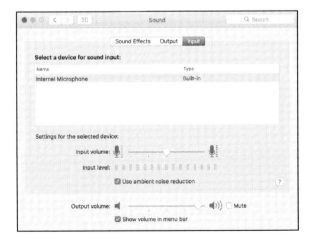

Use this pane to adjust the input volume (sensitivity) of the selected microphone or line input. For mics, select "Use ambient noise reduction" to mute background noise during dictation.

Spotlight

Configures Spotlight search (page 103).

Startup Disk

Sets which drive (page 109) to use when starting (booting) the computer (page 12).

Time Machine

Configures Time Machine (page 188).

Trackpad

Configures the trackpad for multitouch gestures (page 25).

Users & Groups

Configures user accounts (page 13) and login options (page 16).

CHAPTER 4

Files, Folders & Drives

MacOS uses files and folders to organize your information so that you aren't overwhelmed by long file lists and can distinguish one set of content from another. A **file** is the basic unit of computer storage; it can be a program, a program's configuration data, a log that the computer itself maintains, or a document that you create or receive. You organize files in containers called **folders** (or **directories**), which can hold additional folders (called **subfolders** or **subdirectories**) to form a treelike hierarchy. Folders in turn are stored on **drives** (or **volumes**) such as hard drives, USB flash drives, CDs, DVDs, and network servers. macOS creates a few system folders to store its own files and settings but otherwise doesn't care how you structure your tree of folders and files. This chapter explains how to use Finder to navigate and manage your stored information.

System Folders

The drive on which macOS is installed, called the **system drive** or **startup drive**, Macintosh usually is in the desktop's upper-right corner and is labeled *Macintosh*. If this drive icon isn't on your desktop, switch to Finder and then choose Go > Computer (Shift+Command+C) to see a list of available drives. Double-click the system drive to browse the following **system folders** in the macOS folder structure.

Applications contains all the programs— iTunes, Word, Photoshop, and so on—that Applications you, another user, the macOS installer, or an administrator installed, along with all the programs' support files. In general, you shouldn't touch the files in here except to open them or delete (uninstall) them.

Library contains operating-system support files and components (drivers, fonts, preferences, sounds, help files, keyboard layouts, Library and so on).

System contains critical Unix operating-system files that control macOS's basic operations. Most of its contents are invisible. Look System but don't touch.

Users contains the home folder for each user account. These folders contain the users' personal settings and files. If you're not an Users administrator, you can't open or see other users' home folders. The Shared folder (page 164) stores files that are available to every user.

User Guides And Information (or *User Information*) contains links to User Guides User Guides And and other documentation from Apple. Information

Other System Folders

Depending on your setup, you may see other folders with self-explanatory names like Network, Developer, Previous System, or Incompatible Software. If you upgraded from OS 9 or earlier, other folders may appear: your personal files and folders preserved during the upgrade, pre-OS X applications, and old system files.

Home Folder

Your **home folder**, labeled with your user account's short name, stores your files and folders chris in one place. A unique home folder is associated with the user account of whoever is logged in. Other users (besides administrators) can't see what's in your home folder; neither can you see what's in theirs.

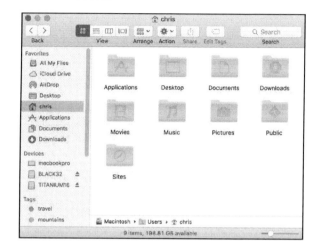

To open your home folder: Do any of the following:

- In Finder, choose Go > Home (Shift+Command+H).

- In a Finder window, click the Home icon in the sidebar.

- Click an empty area on the desktop and then choose Go > Enclosing Folder (Command+↑).

To make new Finder windows open your home folder: In Finder, choose Finder > Preferences > General pane. Select your home folder from the "New Finder windows show" pop-up menu.

Tip: You can create a Home folder shortcut in the dock by dragging the Home folder's proxy icon (page 91) from the title bar to the dock.

Home Subfolders

The home folder contains specialized subfolders, each of which is intended for the type of file that its name suggests:

Applications
> Contains programs that you install. This folder (~/Applications, where ~ denotes your home folder) has more-restrictive sharing permissions (page 156) than the Applications system folder (/Applications). By default, other users can run the programs in this folder but can't delete them.

Desktop
> For desktop files and shortcuts. Anything that you put in here appears on your desktop (and anything that you drag to your desktop lands in the Desktop folder). You can't delete or rename this folder.

Documents
> For word-processing files, spreadsheets, databases, presentations, text files, and other user-created documents.

Downloads
> For files downloaded from the internet.

Library
> For personal preferences, fonts, email, and so on. This folder is hidden by default; to open it in Finder, hold down the Option key and then choose Go > Library. To unhide Library, open your home folder, choose View > Show View Options (Command+J), and then select Show Library Folder.

Movies
> For videos and clips from your digital camera or camcorder, or video files downloaded or ripped (copied) from a DVD.

Music
> For MP3s and digital music, downloaded or ripped from a CD.

Pictures
> For digital pictures from a camera or scanner.

Public
> For files and folders that other users can access without a password, over a network or while sitting at the machine.

Sites
> For websites, if you're using macOS as a web server.

These folders are just helpful anchors to help you organize your files without having to start from scratch, but this storage scheme doesn't work when things get complicated. It's better to ignore file types and nest folders deeply. If you create a shallow or "flat" folder structure, then you're forced to use long, descriptive file names rather than succinct ones. A flat structure also makes you fill each folder with so many subfolders that it's hard to discern the structure quickly. If you're, say, running an advertising campaign, it's more sensible to organize all the photos, graphics, copy, layouts, videos, and spreadsheets in a dedicated project folder rather than disperse them to the factory-installed subfolders.

You don't *have* to store your stuff in your home folder (macOS doesn't care where you put your files), but doing that is a good idea because:

- It's easy to open from Finder.

- It's indexed by macOS automatically so you can find files instantly by using a search box.

- It's where programs expect you to save and open files.

- It segregates your work and programs, preventing accidental document deletion when you remove or upgrade programs.

- It makes it easier to back up your work by archiving only your home folder (and its subfolders) rather than folders scattered about your hard drive.

- It keeps your personal files private.

Finder

Finder is the key tool for working with files and folders on your computer or network. The term "folder window" actually refers to a Finder window. It's common to have several Finder windows or tabs open at the same time, each one looking a little different depending on the settings and filters in effect for that folder. Apple presets folders to show their contents a certain way; you'll see icons grow or shrink or regroup, depending on which folder you click. You can change views globally or by folder. Finder itself always is open, even if no folder windows are. Finder windows work like other windows, but also have specialized parts. Finder supports full-screen view.

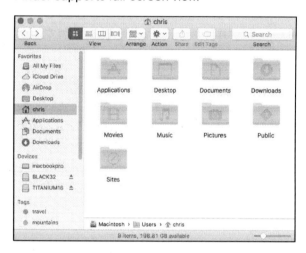

To activate Finder: Do any of the following:

- Click the Finder icon in the dock.
- Click an empty area on the desktop.
- Command+Tab to Finder.
- Click any folder window.

To open a new Finder window: In Finder, choose File > New Finder Window (Command+N). The new window opens the folder set by Finder > Preferences > General pane > "New Finder windows show".

To explore the folder hierarchy: Double-click a folder to open it and explore its contents. Keep double-clicking folders to drill down to the folder you want. To return to a previous folder, click < or right-click the folder name in the title bar.

To print a list of files and folders: Open the desired Finder window, choose Edit > Select All (Command+A), choose Edit > Copy (Command+C), switch to a text editor or word processor (such as TextEdit), and then choose Edit > Paste (Command+V). A list of all the files and folders in the Finder window appears, ready to format and print.

Finder Tabs

Finder **tabs** let you declutter your desktop by consolidating multiple Finder windows into a single, tabbed window (similar to web browsers, where each webpage appears as a separate tab in the same window). Each tab behaves like its own Finder window, so you can change the view of each one independently.

Open tabs are listed in the **tab bar** near the top of a Finder window (under the toolbar). By default, the tab bar is visible only when multiple tabs are open. To always show the tab bar, choose View > Show Tab Bar (Shift+Command+T).

A Finder window can hold an unlimited number of tabs. You can open folders in new tabs, switch among them, move them, close them, drag files between them, and more.

To open a new tab: Do any of the following:

- In Finder, choose File > New Tab (Command+T).

  The new tab opens the folder set by Finder > Preferences > General pane > "New Finder windows show".

- Hold down the Command key and then double-click a folder icon.

- Hold down the Command key and then click a folder in the sidebar.

- Right-click a folder icon in Finder and then choose Open in New Tab in the shortcut menu.

Tip: To choose whether Open in New Tab or Open in New Window appears in the shortcut menu, choose Finder > Preferences > General pane > "Open folders in tabs instead of new windows". To swap between these two options when the shortcut menu is already open, press and hold the Option key.

- Click + on the right edge of the tab bar.

- Right-click a tab in the tab bar and then choose New Tab in the shortcut menu.

- Drag the proxy icon from the title bar of a Finder window to the + on the tab bar of another Finder window.

To view and manage tabs: Do any of the following:

- To view a different tab, click it in the tab bar.

- To cycle forward through tabs, press Ctrl+Tab repeatedly. To cycle backward, press Shift+Ctrl+Tab repeatedly. Alternatively, choose Window > Show Next/Previous Tab.

- To view hidden tabs (if the tab bar is filled with tabs), click the left or right edge of a hidden tab.

- To reorder tabs, drag them left or right in the tab bar.

- To move a tab to its own Finder window, right-click the tab in the tab bar and then choose Move Tab to New Window in the shortcut menu. Alternatively, activate the tab and then choose Window > Move Tab to New Window.

- To consolidate all open Finder windows in a single tabbed window, choose Window > Merge All Windows.

To close a tab: Do any of the following:

- Hover the pointer over the tab in the tab bar and then click × when it appears.

- Activate the tab and then choose File > Close Tab (Command+W).

- Right-click the tab in the tab bar and then choose Close Tab in the shortcut menu.

- To close all tabs but one, right-click the tab that you want to keep in the tab bar and then choose Close Other Tabs in the shortcut menu.

To move or copy files and folders by using tabs:

1 Open tabs for the source and destination folders.

2 Drag files or folders from the source folder and drop them onto the tab of the destination folder in the tab bar.

  To copy an item instead of moving it, hold down Option when you drop it. To alias (page 98) an item instead of moving or copying it, hold down Option+Command when you drop it.

Tip: If you hover over the destination tab before you drop, the destination tab behaves like a spring-loaded folder (page 98) and becomes active, letting you drop items into a nested folder.

Sidebar

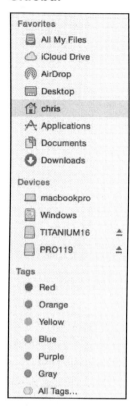

The **sidebar**—on the left side of a Finder window—shows icons for frequently visited locations. Click an icon to show the contents of that location in the main part of the Finder window. An icon in the sidebar is only a pointer; removing it doesn't delete the original, nor does dragging an item to the sidebar move the original. Each sidebar icon has its own shortcut menu, available via a right-click. The sidebar is divided into categories:

Favorites

Lists files, folders, smart folders, programs, drives, and other locations that you use frequently. It's common to customize this section.

Shared

Lists the shared computers on your local network.

Devices

Lists storage devices: internal and external drives, CDs, DVDs, iPods, USB flash drives, and so on. Removable devices are marked with ⏏, which you can click to eject that device.

Tags

Lists recently used tags (page 99).

To add items to the sidebar: Drag the icon of a file, folder, or program to the Favorites section, or select an icon (or group of icons) on the desktop or in any folder window and then choose File > Add to Sidebar (Ctrl+Command+T).

To remove an item: Drag its icon out of the sidebar, or right-click it and then choose Remove from Sidebar. (You can't remove icons from the Shared section.)

To rearrange items: Drag icons or categories up and down to reorder them. (You can't rearrange icons in the Shared category.)

To show or hide the sidebar: Choose View > Show/Hide Sidebar (Option+Command+S).

To change the width of the sidebar: Drag its right edge to the left or right.

To customize the sidebar list: Choose Finder > Preferences > Sidebar pane.

To resize sidebar icons: Choose > System Preferences > General > "Sidebar icon size".

Toolbar

The toolbar—running along the top of a Finder window—works like a normal toolbar and provides a customizable set of Finder-specific buttons:

- Back ⟨ and Forward ⟩ move among previously visited locations (you can click-and-hold these buttons for a location history, letting you jump two or three folders at a time).

- View changes the size or arrangement of the icons in the folder window.

- Arrange sorts icons by the selected criterion.

- Action is a context-sensitive pop-up menu. Its commands change depending on which icons, if any, are selected.

- Share lets you share files via Mail, Messages, AirDrop, and more.

- Edit Tags button lets you assign tags (descriptive labels) to a file or folder.

- Quick Look button previews a file or folder without opening it.

- Path shows the current location in the folder hierarchy.

To show or hide the toolbar: Choose View > Show/Hide Toolbar (Option+Command+T).

To customize the toolbar: Open or activate any Finder window and then choose View > Customize Toolbar, or right-click the toolbar of any Finder window and then choose a command. When the Customize Toolbar panel is open, you can drag icons on or off the toolbar, or drag them left or right to reorder them. Use the Show pop-up menu to show toolbar icons, icon labels, or both.

Proxy Icon

The **proxy icon**—the tiny icon 🏠 chris next to the window's name on the title bar—stands in for the folder or drive itself. Use this icon to manipulate the folder or drive without having to first close its window. To move a folder, hold down the mouse button on the proxy icon until it darkens, and then drag it to a different folder or drive, into the dock, to the sidebar's Favorites section, or into the Trash. To copy the folder, hold down Option while you drag.

Dragging the proxy icon of a *document* window will alias (page 98) the document rather than move or copy it. (Not all document windows have proxy icons.)

Path Bar

The **path bar**—the long strip under the folder contents—appears when you choose View > Show Path Bar (Option+Command+P) and shows your current location in the folder hierarchy as a "breadcrumb trail" of links separated by arrows. These links are

operational: double-click a link to jump to that location, drag items into a tiny folder icon, or right-click a link for a shortcut menu. See also "Paths" on page 2.

Status Bar

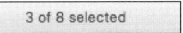

The **status bar**—running along the bottom of a Finder window—appears when you choose View > Show Status Bar (Command+/) and shows the number of icons selected.

Navigating in Finder

Use the Go menu to move among folders on your computer or network.

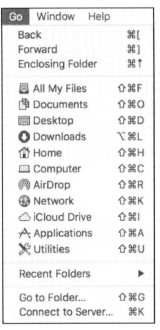

The following commands are available on the Go menu:

- **Back** (Command+[) and Forward (Command+]) move among previously visited locations.

- **Enclosing Folder** (Command+↑) moves up the hierarchy tree to the parent of the current folder.

- **All My Files** (Shift+Command+F) is a smart folder that shows all your files.

- Documents (Shift+Command+O), Desktop (Shift+Command+D), and so on jump to common locations.

- Recent Folders tracks where you've been lately. To cover your tracks, choose Recent Folders > Clear Menu.

- Go to Folder (Shift+Command+G) lets you jump to a folder by typing its Unix path: ~/Downloads, for example (~ denotes your home folder and / separates folder names).

- Connect to Server (Command+K) connects to Macs that have File Sharing turned on (page 156), Windows machines with shared folders, wireless drives, network servers, and other servers (by, say, WebDAV, DNS, NFS, FTP, or IP address).

Tip: To reveal a hidden shortcut to the Library folder in your home folder (~/Library), hold down the Option key when you click the Go menu.

To jump quickly to any folder up the hierarchy tree from the current folder, right-click the name in the folder window's title bar, and then choose a destination from the pop-up menu. (This feature works like the path bar.) When you open a folder, Finder replaces the window's current contents with those of the new folder.

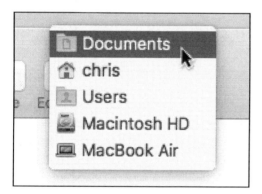

Folder Views

You can change the size and arrangement of the items in a folder by choosing to view them as icons, in a list, in columns, or as large thumbnail images (Cover Flow). Finder lets you fine-tune each view via the View Options dialog box and remembers each folder's view settings independently. In general, the view that you choose for a folder depends on the type and number of files that it contains.

To switch views: In a Finder window or tab, do any of the following:

- In the View menu, choose As Icons (Command+1), As List (Command+2), As Columns (Command+3), or Cover Flow (Command+4).

- Click a view in the toolbar.

- Right-click an empty area in a folder and then choose from the View submenu.

To set view options: In a Finder window or tab, do any of the following:

- Choose View > Show View Options.

- Press Command+J (this keyboard shortcut also closes the View Options dialog box).

- Click > Show View Options.

- Right-click an empty area in a folder and then choose Show View Options.

Tip: The available options change depending on which view is active and apply to only the active folder.

To apply the current view options as defaults for all windows: In the View Options dialog box, click Use as Defaults. To undo this action, hold down the Option key and then click Restore to Defaults.

To override the default view for the active window: Select a view and then, in the View Options dialog box, select the "Always open" checkbox.

Icon View

⊞ This view shows items as icons and works best for sparsely populated folders or folders containing mostly pictures.

To align icons to a grid: To align an individual icon, Command-drag it. To align some or all icons, choose View > Clean Up Selection (with some icons selected) or View > Clean Up (nothing selected). These commands also appear in the shortcut menu when you right-click an empty area in a folder window. To swap commands or show alternative commands temporarily, hold down Option when you right-click or open a menu. To lock all icons to the grid, in the View Options dialog box (Command+J), choose Snap to Grid from the "Sort By" pop-up menu. To override the Snap to Grid setting for an individual icon, Command-drag it.

To sort icons: To sort temporarily, choose View > Arrange By submenu (Ctrl+Command+[0–7]). To sort permanently, hold down the Option key and choose View > Sort By submenu (Option+Ctrl+Command+[0–7]). Alternatively, use the "Arrange By" or "Sort By" pop-up menu in the View Options dialog box (Command+J). These commands also appear in the shortcut menu when you right-click an empty area in a folder window. To swap commands or show alternative commands temporarily, hold down the Option key when you right-click or choose a menu command.

List View

⊟ This view shows a columnar list of files, folders, and their attributes indicated by column headings (Name, Date Modified, Size, Kind, and so on). This view works best for general file management and crowded folders.

To set up columns: To choose which columns appear, right-click any column heading to open its shortcut menu, or use the "Show Columns" checkboxes in the View Options dialog box (Command+J). To reorder columns, drag the column headings left or right (the Name column must be first). To resize a column, drag the right edge of its column heading left or right. To resize a column to fit its widest entry, double-click its right edge.

To sort the list: Click the heading of the column to sort by. To reverse the sort order, click it again. A small arrowhead near the column name points up ⌃ for an ascending sort or down ⌄ for a descending sort. Alternatively, use the "Arrange By" or "Sort By" commands in the View menu. To swap commands or show alternative commands temporarily, hold down the Option key when you choose a menu command.

Tip: To make folders appear at the top of a list that's sorted by name, instead of mixed into the list alphabetically, choose Finder > Preferences > Advanced > "Keep folders on top when sorting by name".

To show or hide the contents of a folder: Click ▶ or ▼ next to the folder icon (or select the folder and then press → or ←). To show all subfolders, hold down the Option key and then click ▶ (or select the folder and then press Option+→).

Column View

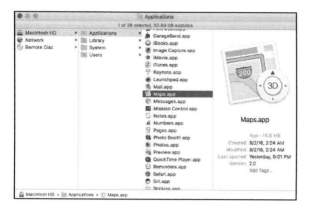

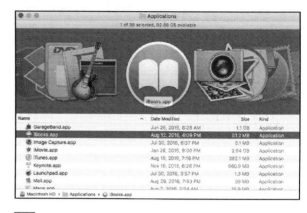

Cover Flow View

▥ This view shows the contents of the current folder and its subfolders in a series of side-by-side vertical panes. The first pane shows the current folder or drive. Clicking a folder in the first pane shows that folder's contents in the second pane, and so on—click a folder in any pane to show its contents in the pane to its right. If panes slide left out of view, use the horizontal scroll bar to show them again. This view works best when you want to see nested folders and their parent folders in the same window.

To resize columns: To view more or fewer columns, resize the window. To change a column's width, drag the column's divider. To change all column widths simultaneously, Option-drag a divider. To resize a column to fit its widest entry (called *right-sizing*), double-click the column's divider. To resize all columns to fit their widest entries, hold down Option and then double-click a divider. Alternatively, right-click a divider to right-size a column or columns.

To navigate columns: To jump from column to column, press → or ←. To go to a specific folder, use the sidebar or Go menu. To choose an item within a column, click it, press ↑ or ↓, or type the first few letters of the item's name. To open a selected item, double-click it (Command+O) or press Command+↓.

To sort columns: Use the "Arrange By" or "Sort By" commands in the View Options dialog box (Command+J), View menu, or shortcut (right-click) menu. To swap commands or show alternative commands temporarily, hold down the Option key when you right-click or choose a menu command.

▥ This view splits the windows into two horizontal panes (to resize the panes, drag the horizontal divider up or down). The top pane shows items as a scrolling row of large preview images that you can "flip" through by using arrow keys, Tab and Shift+Tab, the mouse wheel, or the trackpad (two-finger drag). The bottom pane shows an ordinary list view. Selecting an item in the list view flips to its preview image in the top pane. Special controls appear when you point to certain types of files: a Play button plays a video file in place, for example, and circled arrows page through a PDF document without actually opening the file. This view works best for sparsely populated folders containing pictures or movies.

Quick Look

Quick Look lets you quickly preview the contents of a file or folder without opening it, switching views, or starting a program. The preview appears in a large pop-up window whose contents depend on the type of file that you're viewing. Quick Look supports share sheets and full-screen view.

Tip: To preview the selected file directly in a Finder window panel without using Quick Look, in Finder, choose View > Show Preview (Shift+Command+P).

The types of files that Quick Look natively supports include:

- Photos and graphics (GIF, JPEG, Photoshop, PNG, RAW, and TIFF)

- PDF files

- Text files

- TextEdit files

- Webpages (HTML) and Safari archives

- Audio and video formats (AAC, AIFF, H.264, MP3, MPEG-4, and so on)

- Apple iWork documents (Pages, Numbers, and Keynote)

- Microsoft Office documents (Word, Excel, and PowerPoint)

- Fonts

- vCards

Quick Look is also available in programs other than Finder. For example, you can preview:

- Webpage links in Mail

- Street addresses in Mail, Safari, and Contacts

- Spotlight results (a preview of the selected result appears in the Spotlight window)

- Any item in Mission Control or in a stack

To get third-party plugins that support other file types (such as ZIP or Adobe formats), go to *quicklookplugins.com*. Quick Look works in Finder, Time Machine, Exposé, the Trash, Messages, Spotlight, and elsewhere.

To preview items by using Quick Look: Select the item(s) and then do any of the following:

- Choose File > Quick Look (Command+Y).

- Press Spacebar.

- Click 👁 .

- Click ⚙ˇ > Quick Look.

- Right-click a selected item and then choose Quick Look.

- Tap three fingers.

Tip: To preview full screen instead of in a small window, hold down Option when you choose a Quick Look command (Option+Spacebar or Option+Command+Y, for example).

The Quick Look window opens to show the first item. To preview multiple items, press the arrow keys or click the arrow buttons in the preview window. The other controls in the preview window let you go full screen, scroll through images or pages, open or share files, and so on. To preview items that weren't in the original selection, Command-click their icons in a Finder window. To exit the Quick Look window, click ×, press Esc, or repeat any of the commands listed above.

Managing Files & Folders

To manage your information, create a folder hierarchy in your home folder and organize files within it. You can rename, move, copy, alias, label, and delete files and folders.

Creating Folders

You can create a folder on the desktop, anywhere in your home folder, in a shared location, on a network server, or anywhere you have permission.

To create a folder: On the desktop or in a folder window, choose File > New Folder (Shift+Command+N), or right-click an empty area and then choose New Folder. Type a name for the folder and then press Return. (If the New Folder command is dimmed, then you lack permission to create a folder at the current location.)

Naming Files and Folders

You can rename a file or folder to make its name longer, shorter, or more explicit. The name can contain up to 255 characters, including letters, numbers, spaces, punctuation, and symbols (_, #, &, µ, π, •, and so on). A name can't start with a dot (.) or contain a colon (:) or, in some cases, a slash (/). To use a file with a pre-OS X application, limit its name length to 31 characters. Don't rename applications or system folders.

Finder sorts files that begin with numbers numerically (1, 2, 3, 10, 200) rather than alphabetically (1, 10, 2, 200, 3), so leading zeros aren't required. Punctuation and symbols are significant for sorting; case is not. The usual way to force a file to the top of a sorted list is to start its name with a space, an underscore (_), or a tilde (~).

To rename a file or folder: Right-click it and then choose Rename. Alternatively, select it and then press Return (or click the icon's *name*, wait a moment, and then click it again). When the existing name highlights, type a new name and then press Return (or Enter or Tab) or click outside the name box. Before editing, you can press ← or → to jump to the start or end of the name. While editing, you can use the keyboard shortcuts for Cut (Command+X), Copy (Command+C), Paste (Command+V), Undo (Command+Z), and Select All (Command+A). To cancel and revert to the original name, press Esc. When you rename a file, be careful not change its filename extension accidently.

Tip: You can rename a file from the title bar by using Auto Save (page 117).

To rename a set of files or folders (batch rename): Right-click a set of selected files or folders and then choose Rename Items. You can add custom text and numbers to each filename.

Moving and Copying Files and Folders

You can move or copy files and folders to reorganize your folder structure, make backup copies in a safe location, or move files to the Shared folder to share them with other users. To copy or move items, you must select (highlight) them on the desktop or in a folder window. A progress bar appears during long operations. To cancel mid-operation, press Command+dot (.) or click ×.

Tip: If you're copying files but have to shut down your Mac or put it to sleep, macOS resumes copying later where it left off.

Same-named items can't occupy the same folder. When a naming conflict occurs, macOS asks you what to do: keep both files (under different names), stop the operation, or replace the existing file; an "Apply to All" option applies your chosen action to any further conflicts for the current operation.

You can drag items to the desktop, into an open window, or onto a folder or drive icon. The rules that determine whether an item is copied, moved, or aliased (page 98) are:

- If you drag an item to another place on the same drive, it's moved.

- If you drag an item from one drive to another, it's copied.

- If you drag a drive to another drive (a CD to a hard drive, for example), it's aliased.

- To copy an item instead of moving or aliasing it, hold down Option when you drop it.

- To move an item instead of copying or aliasing it, hold down Command when you drop it.

- To alias an item instead of moving or copying it, hold down Option+Command when you drop it.

To move or copy items by dragging: Make sure that the destination folder or icon is visible. Select the item(s) that you want to move or copy. Drag the items to the destination. As you drag, a translucent image of the selected icons moves with the pointer. The pointer itself sprouts a circled number that indicates how many items you're moving.

To move or copy items by pasting: Select the item(s) that you want to move or copy. Choose Edit > Copy (Command+C), or right-click a selected item and then choose Copy. Open the destination folder. Choose Edit > Paste (Command+V), or right-click an empty area and then choose Paste. The Copy and Paste commands are also available in the ⚙⌄ menu in the toolbar and are labeled with the selection ("Copy 2 Items" or "Paste Item", for example). To move items instead of copying them, hold down the Option key when you paste.

To move or copy items by using Finder tabs: In a Finder window, open tabs for the source and destination folders, and then drag items from the source folder and drop them onto the tab for the destination folder in the tab bar. To copy items instead of moving them, hold down the Option key when you drop. For details, see "Finder Tabs" on page 88.

To move or copy a folder by dragging its proxy icon: Make sure that the destination folder or icon is visible. Drag the proxy icon from the title bar to the destination.

To duplicate items: Select the item(s) that you want to duplicate and then do any of the following:

- Choose File > Duplicate (Command+D).

- Right-click a selected item and then choose Duplicate.

- Click ⚙⌄ > Duplicate.

- Option-drag a selected item.

To merge items: If you drag a file or folder into a folder that already contains a file or folder with the same name, Finder gives you three options:

- Cancel the operation (Stop).

- Replace the existing items with the ones that you're dragging (Replace or Replace All).

- Keep everything (Keep Both Files or Keep Both).

If you're dragging or pasting *files*, then Keep Both renames the incoming files by appending a number (2, 3,...) to their file names (the names of the existing files in the destination aren't changed). If you're pasting *folders*, then Keep Both merges the contents of the folders (renaming the files inside, if necessary). When merging folders, the Keep Both options appear when you're *pasting* a folder into a new window—not dragging it. The Keep Both options also appear when you Option-drag a folder into a new window to copy it there, or when you drag it to a different drive.

Spring-Loaded Folders

The spring-loaded folders feature pops open closed folders automatically so that you can drop items into a nested folder without first opening it.

To set up spring-loaded folders: Choose > System Preferences > Accessibility > Mouse & Trackpad. Select the "Spring-loading delay" checkbox and then drag the slider to adjust the delay until a folder opens automatically.

To use spring-loaded folders: Drag an item (or group of items) onto a folder or drive icon (or onto a location in the sidebar). Keep the mouse button pressed and hover the pointer over the icon until it opens automatically (or press Spacebar to open it immediately). Either release the mouse button to drop the selection in the current folder or hover the pointer over an inner folder to open it automatically, and so on. If a target folder isn't visible, drag near the window's edge to autoscroll to it.

Tip: Even when spring-loaded folders is turned off, you still can press Spacebar to open a folder that you're dragging to.

Aliases

An **alias** is a convenient link to a file, folder, drive, or program. When you double-click an alias, its linked item opens. You can create an alias to any item and store it anywhere; it's a tiny file. A small curved arrow distinguishes an alias from the original item to which it's linked.

Memo to self.txt

Moving or renaming an alias or the original won't break the link. Deleting an alias has no effect on the original. (An alias is the same as a Windows *shortcut*.)

To alias items: Select the item(s) that you want to alias and then do any of the following:

- Choose File > Make Alias (Command+L).

- Right-click a selected item and then choose Make Alias.

- Click ⚙ˇ > Make Alias.

- Option-Command-drag a selected item.

To show the original items linked to aliases: Select an alias (or group of aliases) and then do any of the following:

- Choose File > Show Original (Command+R).

- Right-click a selected alias and then choose Show Original.

- Click ⚙ˇ > Show Original.

To alias a webpage: In your web browser, go to the page that you want to alias. Drag the address (URL) text or the small icon on the left end of the address bar to the desktop or a folder window. (The resulting file isn't a true alias, but it acts like one.)

Tags

Tags are meaningful words and phrases that you can assign to files and folders to make them easy to sort and find—tag a batch of photos with *san francisco* and *2015*, for example. macOS comes with some sample tags (Red, Green, Home, Work, Important, and so on) that you can use, edit, or delete, and you can create your own tags to describe and organize your files.

Tip: The built-in colored tags (Red, Orange, and so on) are holdovers from earlier versions of macOS, where they were called colored labels. On pre-Mavericks Macs (OS X 10.9 or earlier), files with colored tags behave like files with colored labels. If a file has more than one colored tag assigned to it, only the most recently applied colored tag is visible.

Finding tagged files. In the sidebar of every Finder window (and in some Open dialog boxes), is a Tags list showing recently used tags. Click a tag to show all the files on your Mac that have that tag. Or click All Tags to open a complete list of tags. If you start typing the name of a tag in a Finder window's search box, an option to search for files that have that tag appears. Note that you can't select multiple tags in the sidebar; instead, use Spotlight search (page 103) to find files with any or all of a set of tags.

Tip: You can drag a tag from the Finder sidebar to the dock for quick access to all the files with that tag.

Setting up tags in Finder. You can identify tagged files by color as well as by keyword. To set up tags in Finder, choose Finder > Preferences > Tags pane.

To rename, delete, or assign a color to a tag, right-click the tag in the list. To reorder tags in the sidebar, drag tags up or down the list. To choose which tags appear in the sidebar, select or clear the checkboxes in the list. To choose which tags appear in Finder's File, shortcut (right-click), and ⚙︎⌄ menus, drag tags from the list to the Favorite Tags box.

When a tag that's never been added to any file is added to a file for the first time, that tag appears automatically in the Finder sidebar and a crossbar (instead of a checkmark) appears in its checkbox in Finder Preferences.

Tip: You can also edit or reorder tags by right-clicking or dragging them directly in the sidebar. To show or hide the Tags list in the sidebar, choose Finder > Preferences > Sidebar pane > Tags.

Tag indicators in file lists. In file lists in Finder windows, a small colored circle appears next to the name of each file tagged with a color. If a file has multiple colored tags, an overlapping stack of colored circles appears, up to a maximum of three, showing the three most recently applied thereafter. (No circle appears for tags assigned no color.)

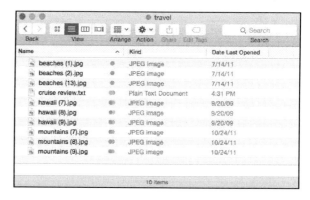

Tagging files in apps. You can add tags to a file when you first save it in an app. The standard Save dialog box (page 117) has a Tags box where you can tag the file. You can choose an existing tag in the pop-up suggestions list, or type to create a new tag.

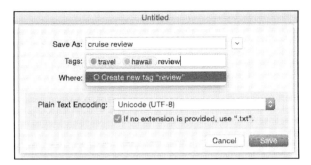

To accept a suggestion, click it or press Return. If you're typing a new tag, select Create New Tag or type a comma—tags are essentially lists of comma-separated items, meaning your tags can be more than one word long, if you like. macOS remembers the tags that you've already created and offers them as autocomplete suggestions. After naming and tagging your file, click Save. The tags live with the file, whether you copy, move, or rename it.

You can also hover the pointer over the document name in a window's title bar and then click the small arrowhead ▼ that appears. The pop-up menu lets you edit that document's tags. For details, see "Auto Save and Versions" on page 117.

Tagging files in Finder. You can also tag selected files and folders via Finder:

- Click the Edit Tags button ⬭ in the toolbar. The process of adding or creating tags here is the same as that for the Save dialog box.

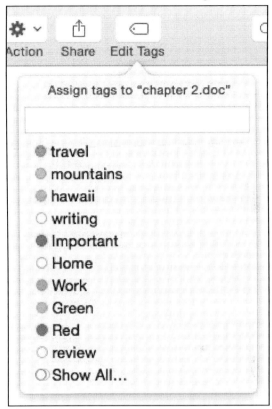

- Drag files or folders onto a tag in the sidebar to add that tag to those items.

- Choose the Tags command in the File, shortcut (right-click), or ⚙ ˅ menu.

- Add tags in an item's Info window (select the file or folder and then choose File > Get Info or press Command+I).

Tip: You can also tag documents stored in iCloud Drive.

Deleting Files and Folders

 When you delete a file or folder, it's not actually erased but moved to the Trash (in the dock). The Trash is a safeguard from which you can recover (undelete) items if you change your mind or delete them permanently. The Trash's icon tells you whether it contains deleted items or is empty.

Emptying the Trash doesn't actually destroy data; it just makes those data harder to find. macOS doesn't erase files but *marks* them as deleted, making them invisible to you and to programs but leaving their data intact. Only when macOS needs drive space later will it overwrite deleted files with newly created ones.

To protect a file or folder from accidental deletion, lock it by selecting the Locked checkbox in its Info window (page 32).

To set up the Trash: In Finder, choose Finder > Preferences > Advanced pane. To autodelete old items, select "Remove items from the Trash after 30 days". To suppress confirmation messages, clear "Show warning before emptying the Trash". (Even if this option is turned on, you can suppress warnings by holding down Option when you empty the Trash.)

To move files and folders to the Trash: Select the item(s) to trash and then do any of the following:

- Choose File > Move to Trash (Command+Delete).

- Right-click a selected item and then choose Move to Trash.

- Click ⚙ ⌄ > Move to Trash.

- Drag a selected item to the Trash icon in the dock.

To recover items from the Trash: Click the Trash icon to open it and then drag the desired items out of the Trash window. To recover an item that you *just* deleted, choose Edit > Undo (Command+Z). To restore selected items to their original locations, choose Put Back (Command+Delete) from the File menu, shortcut (right-click) menu, or ⚙ ⌄ menu.

To empty the Trash: Choose Finder > Empty Trash (Shift+Command+Delete), or right-click (or click-and-hold) the Trash icon in the dock and then choose Empty Trash.

To erase a drive securely: Choose Applications > Utilities > Disk Utility > select the drive > Erase > Security Options.

Compressing Files and Folders

 Compressing files and folders reduces the space they occupy on your drives (fixed or removable). macOS uses the standard **ZIP** compression scheme, Archive.zip which is useful for emailing large attachments, archiving files that you no longer use regularly, transferring files over the internet or via FTP, and gaining the maximum amount of drive space.

To compress files and folders: Select the item(s) that you want to compress and then do any of the following:

- Choose File > Compress.

- Right-click a selected item and then choose Compress.

- Click ⚙ ⌄ > Compress.

A single item is compressed into a file of the same name, but with the extension .zip. Multiple items are compressed into a file named Archive.zip (you can rename it).

To uncompress a ZIP archive: Double-click it. If the ZIP archive contains multiple items, a folder with the same name as the archive appears, containing uncompressed copies of the original items.

Spotlight

> 🔍 Spotlight Search

Spotlight, macOS's search feature, returns results instantly and is available systemwide. You can trigger the main Spotlight window from the menu bar or use Spotlight search boxes in search windows, the System Preferences window, any Finder window, Open and Save dialog boxes, and Help menus. Spotlight is also available in some applications, including Photos, iTunes, and Mail.

You can find all files that meet certain criteria, including:

- File names containing specific text
- Files containing a specific phrase
- Files of a given file type (type *.doc* or *.docx* for Word files, for example)
- Files with specific tags (page 99)
- Documents written by a given author
- Photos taken before or after a certain date
- Photos of certain people (using the Faces feature in the Photos application)
- Photos taken at a certain place (using the Places feature in the Photos application)
- Graphics wider than a fixed number of pixels
- People in your Messages buddy lists
- Files downloaded from a specific source (type *google.com*, for example, to find programs that you downloaded from that site)
- Messages from a specific sender (a name or email address)

Tip: Spotlight can find words inside files on other computers on your network, provided they're Macs running Leopard (OS X 10.5) or later. If not, Spotlight can search for only the names of files on other networked computers.

When you type in a search box 🔍 Search , Spotlight returns a results list or filters the view based on what you're typing. You can type things like file and folder names, tags, program names, text contained within a file, file types, and file attributes (metadata).

Spotlight can find:

- Files and folders
- Installed applications
- Media files (video, audio, and images)
- PDF documents
- iWork documents (Pages, Numbers, and Keynote)
- Microsoft Office documents (Word, Excel, PowerPoint, Outlook, OneNote, and Entourage)
- Safari bookmarks and history
- System Preferences
- Email
- Messages transcripts
- Contacts
- Calendar events
- Reminders
- Dictionary definitions
- Fonts
- Recently used documents (type the name of the application that you were working in)

You can set preferences to expand or limit the scope of the search.

In some cases, Spotlight is context sensitive, basing its results on your current location and activity. Searching from the System Preferences window, for example, finds only relevant System Preferences tasks; and searching from Photos finds matching pictures only in your photo library.

Tip: You can also find files by using the **mdfind** command in Terminal.

Other Types of Search Results

In addition to files, folders, applications, and settings, Spotlight can find:

- Locations in Apple Maps

- Digital media in the iTunes and iBooks stores

- Software in the Mac App Store

- Wikipedia articles

- Bing.com search results and Safari Top Hit

- Unit conversions (type *100 yards* to get 91.44 meters or type *2 square miles in acres*)

- Currency conversions (type *100 euros* or *100 USD in yen*)

- Mathematical calculations (type *6*7* to get 42)

- Movie information and local showtimes (type *movies* or the name of a movie)

- Local restaurants (type *pizza*)

- Weather (type *chicago weather*)

- Sports scores, rosters, and schedules (type *giants vs dolphins* or *yankees roster*)

- Stock prices (type *AAPL*)

- Web videos from YouTube, Vimeo, and Vevo (type *baby panda sneezing*)

- Transit information for certain major cities (type *7th ave subway* or *grand central*)

Tip: You can toggle and reorder Spotlight's search categories in > System Preferences > Spotlight > Search Results pane.

Search Tips

- Search text is case-insensitive: Spotlight considers *Egg*, *egg*, and *EGG* to be the same search term.

- In a search box, you can use the keyboard shortcuts for Cut (Command+X), Copy (Command+C), Paste (Command+V), Undo (Command+Z), and Select All (Command+A).

- Spotlight usually lists results instantly, but you don't have to wait until a search ends to open an item in the results list.

- When searching for a partial word, search for the initial letters. If you're searching for *bicycle*, for example, type *bic* rather than *cyc*.

- Spotlight lists results from only your user account and the public system folders; not anyone else's home folder.

- If a search spans multiple drives, drive names appear in the results list.

- Typing the first few letters of a program's name in Spotlight is often the fastest way to open that program.

- Spotlight can evaluate mathematical expressions like *2.3+3* and *pow(exp(sqrt(pi)), log(3))*. Press Command+C to copy the result to the clipboard. For a list of functions, type the command **man math** in Terminal.

- Unit conversions support **volume** (teaspoons, tablespoons, cups, pints, quarts, gallons, cubic feet, fluid ounces, centiliters, milliliters, liters, cubic feet, cubic inches, cubic meters); **weight and mass** (pounds, ounces, kilograms, grams, milligrams, short tons, metric tonnes, long tons); **area** (acres, hectares, square feet, square yards, square meters, square kilometers); **temperature** (Fahrenheit, Celsius, Kelvin, abbreviated F, C, or K); **force** (joules, calories, foot pounds, newton meters, British thermal units); and **power** (watts, kilowatts, BTUs per minute). To name a few.

- Spotlight (and Mail) respond to searches phrased in **natural language**, but it can be hit-or-miss. Experiment. Some examples: "pictures that I took in Yellowstone National Park in June 2015", "emails from July", "files that I worked on yesterday", "photos from yesterday", "slides from 2014 containing IniTech", and "images from last year". In general, Spotlight understands file types ("documents", "movies", "images", "presentations", "email", and so on), the words and phrases inside each file, dates and times, and the names of email senders or recipients.

Advanced Searches

If a search returns too many results, you can refine it by specifying quoted phrases, metadata (data about data) attributes, and boolean operators:

Quotes

Surround a search phrase with quotes to find files or attributes that contain that exact phrase. *"aspen tree"* finds files in which *aspen* and *tree* are right next to each other, in that order. Without the quotes, the results would include items that contain any of those words, in any order, not necessarily next to each other.

Attributes

Most items contain metadata attributes about their own content (the creation date of a document or the resolution of a photo, for example). Separate the attribute name and the search value with a colon (:). For example, *author:stewart* finds only files with *stewart* in the Author field; *kind:pdf* finds PDF files; and *kind:folder* finds only folders.

Use the <, <=, >, >=, and - operators to specify numerical and date ranges. For example, *modified:1/1/2014-1/1/2015* finds files modified during a one-year date range. *width:>=800* finds all images that are 800 or more pixels wide.

For yes/no (or true/false) attributes, use 1 (one) for yes and 0 (zero) for no. For example, *flash:1* finds all photos that were taken with the camera's flash on and *flash:0* finds photos taken with the flash off.

For Finder tag values (page 99), use the *tag:* search prefix. For example, search for *tag:important* to find files that you've tagged as Important.

To restrict a search chronologically, use a date keyword: *this year, this month, this week, yesterday, today, tomorrow, next week, next month,* or *next year*. The latter four items, which specify future dates, are useful for finding upcoming Calendar events. For example, *date:yesterday* finds files that you last opened yesterday; *modified:today* finds files that you changed today; and *created:this year* finds files that you created since January 1.

You can string words together. For example, *created:today kind:pdf* finds all PDFs that you created today, and *created:today kind:pdf coastal* further restricts the search to PDFs created today that contain the word *coastal*.

You can view a file's metadata attributes in its Info window (page 32). If an attribute has a space in its name—*pixel width, musical genre,* or *phone number*, for example—then omit the space in the Spotlight search (*pixelwidth:, musicalgenre:,* or *phonenumber:*).

Boolean operators

Type AND, OR, and NOT in uppercase to combine search words by using boolean logic. *word1 AND word2* finds both *word1* and *word2*, even if those words aren't next to each other. *word1 OR word2* finds either *word1* or *word2* (or both). NOT *word* excludes *word* from the search; *aspen NOT tree*, for example, finds files or attributes that contain *aspen* but not *tree*. A hyphen (-) is shorthand for AND NOT: *aspen -tree* is the same as *aspen AND NOT tree*. Parentheses are shorthand for AND: *(word1 word2)* is the same as *word1* AND *word2*. Booleans work with attribute searches: *kind:pdf OR kind:jpeg* shows both PDF files and JPEG photos in a single results list.

Using Spotlight

To set up Spotlight: Choose > System Preferences > Spotlight. In the Search Results pane, specify the categories and order in which results appear, and the keystrokes that activate Spotlight. In the Privacy pane, specify any drives or folders that you don't want Spotlight to track for privacy reasons (Spotlight rebuilds its entire search index whenever you modify this list).

Tip: For privacy, turn off Spotlight Suggestions in Spotlight (> System Preferences > Spotlight > Search Results) and in Safari (Safari > Preferences > Search > Safari Suggestions). Turning off this setting prevents your search terms and location from being sent to Apple and third parties.

To search from the Spotlight window: Click Q in the menu bar or press Command+Spacebar. Type text in the Spotlight Search box. As you type, items that match your text appear in the results list, grouped by category (Top Hit, Applications, Definition, System Preferences, Documents, Folders, PDF Documents, Images, and so on). A preview of the selected result appears to the right of the results list.

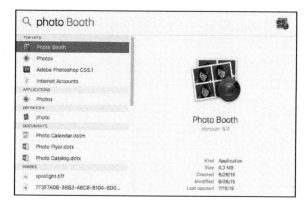

In the Spotlight window, do any of the following:

- To see a preview of an item in the results list, click it, or use the arrow keys to select it.

Tip: Your search might *end* with a glance at the preview pane if you're looking for a simple bit of info like a phone number or unit conversion. To copy content from the preview pane, drag through it and then press Command+C.

- To open an item in the results list, double-click it, or use the arrow keys to select it and then press Return.

- To open the item that Spotlight has autoselected (the Top Hit), press Return. Spotlight chooses the Top Hit based on its relevance (the importance of your search term inside that item) and timeliness (when you last opened it).

- To show an item's location, hold down Command and then click it. The folder path appears at the bottom of the preview pane.

- To show an item in a Finder window instead of opening it, hold down Command and then double-click it, or use the arrow keys to select it and then press Command+Return.

- To see a complete list of results instead of only the best matches, double-click "Show all in Finder" at the bottom of the results list.

- To jump from category to category in the results list, press Command+↓ or Command+↑.

- Drag and drop an item from the Spotlight window (onto the desktop, into a window or a folder, into the Trash, to an email message, onto the AirDrop icon in the sidebar, to another drive, and so on).

- To get Info about an item, select it and then press Command+I.

- To clear the search text, backspace over it or press Esc.

- To cancel the search, press Command+Spacebar, press Esc twice, or click off the Spotlight window.

Tip: You can resize and move the Spotlight window. To restore the window to its original size and position, click-and-hold Q in the menu bar.

To search from a search window: Do any of the following:

- To search from the current folder, in Finder, choose File > Find (Command+F) or File > New Smart Folder (Option+Command+N).

- To search all your files starting from a new window, press Option+Command+Spacebar.

- To start from any Finder window, click in the search box in the upper-right corner (the window will change into a search window when you start to type).

The search results will be the same for all the preceding starting points.

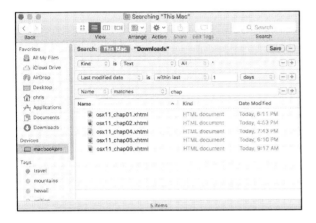

In the search window, do any of the following:

- To do a basic search, type text in the search box. As you type, items that match your text appear in the window. To clear the search text, click × or backspace over it.

- To change the scope of the search, click a location in the location bar: This Mac (includes external drives), *"current_folder"*, or Shared (includes networked computers). To change the default scope, choose Finder > Preferences > Advanced pane > "When performing a search".

- To specify search criteria, click + on the right side of the location bar. Use the menus and controls on the criteria bar to refine the search results. Click + or − to add or remove rows as needed. Each row is connected with the preceding one by using AND logic (that is, the results must match all rows).

- To find hidden files, set a criteria bar to Other > File invisible > Invisible items.

- To save the search results as a smart folder, click Save in the location bar.

Smart Folders

If you work regularly with a certain group of files and do the same search repeatedly to find them, you can save your search as a **smart folder**. When you open a smart folder, Spotlight repeats the search and then lists the most-current files that match the original search criteria. Finder includes the All My Files smart folder in the sidebar's Favorites section, where you can add your own smart folders. Smart folders are actually files with the extension .savedSearch, stored by default in ~/Library/Saved Searches (~ denotes your home folder). They can be copied, moved, renamed, and deleted like any other files.

To create a smart folder: Use a Spotlight search window to find your files. Click Save on the right side of the location bar. Specify the folder's name and location, and choose whether it appears in the sidebar. (You can drag smart folders on or off the sidebar at any time.)

To open a smart folder (run the search): Click the smart folder in the sidebar, or double-click it on the desktop or in a folder window.

To edit a smart folder: Open the smart folder (run the search), choose ⚙ ˅ > Show Search Criteria, make the desired changes, and then resave the folder.

Burning CDs & DVDs

If your Mac has an internal or external Combo drive or SuperDrive, you can **burn** (copy) files to a writable disc. Combo drives can burn to writable CDs (but not DVDs). SuperDrives can burn to most writable CDs and DVDs. You can burn a disc quickly by dragging files to it and then using the Burn command, or you can create a burn folder. The burn-folder method saves space (because it doesn't make temporary copies of the files to burn), lets you burn the same disc multiple times (each time with the latest versions of your files), and doesn't require you to have a blank disc on hand. You can't burn discs on a remote (networked) drive. macOS might not recognize an inserted disc if you're running VMware or Parallels virtual-machine software. iTunes can also burn discs. To set the default action for an inserted disc, use CDs & DVDs preferences (page 64).

To determine which kinds of discs you can burn: Choose Applications > Utilities > System Information > Hardware > Disc Burning.

To burn a disc by dragging files to it: Insert a writable CD or DVD into the disc burner. If a dialog box appears, choose Open Finder and then click OK. Double-click the disc's icon on the desktop. Drag to the disc's window the files and folders that you want to burn (alternatively, you can drop items on the disc icon without opening it). The items appear as aliases, which you can add, delete, or rename (the original files aren't changed). The status bar shows the remaining disc space. To burn the disc, do any of the following, and then follow the on-screen instructions:

- Choose File > Burn.
- Drag the disc icon to the Trash.
- Click the Burn icon next to the disc's name in the sidebar.
- Click the Burn button in the disc window.

To create a burn folder: In Finder, choose File > New Burn Folder. Type a name for the folder, and then press Return.

To add items to a burn folder: Drag the files and folders that you want to burn to the burn folder. The items appear as aliases, which you can add, delete, and rename (the original files aren't changed). The status bar shows the total size of the items.

To burn a disc: Select the burn folder and then do any of the following:

- Choose File > Burn.
- Click the Burn button in the burn-folder window.
- If the burn folder is in the sidebar, click the burn icon beside it. Insert a writable CD or DVD into the disc burner, and then follow the onscreen instructions.

To eject a disc: Quit any programs that are using files on the disc and then do any of the following:

- Select the disc's icon and then choose File > Eject (Command+E).
- Drag the disc's icon to the Trash.
- Click the Eject button ⏏ next to the disc's name in the sidebar.
- Hold down the Eject key ⏏ until the disc ejects.
- Right-click the disc's icon and then choose Eject.
- Click the Eject icon (if there is one) in the menu bar.
- Hold down the left mouse button or F12 key when you start or restart your computer.
- If your drive has an eject hole, put the computer to sleep and then firmly push a straightened paper clip into the hole.

If a busy disc won't eject, macOS will open a dialog box telling you which program is using the disc. Switch to that program, quit it, and then eject the disc.

To duplicate a disc: Choose Applications > Utilities > Disk Utility > select the disc > Restore.

Drives

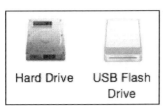

Hard Drive   USB Flash Drive

Macs recognize internal and external hard drives (spinning disk or solid state), USB flash drives, CDs, DVDs, network servers, and mobile devices such as smartphones, media players, ereaders, and iOS Devices (in their role as removable storage). When you insert a disc or connect a drive or device, its icon appears on the right side of the desktop, in the sidebar, and in the Computer window (Shift+Command+C). To see what's on a drive, double-click its icon.

When you start your Mac, it looks for a system or startup drive (that is, one that has a System folder). If it can't find one, it waits until you insert a disc or connect a drive with a bootable System folder. Installing macOS onto a hard drive (internal or external) or DVD turns it into a startup drive. If multiple startup drives are connected, you can choose which one to boot from. You can also use Disk Utility (page 126) to manage drives.

To show or hide drives on the desktop: In Finder, choose Finder > Preferences > General pane > "Show these items on the desktop".

To eject a removable drive: Quit all programs that are using files on the drive and then do any of the following:

- Select the drive icon and then choose File > Eject (Command+E).

- Drag the drive's icon to the Trash.

- Click the Eject button ⏏ next to the drive's name in the sidebar.

- Right-click the drive's icon and then choose Eject.

Tip: For more ways to eject CDs and DVDs, see "Burning CDs & DVDs" on page 108.

To choose a startup drive: Choose > System Preferences > Startup Disk (click 🔒 if the settings are dimmed). See also "Startup" on page 12.

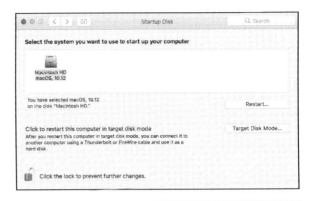

Tip: To select the current startup drive, in Finder, hold down the Shift key and then choose Go > Select Startup Disk on Desktop.

To repair a drive: Choose Applications > Utilities > Disk Utility > select the drive > First Aid.

To erase a drive: Choose Applications > Utilities > Disk Utility > select the drive > Erase. To secure-erase the drive (to make its contents unrecoverable), click Security Options. You can't erase the current startup drive or write-only CDs and DVDs.

To copy or restore a drive image: Choose Applications > Utilities > Disk Utility > select the drive > Restore.

To encrypt a (nonsystem) drive: In Finder or on the desktop, right-click the drive icon and then choose Encrypt. See also "FileVault" on page 179.

CHAPTER 5

Programs & Documents

MacOS is a launching pad for programs, or **applications** (or **apps**, for short). Apple and sound design enforce substantial consistency, so you can apply knowledge of a few common operations to many programs. Most programs share user-interface elements—scrollbars, copy-and-paste operations, menus, buttons, dialog boxes, and so on—as well as setup and management options. macOS provides consistent ways to manage programs and **documents**, which are self-contained pieces of work (files) that you create with programs.

Installing & Removing Programs

How you install a program depends on where its installation files are located. Most shrink-wrapped programs are installed from a CD or DVD. You can also install programs that you've downloaded from the internet, a local network, or the Mac App Store (> App Store). Programs from the App Store are downloaded, installed, and updated automatically; programs from other sources require some manual labor. macOS's **Gatekeeper** security feature helps prevent you from inadvertently installing viruses, spyware, and other **malware** (malicious software). Gatekeeper works by restricting which downloaded apps you can install.

TextWrangler.dmg

A downloaded program lands by default in your Downloads folder (which is in your home folder). If the file arrives as a **disk image** (.dmg file), then you can start the installation.

If the program arrives as a compressed file, then you must decompress it before you install. The usual compression formats are:

ZIP (.zip files)
A standard format that macOS can decompress natively (double-click the file to decompress it).

StuffIt (.sit files)
A proprietary format that the widely available, free program StuffIt Expander (*stuffit.com/mac-expander.html*) can decompress.

Unix formats (.tar, .gz, .tar.gz, and .tgz files)
Standard formats that macOS can decompress natively (double-click the file to decompress it).

The decompressed file will contain a .dmg file and possibly other files, such as release notes, readme files, special instructions, or companion utilities.

To enable app installations (Gatekeeper): Choose > System Preferences > Security & Privacy > General pane (click if the settings are dimmed).

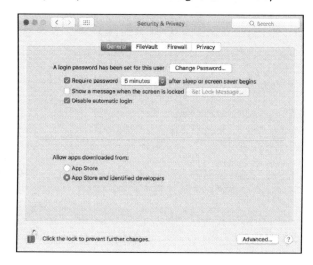

Under "Allow apps downloaded from", choose one of the following options:

App Store
Download and run apps from only the Mac App Store. The App Store is the safest place to get apps because it's curated, meaning that Apple vets the developers and reviews their apps before accepting them to the store. If there's a problem with an app, Apple removes it from the store. Before you download and install an app, you can read reviews from other users.

App Store and identified developers

Download and run App Store apps and non-App Store apps that have a Developer ID. Developers that register with Apple get a unique Developer ID, which they can use to digitally sign the apps that they create. This digital signature is cryptographically secure and lets Gatekeeper verify that the app hasn't been tampered with since it left the hands of the developer. Signed apps aren't necessarily sold through the App Store and aren't pre-screened by Apple, but if Apple discovers any problems with apps created by a registered developer, they can block that developer's apps and revoke their credentials. macOS updates its list of blacklisted developers once each day.

Tip: You can also set security policy by using the `spctl` command in Terminal. The command `sudo spctl --master-disable` disables Gatekeeper and brings back the "Anywhere" option, which lets you download and run apps from anywhere.

Gatekeeper works only the first time that you try to launch an app, and only when that app has been downloaded via a web browser, an email client, or a similar program (Gatekeeper doesn't check apps copied from USB or network drives, and won't stop Flash and Java programs). After an app has been launched once, it's beyond the reach of Gatekeeper.

Tip: To manually override your Gatekeeper setting, right-click an unsigned app in Finder and then choose Open.

To install a program: If you have an installation CD or DVD, insert it, double-click its desktop icon if it doesn't auto-open, and
Installer then follow the onscreen instructions. If you have a .dmg file, double-click it. The disk image will appear as a new drive icon on the desktop.

Double-click the drive icon to open the installer window. Drag the program's icon to the Applications folder or to your home folder, or double-click the installer (if it appears) and then follow the onscreen instructions.

If you're an administrator, you can install a program in:

- The Applications system folder (page 121), where everyone can use it.

- Your home folder (page 86), where only you can see and use it.

- The Applications subfolder in your home folder, where everyone can see and use it but only you can uninstall it.

Nonadministrators can install in only their home folder (or its subfolders).

After installation, you can eject the disk-image (drive) icon and delete the original compressed file and the .dmg file (unless you need to reinstall someday).

To uninstall a program: Drag it (or its folder) from the Applications folder (or your home folder) to the Trash. (Unlike Windows programs, macOS programs usually don't have separate uninstall utilities.) Uninstalled programs sometimes leave minor parts of themselves behind, typically in /Library/Application Support and /Library/Preferences in the system folder and in your home folder. If you downloaded a program from the App Store, you can use Launchpad (page 115) to uninstall it.

To see a program's support files: Right-click its icon in a Finder window, and then choose Show Package Contents.

Opening, Switching & Quitting Programs

An open program appears in the dock (with a dot next to its icon if you've selected > System Preferences > Dock > "Show indicators for open applications"). Only one program at a time is **active** (frontmost, receiving your keystrokes). The bolded application menu, next to the menu, identifies the active program. Quitting a program lets macOS reclaim its memory for other use. If an individual program **freezes** ("hangs"), you can **force-quit** (and then re-open) it without destabilizing or restarting macOS. The "spinning beachball" cursor is a sign of a frozen program. Force-quitting loses any unsaved changes.

To open a program: Do any of the following:

- Click its icon in the dock or sidebar.
- Click the Applications stack in the dock and then click the program's icon.
- Press Command+Spacebar to open the Spotlight search window, type the first few letters of the program's name until it highlights, and then press Return. (This is usually the *fastest* way to open a program, especially if the program has no dock icon.)
- Choose > Recent Items > Applications submenu.
- Double-click its icon in a Finder window (hold down Option to autoclose the window).
- Select its icon and then choose File > Open (Command+O or Command+ ↓).
- Open any document associated with the program.
- Use Launchpad (page 115).
- Use the **open** command in Terminal.

To restore your previous document windows when re-opening programs: Choose > System Preferences > General > clear "Close windows when quitting an app". See also "Auto Save and Versions" on page 117.

To open a program automatically at login: Choose > System Preferences > Users & Groups > Login Items pane.

To switch to an open program: Do any of the following:

- If any of the program's windows is visible in the background, click it.
- Click its dock icon.
- Use Exposé or Spaces.
- Command+Tab to it.

To use Command+Tab: Hold down Command and press Tab repeatedly until the desired program highlights in the pop-up list, and then release both keys (to cycle backward, press Shift+Command+Tab). If you release Tab but keep Command pressed, you can click an icon in the list. If you press and release Command+Tab quickly, you swap between only two programs instead of cycling through them all.

To switch to the next window of the active program: Press Command+~ (or Shift+Command+~).

To quit a program: Do any of the following:

- Choose Quit from the program's application menu (Command+Q).
- Right-click (or click-and-hold) its dock icon, and then choose Quit.
- Command+Tab to highlight its icon, and then press Q without releasing the Command key.

To force-quit a program: Do any of the following:

- Choose > Force Quit (Option+Command+Esc).
- Right-click (or click-and-hold) its dock icon, hold down Option, and then choose Force Quit.
- In Terminal, use the `kill` command (type `man kill` for usage).

Launchpad

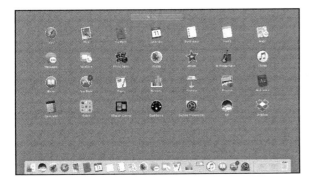

Launchpad displays a full-screen grid of application icons that lets you open, switch, or (in some cases) delete apps. All apps installed on your computer—specifically, in the /Applications and ~/Applications folders—appear automatically, including those downloaded from the App Store. New Launchpad pages sprout automatically to accommodate an icon overflow as you add more apps. (Launchpad mimics the Home screen of iOS devices like the iPad or iPhone.)

To show Launchpad: Do any of the following:

- Click the Launchpad (rocket ship) icon in the dock or in the Applications folder.

- Pinch three fingers and your thumb (**🍎** > System Preferences > Trackpad > More Gestures pane).

- Press the Launchpad key F4 ▦ (on newer Macs).

- Press the Launchpad keyboard shortcut (**🍎** > System Preferences > Keyboard > Shortcuts pane > Launchpad & Dock > Show Launchpad).

- Move the pointer into one of the screen's four corners (**🍎** > System Preferences > Mission Control > Hot Corners > Launchpad).

To dismiss Launchpad without opening an app, press the keyboard shortcut again, reverse the multitouch gesture, press Esc, or click an empty area.

To open or activate an app from Launchpad: Do any of the following:

- Click or tap the app's icon.

- Use the arrow keys to highlight the target app and then press Return.

- In the search box at the top of the screen, type the first few letters of the app's name until it highlights, and then press Return. (You don't need to click in the search box; just start typing as soon as Launchpad opens.)

To switch among Launchpad pages: Do any of the following:

- Drag the pointer left or right on an empty area.

- Flick two fingers left or right.

- Hold down Command and then press the left or right arrow key.

To rearrange Launchpad icons: Drag icons within a page or off the edge of one page and onto the next. (You can also drag icons from Launchpad to the dock).

To group apps into folders in Launchpad: To create a folder, drag one app's icon over another, and then drag other apps to add to the folder. To change a folder's name, click the folder to open it, click the current name, and then type the new name. To move an app out of a folder, click the folder to open it, and then drag the app out of the folder.

To uninstall an app from Launchpad: Click-and-hold any app icon (or press-and-hold the Option key) until all the icons wiggle. Click the target app's ⊗ button to uninstall the app. If an icon doesn't have a ⊗ button, you can't uninstall it by using Launchpad. You can always uninstall apps downloaded from the App Store and reinstall them for free at any time.

Resume

When you open an app, it starts where you left off the last time you ran it, with the same windows open in the same positions. Resume also works when you log out of macOS or shut down your Mac: log back in or restart and all the apps that you were using automatically relaunch with the same open windows.

If you prefer a clean desktop, you can turn off this feature: choose > System Preferences > General > select "Close windows when quitting an app". This setting stops macOS from opening windows when you open an app, but doesn't affect how Resume works when you log in or restart. To turn off Resume, when you log out or restart, clear "Reopen windows when logging back in".

Running Older Programs

If you're upgrading from an older version of macOS, consider the following changes that have been made to macOS over the years:

- OS X 10.8 (Mountain Lion) and later don't include **X11**, an environment used to host X Window System programs (graphical Unix apps that don't supply a native macOS interface). If you launch an X11-dependent program, macOS prompts you to install X11 separately.

- In OS X 10.7 (Lion), Apple stopped supporting all **PowerPC** applications, including Photoshop CS2, Quicken 2007, Microsoft Office 2004, AppleWorks, and many classic games. The translation software that runs PowerPC apps, called **Rosetta**, isn't available as an optional add-on; to run PowerPC apps, partition your hard drive and dual boot to OS X 10.6 (Snow Leopard) or earlier. Lion also doesn't include the **Java Development Kit** (JDK), which must be installed separately.

- In OS X 10.5 (Leopard), Apple stopped supporting "Classic" mode, which ran pre-Intel, pre-2001, OS 9 programs.

- **Cocoa** and **Carbon** refer to the programming libraries ("APIs") that the program's developers used to create it. Cocoa programs are true macOS programs. Carbon programs look (and mostly behave) like true macOS programs but really are repackaged versions of older OS 9 programs—"Carbonized" programs can't use all macOS's special features. With each new version of macOS, Apple deprecates (phases out) more parts of Carbon.

Saving Documents

Most applications let you save your work as documents, which you can return to later, print, send to other people, back up, delete, and so on. Nearly all programs use macOS's standard Save dialog box. The first time that you save a document, macOS asks you to name it and pick a location to store it in. (Two files in the same folder can't have the same name.)

Tip: To perform common file operations, you can right-click, drag, Command-drag (move), or Option-drag (copy) files in the Save dialog box.

To save a document: To save the document in its current state, choose File > Save (Command+S). To save a copy of a file under a different name or in a different folder, choose File > Save As (Option+Shift+Command+S) or File > Duplicate (Shift+Command+S).

Tip: If the Save As command doesn't appear in the File menu, hold down the Option key when the menu is open.

To use Finder-like navigation to choose a destination for the file, click ⌄ to expand the dialog box (you can drag a folder icon from the desktop or a Finder window to the expanded dialog box to jump to that location). You can use the search box to find a destination folder quickly. If the application

supports iCloud storage, you can choose it in the iCloud section of the sidebar. In the Save As box, type the name of the file. While editing, you can use the keyboard shortcuts for Cut (Command+X), Copy (Command+C), Paste (Command+V), Undo (Command+Z), and Select All (Command+A). Name the file according to macOS's file-naming rules (page 96). Many programs offer the option to save a file in a format other than the program's default (native) format.

Tip: The standard Save dialog box also lets you add tags to documents (page 99).

Auto Save and Versions

Documents in applications that support macOS's **Auto Save** feature are saved automatically in the background, without pauses or progress bars (meaning you don't have to press Command+S every few minutes). Auto Save saves during pauses in your work and, if you work continuously, it will save after 5 minutes.

Tip: If you prefer to be prompted to save changes, choose > System Preferences > General > select "Ask to keep changes when closing documents".

The **Versions** feature lets you save and browse past versions of documents by using a Time Machine-like interface (page 188) that shows document snapshots cascading back to earlier versions. Versions automatically creates a new version of a document each time that you open it and every hour while you're working on it. You can also create versions manually (choose File > Save or press Command+S). Versions doesn't actually create a copy of a document for each new version (otherwise, your drive would quickly fill to capacity); instead, Versions saves only the *changes* ("deltas", in geekspeak) to the document over time and applies them as needed to show different versions of the original. When you share a document with someone, you share only the most recent version.

Applications that support Auto Save and Versions include some built-in macOS apps (TextEdit, Preview, and Automator, for example) and Apple iWork (Pages, Numbers, and Keynote). Third-party developers are free to update their own apps to support Auto Save and Versions. To use Auto Save and Versions, you can:

- Use File menu commands (Save, Duplicate, Move To, Revert To, and so on).

- Hover the pointer over the document name in the window's title bar until a small arrowhead Down-pointing arrowhead appears, and then click to open the menu.

Tip: To use the Save As command in an application that supports Auto Save, hold down the Option key when you click the File menu, or press Option+Shift+Command+S.

Do any of the following:

- Tag the document.

- Rename the document.

- Move the document to iCloud storage.

- Move the document to a different folder or drive.

- Create a duplicate of the document next to the original (type a new name for the copy).

- Lock the document to prevent inadvertent changes (if you try to change a locked document, you're prompted to unlock it or copy it). Two weeks after the last edit, macOS automatically locks the document for you.

- Revert (roll back) the document to the state it was in when you last opened or saved it (if you're unhappy with your recent changes).

- Bring up the Versions interface (choose Revert To > Browse All Versions).

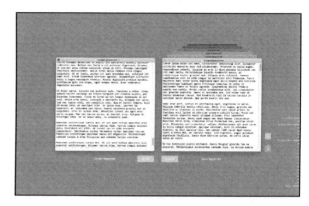

The Versions interface lets you:

- See your document in its current state (on the left) and past incarnations (use the timeline on the right edge of the screen to scroll through old versions).

- Copy and paste between versions.

- Delete old versions.

- Make side-by-side version comparisons.

- Revert to an earlier version.

Opening Documents

To open a document: Do any of the following:

- In the program that created the document, choose File > Open (Command+O). The standard Open dialog box works like the Save dialog box (page 117). You can use the search box to find a document quickly. If the application supports iCloud, you can open documents from iCloud storage.

- Click its icon in the dock or sidebar.

- Click its stack in the dock, and then click the document's icon.

- Press Command+Spacebar to open the Spotlight search window, type the first few letters of the document's name until it highlights, and then press Return.

- Choose > Recent Items > Documents submenu.

- Double-click its icon in a Finder window (hold down Option to autoclose the folder window when the document opens).

- Select its icon and then choose File > Open (Command+O or Command+↓).

- Drag its icon onto the icon of any program that can open it (in the dock, the sidebar, or in a Finder window).

- Use the **open** command in Terminal.

To open a document automatically at login: Choose > System Preferences > Users & Groups > Login Items pane.

Tip: To perform common file operations, you can right-click, drag, Command-drag (move), or Option-drag (copy) files in the Open dialog box.

Associating Documents with Programs

macOS tracks file types to determine which program to launch when you open a document. If you haven't set a default program with "Always Open With", macOS consults its own database. Finally, it checks the document's filename **extension**—the few characters appearing after the filename's last dot (.txt for text files, for example). The Info window (page 32) shows a file's type and default program. Note that setting your preferences with "Always Open With" overrides filename extensions.

macOS hides extensions by default to appear friendlier. But you should show extensions because they impart the types of like-named files quickly (readme.doc vs. readme.txt vs. readme.html, for example) without making you discern icons or read the Kind column in Finder. If a newly installed program hijacks an extension's association without asking your permission, you can reassociate the extension with your preferred program.

To show or hide filename extensions in Finder: In Finder, choose Finder > Preferences > Advanced pane > "Show all filename extensions".

To show or suppress warnings when you change filename extensions: In Finder, choose Finder > Preferences > Advanced pane > "Show warning before changing an extension".

To open specific document(s) in a nondefault program: In Finder, select the document(s) that you want to open and then do any of the following:

- Choose File > Open With.

- Right-click a selected icon and then choose Open With.

- Click $\boxed{\text{\#} \vee}$ > Open With.

- Drag a selected icon onto the program's icon in Finder or the dock.

Tip: If a program isn't listed in the "Open With" menu, choose Other to locate it, or choose App Store to find a compatible app. Alternatively, you can open the desired program and then choose File > Open (Command+O).

To change the default program for specific document(s): In Finder, select the document(s) whose default program you want to change and then do any of the following:

- Hold down Option and then choose File > Always Open With.

- Hold down Option, right-click a selected icon, and then choose Always Open With.

- Hold down Option and then click $\boxed{\text{\#} \vee}$ > Always Open With.

- If only one document is selected, choose File > Get Info (Command+I) > "Open with" pop-up menu. If multiple documents are selected, hold down Option and then choose File > Show Inspector (Option+Command+I) > "Open with" pop-up menu (don't click Change All).

Tip: If a program isn't listed in the "Always Open With" menu, choose Other to locate it.

To change the default program for all documents of a specific file type: In Finder, select any document of the target file type, choose File > Get Info (Command+I), select the desired program from the "Open with" pop-up menu, and then click Change All.

Tip: If a program isn't listed in the "Open with" pop-up menu, choose Other to locate it.

To open a file that has an unknown extension (or no extension): Double-click the mystery file and then click Choose Application.

Applications & Utilities

The Applications folder teems with free programs (.app files) that are part of the standard macOS installation. Inside the Applications folder is the Utilities folder, which holds smaller-scale tools for more-technical tasks. To get help for a specific program, open it and use its Help menu.

To open the Applications folder: In Finder, choose Go > Applications (Shift+Command+A) or click Applications in the sidebar. Alternatively, click the Applications stack in the dock and then choose Open in Finder.

To open the Utilities folder: In Finder, choose Go > Utilities (Shift+Command+U). You can add a Utilities icon to the sidebar or create a Utilities stack in the dock.

Activity Monitor

Use the Activity Monitor utility to identify the programs and processes running on your computer, monitor their activity, and show statistics and graphs about CPU load, memory allocation, power consumption, drive activity, drive usage, and network traffic. If you select a process, you can inspect its details (View > Inspect Process or Command+I) or kill it (View > Quit Process or Option+Command+Q). The Activity Monitor dock icon shows a real-time activity graph (View > Dock Icon).

AirPort Utility

Use AirPort Utility to set up and manage AirPort base stations (Apple's wireless routers). Click Continue to step through a series of setup screens, or click Manual Setup to skip the hand-holding interview and configure the router manually. A free AirPort Utility app is also available for iOS devices.

App Store

Use the App Store application to find, buy, download, install, and update macOS system software and applications directly from Apple's online store. The Mac App Store works like the iOS App Store for iPhone, iPad, and iPod touch. To open App Store, choose > App Store. Thousands of free or paid apps from Apple and third-party developers are available, with new or updated apps arriving every day. App Store supports notifications and parental controls.

The store is curated, meaning that Apple must approve every app. Apple can also yank an app from the store if it crashes too much, violates store policy, is complained about excessively, or whatever. Yanked apps disappear from the store but not from your Mac; after you download an app and back it up, it's yours.

You can read program descriptions and customer reviews before you buy. App Store programs have cost advantages (no box, no disc, and no shipping) and tend to be cheaper than traditionally distributed software (many programs in the store are free). Apple controls the transaction as middleman between you and the developer and identifies you by your Apple ID. If you uninstall an app that you bought from the App Store, you can reinstall it for free at any time on any of your Macs.

Tip: To set a password policy for additional downloads from the Mac App Store, choose > System Preferences > App Store > Password Settings.

You can find apps by using the store's browse and search tools. Apps are available in many languages, though store content varies by country. In App Store, click one of the following buttons in the toolbar:

Featured
> The Featured pane (Command+1) shows new and notable apps spotlighted by Apple's staff (via editorial fiat or paid placement). Scroll down to see apps organized in various special categories.

Top Charts

The Top Charts pane (Command+2) lists the currently most popular paid, free, and top-grossing apps in the store. To show more apps, click See All. To show only a certain type of top apps, click an item in the Top Charts Categories list. These lists are updated many times each day.

Categories

The Categories pane (Command+3) lists apps by type (Games, Productivity, Weather, and so on). Click a category name or icon to see new, popular, or featured apps in that category.

Purchases

The Purchases pane (Command+4) lists the apps (paid or free) that you've downloaded previously. To restore an app that you uninstalled, find it in the list and then click Install. You don't have to pay again for previously purchased apps, though substantial revisions may cost money.

Updates

The Updates pane (Command+5) lists apps that have been updated by their developers since you downloaded or last updated them. All macOS and other Apple software updates (page 186) are also available here.

Tip: Flick two fingers left or right on the trackpad to navigate through your history in App Store.

Audio MIDI Setup

Use the Audio MIDI Setup utility to add and configure MIDI (Musical Instrument Digital Interface) devices connected to your computer. You can select audio-channel input and output devices, configure output speakers, set clock rates, and control levels. In GarageBand, Audio MIDI Setup helps connect your guitar, keyboard, and other instruments.

Automator

Use the Automator application to create drag-and-drop workflows that automate repetitive tasks such as renaming groups of files and converting image formats. Automator works with Apple programs (Finder, Calendar, Contacts, iTunes, Safari, Mail, iWork, and so on) and third-party programs such as those in Microsoft Office and Adobe Creative Suite. Automator doesn't require programming knowledge, as does AppleScript. To use Automator, drag Actions for programs to the Workflow area, and then save the actions as a workflow or application to run whenever you want. You can also save workflows as services, plugins, and other types of documents. To download and share Automator Actions, choose Automator > Display Automator Website.

Bluetooth File Exchange

Use the Bluetooth File Exchange utility to share files with Bluetooth-enabled devices. You can receive a photo from a mobile phone, for example, or send multiple selected documents to an iPad or tablet. To send a file, drag its icon from a Finder window to the Bluetooth File Exchange icon in the dock. You can create remote folders and double-click to navigate folders.

Bluetooth Firmware Update

Use the Bluetooth Firmware Update utility to update low-level Bluetooth software.

Boot Camp Assistant

Use the Boot Camp Assistant utility to install Windows 7 or later on an Intel-based Mac. (For upgraders, existing Boot Camp installations support Windows XP Service Pack 2 or later.) Boot Camp Assistant partitions your Mac's hard drive and steps you through installing Windows on the new partition.

After you install Windows on a Boot Camp partition, you can choose to boot either macOS or Windows at startup. To choose, hold down the Option key during the startup process, and then select the desired system when the partition list appears. To set the default partition for future startups, choose > System Preferences > Startup Disk.

As an alternative to (or in addition to) Boot Camp, you can use VMware Fusion (*vmware.com*), Parallels

Desktop (*parallels.com*), or VirtualBox (*virtualbox. org*) to run Windows (or other operating systems) in a virtual machine simultaneously with macOS.

Calculator

Use the Calculator application to perform the basic operations of arithmetic.

Calculator includes these features:

- Switch among Basic (Command+1), Scientific (Command+2), and Programmer (Command+3) modes.

- To operate Calculator, click the onscreen buttons or press the corresponding number and symbol keys on the keyboard.

- To clear the display, click the C button or press C on the keyboard.

- To make Calculator speak keystrokes aloud, use the Speech menu.

- To convert between standard units of measurement, use the Convert menu.

- To copy the calculated result for pasting into another program, choose Edit > Copy (Command+C).

- To toggle algebraic and RPN entry (like Hewlett–Packard calculators), choose View > RPN Mode (Command+R).

- To view the calculation history, choose Windows > Show Paper Tape (Command+T). To export the calculation history to a text file, choose File > Save Tape As (Shift+Command+S).

Tip: A quick alternative to Calculator: type or paste a mathematical expression in the Spotlight search window (Command+Spacebar); the answer appears in the results list.

Calendar

Use the Calendar application to manage your calendars and events (appointments). Calendar identifies you by your Apple ID (Calendar > Preferences > Accounts pane) and is integrated with Contacts.

Calendar includes these features:

- View individual calendars or multiple color-coded calendars at the same time (choose View > Show Calendar List or click Calendars in the toolbar).

- Add new events (File > New Event).

- Edit existing events (Edit > Edit Event).

- View and search recent and upcoming events.

- Add events such as flights and restaurant reservations found in Mail messages (Calendar > Preferences > General pane).

- Learn when to leave for an appointment based on locations and traffic conditions in Apple Maps (Calendar > Preferences > Alerts pane).

- Enter repeating events (such as birthdays or weekly meetings).

- Specify what hours constitute a workday and what weekday starts the week (Calendar > Preferences > General pane).

- Receive onscreen, audio, email, or message alerts of upcoming events (Edit > Edit Event > Alert).

- Receive notifications for events and invitations (Calendar > Preferences > Alerts pane).

- Create multiple calendars for home, work, and so on (File > New Calendar).

- Set the default calendar for new events (Calendar > Preferences > General pane > Default Calendar).

- Switch among daily (Command+1), weekly (Command+2), monthly (Command+3), and yearly (Command+4) views.

- Import, export, and print calendars (File menu).

- To use iCloud to sync calendars wirelessly across your Macs and iOS devices, choose > System Preferences > iCloud > Calendars.

- To sync Calendar with Gmail, Yahoo, or other services that support calendars, choose > System Preferences > Internet Accounts, select the account, and then turn on Calendars/Reminders.

- To turn on notifications for calendar events, choose > System Preferences > Notifications > Calendar.

- View event locations in Apple Maps.

Calendar also lets you view the online calendars of people who have published them on the internet. You can subscribe to **iCalendar** (.ics) or **CalDAV** calendars, including iCloud, Yahoo, Google, and Calendar for iOS calendars. You can read events from subscribed calendars, but you can't add or edit events. To subscribe to a calendar, choose File > New Calendar Subscription (Option+Command+S).

You can also subscribe to web calendars by clicking a link to the calendar in Safari. Open Safari, go to a site such as *icalshare.com*, find a calendar that you like (holidays, sports schedules, movie releases, and so on), and then click Subscribe to Calendar. The new calendar is added to your subscription list, and its events appear in Calendar. To show or hide those events, click the Calendars button in the toolbar and then toggle the target calendar.

To edit or delete a calendar subscription, right-click the calendar in the Calendars list.

If you get an iCalendar (.ics) file attached to an email message, you can open the attachment to import its events into Calendar.

Chess

Use the Chess application to play chess and chess variants on a 3D board, optionally logging games. To make moves by speaking or to make Chess speak moves aloud (handy if you drift off during slow games), choose Chess > Preferences > Speech. Chess supports Game Center.

ColorSync Utility

Use ColorSync Utility to manage color profiles and filters used in Apple's PDF workflow, and to apply filters to PDF documents. Click one of the buttons in the toolbar:

- Profile First Aid repairs ColorSync profiles so they conform to the ICC specification.

- Profiles browses and compares installed profiles.

- Devices lists registered ColorSync devices and displays and their default profiles.

- Filters builds and modifies systemwide PDF filters.

- Calculator converts among RGB, CMYK, and other color-value schemes.

Console

Use the Console utility to view text logs of interaction messages passed between macOS and programs (useful for software developers).

Contacts

Use the Contacts application to store names, addresses, telephone numbers, email addresses, birthdays, and other contact information.

Contacts includes these features:

- In its default view, Contacts resembles an address book. On the left page, browse contacts by clicking, scrolling, or searching. On the right page, scroll contact info, or click a field or button to perform an action such as sharing a contact or opening a contact's home page.

- To create a new contact, choose File > New Card (Command+N) or click (+). Your contacts are available in Mail, Messages, FaceTime, Calendar, file sharing, AirDrop, and other apps and services that tap into Contacts.

- To edit an existing contact, select the contact and then choose Edit > Edit Card (Command+L) or click the Edit button.

- To view or edit your own information, choose Card > Go to My Card (Shift+Command+M).

- Add and update contacts found in Mail messages (Contacts > Preferences > General pane).

- To specify which fields appear in all cards, choose Contacts > Preferences > Template pane. To add a field to a specific card, select the card and then choose Card > Add Field.

- To change how contacts are sorted and displayed, choose Contacts > Preferences > General pane.

- To sync your contacts with iCloud, Yahoo, or other contact lists, choose Contacts > Preferences > Accounts pane. Alternatively, choose > System Preferences > Internet Accounts, select the account, and then turn on Contacts.

- To use iCloud to sync your contacts across your Macs, Windows PCs, and iOS devices, choose Contacts > Preferences > General pane > Default Account > iCloud. To store your contacts on only your Mac, choose On My Mac as the default account.

- Each Contacts entry is a customizable "card". You can use the File menu to import and export cards in common formats, organize them into fixed or self-updating ("smart") groups, or print contact lists and address labels.

- To display groups, choose View > Show Groups (Command+1).

- Contacts exchanges contact information with other programs (including Windows programs) mainly through **vCards** (.vcf files). If you get a vCard file attached to an email, drag the file into your Contacts window to create a contact. To create a vCard file, drag an entry (or Command-drag multiple entries) out of your Contacts list to the desktop or into an outgoing message. To change the vCard format, choose Contacts > Preferences > vCard pane.

- To control which apps and services can access your contacts, choose > System Preferences > Security & Privacy > Privacy pane > Contacts (click 🔒 if the settings are dimmed).

- Facebook friends appear in Contacts with profile photos and up-to-date information.

- View contact addresses in Apple Maps.

Dashboard

Opens the dashboard (page 46).

Dictionary

Use the Dictionary application to look up word definitions, pronunciations, synonyms, Apple terms, and Wikipedia articles. It includes American, British, Japanese, Simplified Chinese, Spanish, German, and other dictionaries and thesauri (Dictionary > Preferences). Dictionary supports parental controls for profanity.

You can look up a word in any of the following ways:

- In Dictionary, type or paste the word in the search box and then click it in the results list.

- In TextEdit, Notes, Mail, Messages, Safari, and other macOS programs, point to a word and then press Ctrl+Command+D.

- In any program that taps into Dictionary, right-click a word and then choose Look Up or double-tap a word or phrase with three fingers.

- In a web browser, type *dict://word* in the address bar, replacing *word* with the actual word to define.

- Use the Dictionary widget in Dashboard.

Tip: Flick two fingers left or right on the trackpad to navigate through your history in Dictionary.

DigitalColor Meter

Use the DigitalColor Meter utility to show the color value of any onscreen pixel (useful for print and web designers). Open DigitalColor Meter and point anywhere on your screen. A magnified view appears in the meter window, along with the RGB (red-green-blue) color value of the selected pixel(s). To change the format of the color value, click the pop-up menu. To get the *average* color value of multiple pixels, increase the aperture size. To move the pointer precisely, tap the arrow keys.

Disk Utility

Use Disk Utility to perform drive-related tasks.

- Get size, format, hardware, and other information about any drives attached to your Mac.

- Mount, unmount, rename, and eject drives.

- Verify and repair a drive's integrity (First Aid). This feature can fix drives that misbehave or won't appear on your desktop, and solve a number of small, quirky, and disparate problems.

- Erase, secure-erase, format, and partition drives. Partitioning a drive subdivides it into multiple logical **volumes**, each of which appears on the desktop as a separate drive icon.

- View color-coded content maps of drives and partitions.

- Manage partitions (you can create or resize partitions without erasing the entire drive).

- Open disk images.

- Create a blank disk image or a disk image of a folder or partition.

- Restore a disk image to a partition.

- Toggle journaling.

- Manage RAID sets (a cluster of separate drives that acts as a single volume) by using the `diskutil` command in Terminal.

Tip: The command-line interface for Disk Utility is the `diskutil` command in Terminal. This command is more powerful than the Disk Utility app.

DVD Player

Use the DVD Player application to play DVD movies on your computer. It supports multiple audio, video, and subtitle tracks, Dolby audio, closed captions, and other standard DVD features. To circumvent DVD restrictions (such as unskippable warnings and ads), use VLC media player (*videolan.org*) instead. To open a player automatically when you insert a movie DVD, use CDs & DVDs preferences.

FaceTime

Use the FaceTime application to make video calls to other FaceTime users over a high-speed internet connection. The other caller must have an iPhone, iPad, or iPod touch with a forward-facing camera, or a camera-equipped Mac running FaceTime. To use a specific camera or microphone, use the Video menu.

FaceTime identifies you by your Apple ID (FaceTime > Preferences > Settings pane) and is integrated with Contacts. To make a FaceTime call, double-click a contact in the FaceTime window, or right-click the FaceTime dock icon and then choose a contact under Recent Calls.

After you connect, you can:

- Resize the window (drag any window edge, click the green button in the top-left corner, or choose Window > Zoom).

- Go full screen (choose Video > Enter Full Screen, press Ctrl+Command+F, or spread two fingers on the trackpad).

- Drag the small inset picture of you to a different corner of the video window.

- Mute the mike (choose Video > Mute or click the microphone button at the bottom of the video window).

- Pause the call (minimize FaceTime, choose FaceTime > Hide FaceTime, press Command+H, or right-click the FaceTime dock icon and then choose Hide).

- Rotate your picture (choose Video > Portrait/Landscape, press Command+R, rotate two fingers on the trackpad, or click the curved arrow in the inset picture of you).

For incoming FaceTime calls:

- FaceTime doesn't have to be running for you to receive a call.

- When someone calls you, FaceTime posts a message on your screen and plays a ringtone (FaceTime > Preferences > Settings pane > Ringtone).

- If your screen is locked, you can answer the call from the login screen without having to enter your password.

- If iTunes is playing, it pauses automatically.

- You can accept the call and start talking, or decline it to tell the caller that you're unavailable.

- FaceTime can send notifications for missed calls.

- If you don't want to be interrupted, you can turn off FaceTime by choosing FaceTime > Turn FaceTime Off (Command+K), or by signing out of FaceTime or disabling your account (FaceTime > Preferences > Settings pane).

- To stop specific contacts from calling you, choose FaceTime > Preferences > Blocked pane.

- When you receive a FaceTime call while you're having another FaceTime call with someone else, you can put your current conversation on hold and answer the incoming call (call waiting).

Font Book

Opens Font Book (page 150).

Game Center

Use the Game Center application to play games on Apple's online multiplayer social gaming network, which Apple says has more than 100 million

members around the world. You can get Game Center-compatible games from the Mac App Store to play against friends or strangers on iPhones, iPads, iPods, or Macs.

Tip: Chess (page 124) supports Game Center.

Game Center offers features common to most gaming networks:

- You can add people to your friends list or receive friend requests from others.

- Friends can invite each other to play or find equally matched opponents.

- You can earn bonus points for games that reward points for completing certain tasks, and you can see what your friends have achieved.

- Game leaderboards rank the best players.

- In-game voice chat lets you talk with your opponents or team members during multiplayer games.

Game Center supports parental controls and notifications for friend requests and game invitations.

To use Game Center, you need an internet connection and an Apple ID. If you like, you can create a separate Apple ID for gaming and still use your main Apple ID for iCloud, App Store, iTunes, and so on.

The first time that you sign in to Game Center, you must create a **nickname**, which is your unique user name in Game Center. If you pick a nickname that someone is already using, Game Center suggests alternatives, which you're free to ignore. If you see your nickname at the top of the Me pane, you're already signed in. You can change your nickname at any time in account settings, but only one nickname at a time can be associated with an Apple ID. Other players can search for you by using your nickname. Account settings also let you configure privacy-related options, such as whether to accept game invitations or display your real name to nonfriends.

After you sign in, click the buttons in the toolbar to edit your account, play or buy games, or manage your friends:

Me

View or buy top games, add or take a photo, or declare your status, which you define.

Tip: You don't need to sign out each time you quit Game Center.

Friends

Invite people or contacts to be friends, respond to friend requests or search for requests, get friend recommendations, invite friends to play, see games that friends play, buy a game that a friend has, check a friend's scores, search your friends list, list a friend's friends, remove (un-friend) a friend, or report problems or cheaters.

Tip: No friends? Unresponsive friends? Use Auto-Match to have Game Center find another player for you.

Games

Play a game, get game recommendations, search for Game Center games, tell a friend about a game, view leaderboards (rankings) and achievements, or get a game from the App Store. Not all Game Center-compatible games feature multiplayer play.

Challenges

Send or receive challenges to beat friends' scores or earn achievements.

Turns

Keep track of turn-based games.

Tip: Apple maintains and updates your Game Center **profile** automatically. Your profile contains your nickname, friends list, achievement points, photo, status, Game Center-compatible games owned, and more.

In many multiplayer games—racing and cooperative games being obvious examples—all players play at the same time. Other games—particularly board and card games such as backgammon, Scrabble, and poker—are **turn-based**, in that each player waits until the other acts before proceeding. Game Center keeps track of each player's turn and can manage multiple games if you're playing more than one. If it's taking a long time between moves, Game Center can send you notifications when it's your turn.

GarageBand

Use the GarageBand application to create music or podcasts. Its features include audio recording, virtual instruments, MIDI editing, and music lessons. If GarageBand didn't come installed on your Mac, you can buy it from the Mac App Store.

Grab

Use the Grab utility to take screenshots (image files that record what's on your display). Use the Capture menu to take a picture of a selected part of the screen (Shift+Command+A), a selected window (Shift+Command+W), or the entire screen (Command+Z). The Timed Screen command (Shift+Command+Z) waits 10 seconds before snapping the picture, giving you time to set up the shot or open a menu. To show or hide the pointer in screenshots, choose Grab > Preferences.

Grab's image format is TIFF; to convert to another format, use the File > Export command in Preview (page 135). Note that Preview has its own File > Take Screen Shot command.

Instead of Grab, you can use macOS's own built-in keyboard shortcuts to take screenshots:

- To capture the whole screen, press Shift+Command+3. The screenshot appears on the desktop as a PNG-format file named *Screen Shot YYYY-MM-DD at HH.MM.SS*. You can open, edit, and convert these files in Preview.

- To capture part of the screen, press Shift+Command+4, and then drag a rectangular area (hold down Shift to constrain the drag vertically or horizontally, or hold down Option to drag from the center outward), or press Space-bar and then click a screen object. To cancel the screenshot, press Esc.

- To copy a screenshot to the clipboard (ready for pasting), rather than saving it as a file, also hold down Ctrl when you take the shot.

- To change the screenshot keyboard shortcuts, choose > System Preferences > Keyboard > Shortcuts pane > Screen Shots.

You can also take screenshots by using the screencapture command in Terminal.

To create screen recordings—videos of what takes place on your computer screen—open QuickTime Player (page 137) and then choose File > New Screen Recording (Ctrl+Command+N).

Grapher

Use the Grapher utility to create 2D and 3D graphs of equations.

Grapher includes these features:

- To see sample graphs that you can use as starting points, use the Examples menu.

- To fine-tune a graph, use the Format, Object, View, and Window menus, or choose Window > Show Inspectors.

- To move a 2D graph in the window, choose View > Move Tool (Command+2) and then drag. To move a 3D graph, Command-drag it.

- To rotate a 3D graph, drag in any direction, or Option-drag to flip the graph on one axis.

- To export a graph as an image file, choose File > Export.

- To copy an equation for pasting into another program, select the equation in the edit field above the graph, right-click it, and then choose Copy As or Copy LaTeX Expression.

- To create animations and do higher-math calculations, use the Equation menu.

iBooks

The iBooks application is Apple's ebook reader for the Mac, iPad, iPhone, and iPod touch. Like the Amazon Kindle and other ereaders, iBooks lets you download books and read them onscreen.

- Shop for books in Apple's iBooks Store (click iBooks Store in the toolbar, choose Store > Store Home, or press Shift+Command+H). You can browse by title, author, or genre. And click to see details, read reviews, or download a free sample. To return to your bookshelf, click Library in the toolbar.

- Use iCloud to download iBooks Store purchases to all your Macs and iOS devices automatically (iBooks > Preferences > Store pane > "Download new purchases automatically").

- Download EPUB-format books from the internet and add them to your iBooks library (File > Add to Library).

- Add PDF files to your iBooks library to read in Preview (File > Add to Library).

- Sort the books in your library manually or automatically (View > Sort By).

- Organize your books into collections on topics of your choosing (File menu).

- Open multiple books at the same time to view side by side, each in its own window.

- Read books in one-page or two-page view (View > Single Page/Two Pages or Command+1/2).

- Turn pages by clicking, flicking, or using the Go menu keyboard shortcuts.

- Zoom images by double-clicking or pinching.

- Move the pointer to the top of the window to show the reading and navigation controls.

- Annotate books with bookmarks, highlights, and notes (use the Edit menu or drag to select text). Annotations and reading progress (furthest page read) are synced across all your devices.

- Share quotes from books via Mail, Messages, Twitter, or Facebook (File > Share).

- Change a book's typography and layout.

- Use the Night (View menu) theme to make reading in the dark easier on your eyes.

- Change to full-screen view to focus on the words without distraction.

- Find all occurrences of a word or phrase in a book.

- Double-click a word to see its definition in the built-in dictionary.

- Copy text from a book and paste it in other apps.

- Set parental controls (iBooks > Preferences > Parental pane).

Image Capture

Use the Image Capture application to transfer images to and from a digital camera, or grab images from a scanner. Image Capture lacks the organizational tools of Photos but is smaller and faster and lets you create slideshows and rescale images for printing or email. You can also share cameras and scanners attached to your Mac with other users on a network, or control a camera remotely to monitor a room.

To set up photo transfer, connect your camera to your Mac, turn on the camera, select the camera in the Devices list (on the left), and then use the "Connecting this camera opens" pop-up menu.

You can also use Preview (page 135) to import camera images or operate a scanner.

iMovie

Use the iMovie application to edit home movies. If iMovie didn't come installed on your Mac, you can buy it from the Mac App Store.

iMovie lets you:

- Import footage from movie files, tape camcorders, digital video cameras, iPhones, iPads, iPod touches, or DVD camcorders.

- Record live video from a built-in FaceTime/iSight camera, a third-party webcam, or an external camera (via a FireWire or USB connection).

- Storyboard and edit a movie.

- Add transitions, themes, travel maps, and animatics.

- Add video effects.

- Crop, rotate, color-fix, and stabilize video.

- Add titles, subtitles, and credits.

- Add narration, music, and sound.

- Add photos and still images.

- Create trailers.

- Play the final movie in QuickTime Player; share it on the web (YouTube, Facebook, and so on); download it to your iPhone, iPad, or iPod touch.

- Go full screen.

iTunes

Use the iTunes application to buy, play, and organize your digital library of music, video, audiobooks, and other media.

iTunes lets you:

- Play CDs, rip (copy) songs from CDs, burn custom music CDs, and organize and play audio files.

- Create playlists and smart (self-updating) playlists (File > New > Playlist or File > New > Smart Playlist).

- Use Picture in Picture (page 138).

- Download media (free or paid) from Apple's iTunes Store, including music, movies, TV shows, podcasts, audiobooks, iOS apps and games, and ringtones.

- Download free university lectures from iTunes U.

- Get automated Genius recommendations and playlists based on the media in your library (Account > Turn On Genius).

- Share (stream) your media library on your local network (iTunes > Preferences > Sharing pane).

- Copy music and videos from one Mac to another one (File > Home Sharing).

- Sync or back up an iPhone, iPad, or iPod.

- Use iCloud to sync music, iOS app, and book purchases across iOS devices (iTunes > Preferences > Store pane > Automatic Downloads).

- Read, write, and convert between MP3, AIFF, WAV, MPEG-4, AAC, and Apple Lossless audio formats.

- Read CD track names from an online database when a music CD is inserted (iTunes > Preferences > General pane).

- Listen to internet radio stations around the world.

- Listen to Apple's ad-supported internet radio service.

- Set parental controls (iTunes > Preferences > Parental pane).

Java Preferences

The Java Preferences utility holds settings of interest mainly to Java programmers.

Keychain Access

Opens Keychain Access (page 180).

Launchpad

Opens Launchpad (page 115).

Mail

Use the Mail application to send, receive, and manage email. See also "Internet Accounts" on page 81.

Mail includes these features:

- Read, reply to, forward, redirect, print, file, flag, find, archive, or delete messages.

- Open or search attachments.

- Add or edit multiple email accounts (Mail > Add Account or Mail > Preferences > Accounts pane).

- iCloud support (Mail > Preferences > Accounts pane).

- Notification Center support for incoming email from all senders, only contacts, or only VIP senders (Mail > Preferences > General pane > "New message notifications"). To designate a person as a VIP, click the sender's From name at the top of a message and then choose Add to VIPs.

- Contacts integration.

- View locations in messages in Apple Maps.

- Point to a message in the message list and then flick two fingers left or right on the trackpad to delete the message or mark it as read/unread.

- In full-screen view, the New Message window uses tabs, letting you work on several messages at once, and shrinks to the bottom of the screen when you click outside it. You can drag images and other attachments down to a shrunken message.

- Search in Mail responds to natural-language queries like "unread mail from Diane in July" or "emails with attachments from last week".

- Mail can update your calendar and contacts by recognizing meeting suggestions, events, locations, and contact information in your messages (toggle these features in Calendar > Preferences and Contacts > Preferences).

- Import mailboxes from Apple Mail, Netscape/Mozilla, Thunderbird, Eudora, and other email programs that use the mbox format (File > Import Mailboxes).

- Export mailboxes for backups (Mailbox > Export Mailbox).

- Rebuild mailboxes to repair and compact message files (Mailbox > Rebuild).

- Threaded conversations (Mail > Preferences > Viewing pane > "View conversations").

- Data detectors recognize postal addresses, phone numbers, dates, times, flight numbers, and so on.

- Message-filtering rules (Mail > Preferences > Rules pane).

- Rich (formatted)-text or plain-text message composition (Mail > Preferences > Composing pane).

- Junk-mail (spam) filtering (Mail > Preferences > Junk Mail pane).

- Self-updating smart mailboxes or folders (Mailbox > New Smart Mailbox or Mailbox > New Smart Mailbox Folder).

- Spotlight-indexed messages.

- Attachment searches.

- Use Mail Drop to send large attachments (up to 5GB).

- Use Markup to annotate images and fill out forms without leaving Mail.

- Fill out PDF forms without leaving Mail.

- Message-priority flags.

- Photo-resizing tools.

- Slideshow views of received photos.

- Signatures (Mail > Preferences > Signatures pane).

- Stationery templates.

- Inline images.

- Custom fonts and colors (Mail > Preferences > Fonts & Colors pane).

- Microsoft Exchange support.

- Set parental controls.

Maps

The Maps application is Apple's mapping and navigation program for the Mac, iPad, iPhone, and iPod touch.

- Open multiple maps in separate windows.

- Find a location, business, or other point of interest and get the complete address, telephone number, website link, photos, reviews, and more.

- Mark a spot on a map by dropping a pin.

- Find your current location by using Location Services (page 184).

- Get travel directions (walking or driving). You can plan a trip on your Mac and then send the map directly to your iPhone, where Maps can give you turn-by-turn voice navigation as you go.

- Get public-transit directions (train or bus) for certain major cities around the world.

- Switch to transit view to see color-coded train lines and stations. Click a station to see its train lines, schedule, nearest train, and more.

- Show real-time traffic conditions and incident reports.

- Show 3D views and photo-realistic Flyover views (for major cities and landmarks).

- Zoom, pan, tilt, or rotate the map by using the mouse, multitouch gestures, menu commands, or keyboard shortcuts.

- Bookmark your favorite places.

- Switch to satellite view to see satellite imagery.

- Share locations via Mail, Messages, Facebook, Twitter, AirDrop, and more.

- Add locations as new contacts.

- Print a map or export it as a PDF file.

- Reorient to North.

- See maps for addresses within Mail, Contacts, Calendar, Reminders, and more.

Messages

Use the Messages application for instant text messaging, audio/video chatting, and file exchange.

In addition to supporting the ubiquitous SMS and MMS messaging services used on mobile phones and the web, Messages supports Apple's **iMessage** service. iMessage is a free alternative to SMS/MMS that lets you send unlimited free text messages, photos, videos, and more to people who are also running Messages on their iPads, iPhones, iPod touches, or Macs, and with whom you've exchanged email addresses. iMessage identifies you by your Apple ID email address and requires an internet connection. iMessages are displayed on all your Macs and iOS devices logged in to the same account. You can start a conversation on, say, your iPad and then continue it on your Mac. Set up Messages on each device, using the same email address.

Messages includes these features:

- Support for iMessage, AIM (AOL Instant Messenger), Jabber, Google Talk, and Yahoo Messages accounts (Messages > Preferences > Accounts pane).

- Get notifications for new messages.

- Contacts integration.

- One-to-one or group typed conversations.

- Add or remove people in group conversations at any time.

- Leave a group conversation at any time.

- Give group conversations titles to make them easier to find and manage.

- Mute notifications for conversations when you don't want be bothered, and read the messages later.

- Delivery and read receipts (iMessage only).

- End-to-end encryption secures iMessage conversations.

- Search messages by text or recipient.

- Video and audio chat via FaceTime/iSight camera (or other webcam or microphone).

- Soundbites: record your voice in Messages and send the audio clip to others, who can play the recording inside their conversation.

- Automatically find other Messages users on your local network.

- Background, image, and video effects.

- Multiple chats in a single window or in separate windows.

- Message forwarding (right-click selected messages and then choose Forward).

- Inline video playback and link previews.

- Unified buddy list and unified status.

- Buddy search.

- Screen-sharing for getting live help from other Mac users.

- Timestamped chat histories.

- Formatted text and smileys.

- File exchange (Buddies > Send File). iMessage allows attachments of up to 100MB.

- Send email (Buddies > Send Email).

Tip: To sync Messages with Gmail (Google Talk), Yahoo (Yahoo Messages), or other services that support messages, choose > System Preferences > Internet Accounts, select the account, and then turn on Messages.

Migration Assistant

Use the Migration Assistant utility to transfer your user accounts, files, programs, and settings from one Mac to another, or from a Windows PC to a Mac. Migration Assistant is useful when you buy a new Mac or when you need to recover data from Time Machine, a secondary hard drive, or a partition. On-screen instructions guide you through the process.

Mission Control

Opens Mission Control (page 50).

Network Utility

Network Utility is a graphical frontend for standard Unix networking commands: netstat, ping, lookup, traceroute, whois, and finger. (These commands are also available in Terminal.) Network Utility also shows information about network connections and scans open ports for a given domain name or IP address.

Notes

Use the Notes application to type notes on a virtual pad of scratch paper. It's also a handy place to attach text, photos, websites, and other items copied, dragged, or shared from other apps.

Notes includes these features:

- To create a new note, choose File > New Note (Command+N), click New Note in the toolbar, or right-click the notes list and then choose New Note.

  A list of notes appears, and the current note is highlighted. Notes are listed chronologically, with the most recently modified note at the top. Each item in the list shows the first few words of the note.

- To view or edit a note, click it in the notes list.

- Export a note as a PDF file (File > Export as PDF).

- Create checklists (Format > Checklist).

- Invite people to collaborate on a note in real time.

- Share from other apps: Notes appears in share sheets in Safari, Photos, Photo Booth, Maps, Contacts, Finder, and more.

- Paste, drag, or share to attach photos, videos, digital sketches, map locations, websites, audio, and documents to notes.

- To attach a photo or video to a note without leaving Notes, choose Window > Photo Browser or click the photos button in the toolbar.

- Attachments appear as clickable boxes in notes. Use the Attachments Browser (View > Show Attachments Browser) to see everything in one place.

- To format a note, select the target text and then use the Format menu or click the style button (Aa) in the toolbar.

- To find a note, type or paste text in the search box.

- To open a note in a separate window, double-click it in the notes list. These notes stay visible even when Notes is minimized.

- To delete a note, right-click it in the notes list and then choose Delete, or select the note and then press Delete or click the trash button in the toolbar.

- You can organize notes in a hierarchy of folders. To view a list of folders, choose View > Show Folders or click the folders button in the toolbar. To create a new folder, choose File > New Folder (Shift+Command+N) or click New Folder at the bottom of the folders list. To view a folder's notes, click the folder in the folders list. To move a note to a different folder, drag the note from the notes list to the target folder. To nest folders, drag a folder onto another. To delete or rename a folder, right-click it in the folders list (deleting a folder also deletes its notes and subfolders).

- Store notes locally (Notes > Enable Local Notes) or use iCloud to sync notes wirelessly across your Macs and iOS devices (> System Preferences > iCloud > Notes).

- To sync Notes with Gmail, Yahoo, or other services that support notes, choose > System Preferences > Internet Accounts, select the account, and then turn on Notes.

Notification Center

See "Notification Center" on page 52.

Photo Booth

Use the Photo Booth application to take photos or video with an FaceTime/iSight camera, webcam, or camcorder. (Photo Booth won't open if your Mac doesn't have a camera.) Before you shoot, you can apply special effects, distortions, color changes, and background images or video. After you shoot, you can trim video clips.

Photos

Use the Photos application to import, organize, edit, print, and share digital photos. To get started, read the Apple support article "Updating from iPhoto to Photos for macOS" at *support.apple.com/HT204655*.

Photos includes these features:

- Import images in JPEG, TIFF, RAW, and other image formats.

- Import images from digital cameras, iOS devices (iPhone, iPad, and iPod touch), mobile phones, tablets, hard drives, flash drives, CDs, DVDs, SD cards, emails, text messages, webpages, and My Photo Stream.

Tip: Use My Photo Stream (> System Preferences > iCloud > Photos > Options) to sync recently taken and imported photos across Macs, Windows PCs, and iOS devices.

- Import and manage videos.

- Use **iCloud Photo Library** (> System Preferences > iCloud > Photos > Options) to store every photo and video that you take, making them accessible from your Mac, iPhone, iPad, or iPod touch, and on *icloud.com*. For details, read the Apple support article "iCloud Photo Library" at *support.apple.com/HT204264*.

- Use **iCloud Photo Sharing** (> System Preferences > iCloud > Photos > Options) to create shared albums, control who sees what, and see updates to your shared albums across your devices. For details, read the Apple support article "iCloud Photo Sharing" at *support.apple.com/HT202786*.

- Use editing tools to fix red-eye, adjust contrast and brightness, crop and resize images, change saturation and color balance, apply filters, and so on. Install third-party extensions (page 76) to add more editing tools.

- Use Moments, Collections, and Years views to organize your photos and videos automatically by when (timestamp) and where (geolocation)

they were taken. Or use the Faces facial-recognition feature to organize photos by people.

- Use Memories to autocreate themed videos.

- Add geotags to images manually or use geotags embedded in photos taken with a GPS-enabled camera.

- Title, tag, and sort images.

- Create slideshows, albums, and smart (self-updating) albums.

- Make your own prints or order prints online.

- Create photo books, calendars, and cards.

- Use Spotlight (page 103) to find photos based on their Faces and Places information in Photos, as well as their file names and attributes.

- Email photos from within Photos, automatically optimizing your message so that it's not too big to send.

- Publish photos to the web (Facebook, Twitter, Flickr, and so on).

- Set a photo as your desktop picture (wallpaper).

- Use an Apple TV to view photos and videos on your HDTV.

Preview

Use the Preview application to view image files, PDF files, and other documents. Preview has basic image-correction, cropping, and rotation tools. You can view, edit, search, encrypt, annotate, and page-shuffle PDF documents, and much more.

Tip: To preview the selected file directly in a Finder window panel without using Preview, in Finder, choose View > Show Preview (Shift+Command+P).

Preview includes these features:

- To customize the Preview toolbar, choose View > Customize Toolbar. To rearrange toolbar icons, Command-drag them sideways. To remove toolbar icons, Command-drag them downward.

- Like Photos and Image Capture, Preview can import pictures directly from a digital camera, iPhone, or iPod touch. Connect your camera, open Preview, and then choose File > Import from Camera.

- Like Image Capture, Preview can operate a scanner, autostraighten the scanned images, and save or export them to various formats (PDF, JPEG, and so on). Connect your scanner, Open Preview, and then choose File > Import from Scanner.

- To save documents and images in iCloud, choose File > Move To > iCloud.

- Use the Preview sidebar to work with multiple PDF files, multiple photos, multiple fax pages, and so on. You can switch among views by using the View menu or pressing Option+Command+1–6.

  Choose View > Thumbnails to view a scrolling vertical list of miniature pages or photos. Click one of the thumbnails to see it at full size in the main section of the window. To make the thumbnails larger or smaller, drag the right edge of the sidebar.

  Choose View > Table of Contents to view a list of photo names, file names, or PDF chapter and section headings.

  Choose View > Contact Sheet to view a full screen of thumbnail miniatures. To make the images bigger or smaller, click the Zoom buttons in the toolbar.

- To mix and match pages from different PDF documents into a single new one, drag thumbnails from one Preview window's sidebar into another.

- If you select multiple image files in a Finder window and then open them all at the same time (by pressing Command+O, for example), Preview shows the first one and lists the thumbnails of the group in the sidebar. To step through the images, press the arrow keys. To open a full-screen slideshow, choose View > Slideshow (Shift+Command+F). To reorder the photos, drag them in the sidebar (in any sidebar view).

- To crop an image, drag across the part of the image that you want to keep, adjust the crop area by dragging its handles, and then choose Tools > Crop (Command+K). If necessary, you can use Auto Save to return to the original image.

- To rotate or flip images or PDF documents, select one or more thumbnails in the sidebar and then use the Rotate or Flip commands in the Tools menu.

- Preview has a few Photoshop-like tools. To fix up photos, use the Show Inspector, Adjust Color, and Adjust Size commands in the Tools menu.

- To convert file formats, choose File > Export.

- To bookmark your place in a PDF document, choose Tools > Add Bookmark (Command+D).

- To annotate a PDF document or image, you can type notes in a box or a bubble, add clickable links (to web addresses or other parts of the document), or add circles, arrows, rectangles, strikethrough, underlining, or highlighting. To do so, choose Tools > Annotate or use the Edit toolbar (choose View > Show Edit Toolbar or press Shift+Command+A). To see a list of your annotations, choose Tools > Show Inspector (Command+I) or View > Highlights and Notes (Option+Command+4). You can search annotations either by author or by content.

- To inspect part of a graphic or PDF closely, choose Tools > Show Magnifier (or press the ` key).

- You can fill out PDF forms within Preview. Type or paste in text-entry areas such as underlining and textboxes or click to select checkboxes.

- To add your "written" signature to a PDF document, choose View > Show Markup Toolbar (Shift+Command+A), click the Sign button (signature icon), and then choose Trackpad (to sign the trackpad with a stylus or finger) or Camera (to take a photo of your written signature). For Camera, hold up your signature (black ink on white paper) to the FaceTime/iSight camera and then take a snapshot. You can store multiple signatures to sign or initial documents.

- Go full screen.

Preview can open many types of files, including:

- AI (Adobe Illustrator)
- BMP (Windows Bitmap)
- DNG (Digital Negative)
- EPS (Encapsulated PostScript)
- FAX (faxes)
- FPX (FlashPix)
- GIF (Graphics Interchange Format)
- ICNS (Apple Icon Image)
- ICO (Windows icon)
- JPEG (Joint Photographic Experts Group)
- PS (PostScript)
- PSD (Adobe Photoshop)
- PICT (QuickDraw)
- PDF (Portable Document Format)
- PNG (Portable Network Graphics)
- RAW (Raw)
- SGI (Silicon Graphics Image)
- TGA (Targa Graphic)
- TIFF (Tagged Image File Format)
- Apple iWork (Pages, Numbers, and Keynote)
- Microsoft Office (Word, Excel, and PowerPoint)

QuickTime Player

Use the QuickTime Player application to:

- Play or edit QuickTime movie files (File, Edit, and View menus).
- Convert (export) media to a web-friendly format (File menu).
- Stream audio and video in your web browser.

- Make audio, video, and screen recordings (File menu).
- Export, stream, or share video via YouTube, iTunes, Facebook, Vimeo, Flickr, iMovie, Mail, Messages, or AirDrop (File > Share).
- Go full screen.

RAID Utility

Use RAID Utility to create a RAID array (multiple-drive system), provided you have a RAID card and can access a system running macOS Server.

Reminders

The Reminders application lets you create and manage to-do lists. You can add reminders to custom lists, assign them to future due dates, receive notifications when they come due, and mark them as completed to hide them from view. You can create multiple to-do lists to keep your work, personal, and other tasks separate. Reminders comes with two lists: Reminders for active reminders and Completed for finished tasks.

Reminders includes these features:

- To view reminder lists, choose View > Show Sidebar (Option+Command+S). To create a new list, choose File > New List (Command+L). To view a list's reminders, click the list in the sidebar. To move a reminder to a different list, drag the reminder to the target list or right-click it and then choose Move to List. To reorder lists, drag them up or down. To delete or rename a list, right-click it in the sidebar (deleting a list also deletes its reminders).
- To create a new reminder, click the target list and then choose File > New Reminder (Command+N) or click (+).
- To edit a reminder, right-click it and then choose Show Info, or click the reminder's *i* button, which appears when you point to a reminder. You can add a due date, set a priority, add a location-based (geofenced) alert, and more.

- To delete a reminder, right-click it and then choose Delete.

- To mark a reminder as completed, select its checkbox or right-click it and then choose Mark as Completed. Completed reminders are moved to the Completed list.

- To reorder reminders, drag them up or down.

- To import or export reminders as iCalendar (.ics) files, use Import or Export commands in the File menu. iCalendar is a standard format that many email and calendar programs can read.

- To show a calendar in the sidebar, choose View > Show Calendar (Option+Command+K). Days with active reminders are marked with dots. To jump to today's date, choose View > Go to Today (Command+T).

- To use iCloud to sync reminders wirelessly across your Macs and iOS devices, choose > System Preferences > iCloud > Reminders.

- To sync Reminders with Gmail, Yahoo, or other services that support reminders, choose > System Preferences > Internet Accounts, select the account, and then turn on Calendars/ Reminders.

- To turn on notifications for reminders, choose > System Preferences > Notifications > Reminders.

- View reminder locations in Apple Maps.

- Flick two fingers left or right on the trackpad to scroll reminder lists or calendar dates.

Safari

Use the Safari application to browse the web. Safari has features common to most browsers, as well as a few Apple touches.

Safari includes these features:

- Tabbed browsing.

- Top Sites (Bookmarks > Show Top Sites) shows a thumbnail array of frequently visited sites. You can add sites from your bookmarks and rearrange the thumbnails by dragging them.

- To use **Picture in Picture** (PiP), click the Picture-in-Picture button ⊡ at the bottom of a video. A small, borderless, floating video window pops out of the page and hovers over all other windows and apps (including full-screen apps). You can drag the PiP video to any corner of the screen, drag its edges to resize it (within limits), or point to it to use its playback controls. Click the Picture-in-Picture button again to return the video to its original page. If the Picture-in-Picture button doesn't appear on a video (on YouTube, for example), right-click the video *twice* and then choose Enter Picture-in-Picture.

- The sidebar (View > Show Sidebar) lists your bookmarks, Reading List, or Shared Links alongside the page you're currently on. You can also add pages to your Reading List with one click.

- Shared Links shows you links from people you follow on Twitter, LinkedIn, and other feeds.

- Tab View (View > Show All Tabs) shows your open tabs (pinch to see them all or flick to switch among them).

- Pin your favorite websites to the left side of the tab bar. To pin a site, drag its tab to the left side of the tab bar (the tab will narrow to an icon). Pinned sites stay pinned even after you quit and reopen Safari. To unpin a site, drag its tab to the right.

- Quickly mute tabs that play audio: click the speaker icon in the address bar or on the noisy tab. For more options, click-and-hold the speaker icon.

- Stream video from a webpage (YouTube or Vimeo, for example) to your HDTV via Apple TV and AirPlay (page 168) without showing everything else on your desktop.

- Launch with previously open webpages.

- Bookmark management.

- Multitouch gestures (pinch or spread to zoom; two-finger double-tap to magnify a block; and two-finger flick for Back or Forward).

- Download manager.

- AutoFill automatically fills in your name, address, contact info, user names, and passwords.

- View PDF pages in the browser window.

- Resume webpages you had open last.

- Pop-up blocking.

- History and bookmark search.

- Text search.

- Unified search/address bar.

- Integration with Photos, Mail, and Contacts.

- Web Clips for Dashboard.

- Reader view for distraction-free reading.

- Reading List saves webpages for later reading offline.

- HTML5 and CSS3 technologies.

- MathML support.

- Private Browsing mode.

- Sandboxing (personal data protection).

- Third-party extensions.

- iCloud support for bookmarks, Reading List, and open tabs. To view synced tabs in Safari, click the iCloud button ☁ in the toolbar.

- Set parental controls.

Script Editor

Use the Script Editor utility to write programs (.scpt files) in AppleScript, a natural-language-like scripting language with macOS-specific commands that automate tasks such as renaming groups of files and converting image formats. To set the default editor or toggle the Script menu in the menu bar, choose Script Editor > Preferences > General pane. To see sample scripts to get you started, choose Help > Open Example Scripts Folder. To open the online reference to the AppleScript language, which includes syntax and sample code, choose Help > Show AppleScript Language Guide. To set up AppleScript folder actions, right-click a folder icon in Finder and then choose Folder Actions Setup.

Script Editor also supports JavaScript for Automation, which provides the ability to use JavaScript for interapplication communication between apps in macOS.

Tip: To automate tasks without programming, use Automator (page 122).

Stickies

Use the Stickies application to post virtual notes on your screen, similar to the paper reminders that you stick to the edge of your actual monitor.

System Information

Use the System Information utility to get detailed technical information about your Mac's hardware, software, and network. You can save this report to a file or use it to diagnose problems. Shortcut: hold down the Option key and choose > System Information.

System Preferences

Opens System Preferences (Chapter 3).

Terminal

Use the Terminal utility to interact with macOS through a command-line interface. Running invisibly beneath macOS's graphical interface is a complete Unix operating system.

Terminal includes these features:

- Type Unix commands at the Terminal prompt (to list the contents of the current directory, for example, type ls).

- Copy or paste text commands in a Terminal window.

- Drag a file, folder, or proxy icon into Terminal to enter its path on the command line. Or drag an icon onto Terminal's icon in the dock or in a Finder window.

- Use multiple tabs in the same Terminal window (Shell > New Tab and View > Show Tab Bar).

- Customize Terminal (Terminal > Preferences).

- Import or export Terminal settings (Shell menu).

macOS includes hundreds of standard Unix commands (derived from BSD Unix), common tools, and scripting languages such as Perl and Python. To learn how to use a command, read the command's manual page by typing man *command_name*. (man ls, for example). To learn how to use man, type man man. Manual pages are written by programmers for programmers, so they may take some deciphering.

TextEdit

Use the TextEdit application as a text editor or word processor. TextEdit has some high-end word-processing and typography features, supports Auto Save, and can share selected text. You can use TextEdit to read and write the following types of files:

- Plain text (.txt)

- Rich Text Format (.rtf)

- Rich Text Format with Attachments (.rtfd)

- HTML (.htm or .html)

- Web Archive (.webarchive)

- Microsoft Word (.doc, .docx, or .xml)

- Open Document Text (.odt) files

To save documents in iCloud, choose File > Move To > iCloud.

Tip: Pinch the trackpad to zoom a document.

Time Machine

Opens Time Machine (page 188).

VoiceOver Utility

Use VoiceOver Utility, an Accessibility feature (page 63), to make your Mac describe aloud what appears onscreen and speak the text in documents and windows.

X11

See "Running Older Programs" on page 116.

Services

Services lets you apply the features of other programs to content selected in the current program (the service-providing program doesn't have to be open). In TextEdit, for example, you can define the selected word by using the service provided by Dictionary. TextEdit, in turn, provides its own services to other programs: you can highlight webpage text in Safari and then send it to a new TextEdit document. Services commands are contextual (text-related commands won't appear when a photo is selected, for example) and some programs neither provide nor accept services. macOS comes with built-in services and third-party programs—Skype, for example—can add their own services. You can also create custom services by using Automator (page 122).

To choose a service: In any Services-compatible program, select the content that you want to apply a service to (text, pictures, or Finder icons, for example) and then do any of the following:

- Choose from the Services submenu, which is in the program's application menu.

- In Finder, choose a service from the ⚙ˇ menu in the toolbar.

- Right-click the selection and then choose a service. (Services commands usually appear at the bottom of menus, sometimes grouped into a Services submenu.)

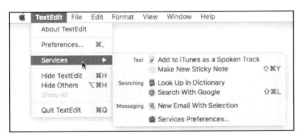

To configure Services: Choose > System Preferences > Keyboard > Shortcuts pane > Services. Alternatively, choose Services > Services Preferences from the application menu.

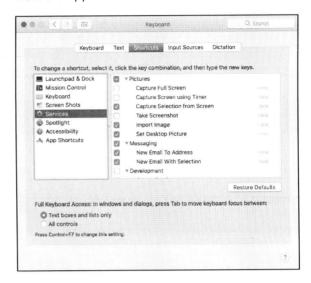

To assign or change keyboard shortcuts, click a service's name and press Return (or double-click to the right of a service's name), and then type the new keystroke. Use the checkboxes to toggle services (many are turned off by default). Commonly used services include:

Pictures

The Capture services use Grab to take a picture of all or part of the screen. The Import Image service imports a digital photo from an attached scanner, digital camera, or webcam. These services are available only in programs that accept pasted graphics. The Set Desktop Picture service makes the selected picture your desktop wallpaper.

Messaging

These services open Mail with a newly created message containing the selected file or text or addressed to the selected email address in a text document.

Development

These services invoke Automator and AppleScript.

Files and Folders

The Open Selected File in TextEdit service opens the TextEdit document specified by the selected path (~/Documents/readme.txt, for example). The New Terminal services open a Terminal window or tab with the selected folder as the working directory. The Encode services encode (convert) selected video or audio files. The Folder Actions Setup service configures AppleScript folder actions for the folder specified by the selected path. The Open, Reveal, and Show Info services invoke Finder for the file specified by the selected path. The Send File to Bluetooth Device service (Shift+Command+B) transfers the selected file wirelessly via Bluetooth to a laptop or other Bluetooth device; you can select a file icon in Finder or a file path in a text document. For all these services, an error message appears if the selected text is an invalid path.

Searching

The Look Up in Dictionary service defines the selected word. The Search with Google service (Shift+Command+L) opens the default browser and then searches for the selected text by using Google. The Spotlight service (Shift+Command+F) searches systemwide for the selected text by using Spotlight.

Text

The Add Contact service adds the selected text as a new contact. The Call and Send services call or send messages to the highlighted recipient. The Add to iTunes as a Spoken Track service saves the selected text or the path of the selected icon as an audio file by using Speech. The Convert services convert the selected file or text from Simplified Chinese to Traditional Chinese, or vice versa. The Create services create a Font Book collection or library of fonts used for the selected text. The Make New Sticky Note service (Shift+Command+Y) opens Stickies with a newly created sticky note containing the selected text. The New TextEdit Window Containing Selection service opens TextEdit with a newly created document containing the selected text. The Open man Page and Search man Page Index services display help in Terminal for the selected Unix command (mkdir, for example). The Show Address in Google Maps service opens the default browser with the selected text address or location highlighted in Google Maps. The Show Map service opens Apple Maps to the selected text address or location. The Summarize service creates a concise version of a selected passage (as if someone had highlighted the important bits); to vary the length of the summary, use the slider that appears in the pop-up Summary window.

Internet

The Add to Reading List service adds the selected URL to the Safari reading list. The Open URL service opens the selected web address (google.com, for example) in the default browser.

CHAPTER 6

Printing, Faxing & Fonts

In macOS, the operating system—not individual programs—handles printing. When you print something in any program, you activate macOS's intermediary printing system, which accepts print jobs from programs and feeds them to the printer. This process, called **background printing**, lets you keep working in your program while your documents print.

Installing and configuring a printer is easy. After connecting and setting up your hardware, you can print individual documents with the default settings or override them for special printouts. If you have an analog modem, you can fax documents as easily as print them. You can use Font Book to install and manage font files.

Setting Up a Printer

A printer connects to your computer through a USB or FireWire port, an Ethernet jack, or a wireless signal (wi-fi, Bluetooth, or Bonjour). Computers on a network can share a network printer.

When you connect a printer to your computer, macOS often recognizes it and searches its extensive collection of built-in drivers. A **printer driver** is software that lets programs send commands to a particular printer. If your printer isn't in macOS's library, you can use the driver on the disc that came with the printer or download the driver from the manufacturer's website. If you upgraded from an earlier version of macOS, you inherited the existing printer driver and settings, and your printer will usually work fine.

If you have several printers, you can designate one to be the default printer—the one selected automatically when the Print dialog box opens. You can save drive space by deleting unneeded printer drivers from /Library/Printers. Printers that you add manually are stored in ~/Library/Printers (~ denotes your home folder).

To set up a printer: Connect the printer to your computer and then turn on the printer. Open a document to print (any document will do) and then choose File > Print (Command+P). In the Print dialog box, choose the printer's name from the Printer pop-up menu. (If the printer isn't listed in the menu, then macOS couldn't detect and autoconfigure it—you have to add it manually.)

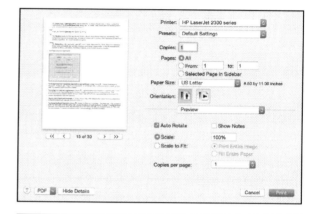

Tip: "Nearby Printers" refers to printers that aren't connected directly to your Mac, but are still accessible. For example, a shared printer connected to another Mac, a network printer that speaks Bonjour, or a printer connected to an AirPort base station or an Apple Time Capsule.

To add a printer manually: Open a document to print (any document will do) and then choose File > Print (Command+P). In the Print dialog box, choose Add Printer from the Printer pop-up menu. If your printer is listed in the "Default" pane, click it and then click Add. If your printer isn't listed, click the icon in the toolbar for your type of printer:

- Click "IP" if you have an internet printer, a network printer, an LPR (Line Printer Remote) printer, a wireless (wi-fi or Bluetooth) printer, or an old AppleTalk printer.

- Click "Windows" if you have a Windows-only network printer.

In the list, click the printer that you want to use (only connected and turned-on printers appear). Optional: to use a specific printer driver, choose "Select Printer Software" from the Use pop-up menu. When you're done, click Add.

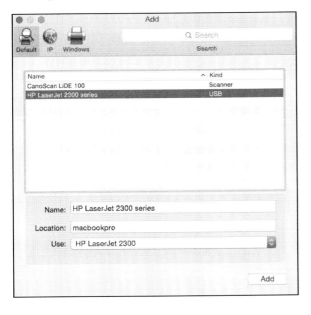

To designate a default printer: Choose > System Preferences > Printers & Scanners > "Default printer" pop-up menu.

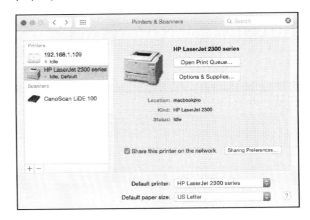

 To create a desktop printer icon: Choose > System Preferences > Printers & HP LaserJet 2300 Scanners. Drag a printer icon from the Printers list to the desktop, to a Finder window, or to the dock. You can drag documents to this icon to print them.

To delete a printer: Choose > System Preferences > Printers & Scanners. Select a printer in the Printers list and then click (–).

Printing Documents

Most programs have a Print command, which prints a document, and a Page Setup command, which sets basic printer options. The Print and Page Setup dialog boxes vary by program and printer model, but they have some common settings.

To set up a printout: Choose File > Page Setup (Shift+Command+P). Choose a paper size, change the orientation (landscape or portrait), or reduce or enlarge the pages' content (the standard Print dialog box actually has better scaling controls than the Page Setup dialog box). You must configure Page Setup independently in each program.

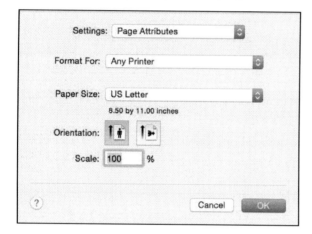

To set the default paper size: Choose > System Preferences > Printers & Scanners > "Default paper size" pop-up menu.

To print a document: Open the document and then choose File > Print (Command+P). To print using the default settings, click Print.

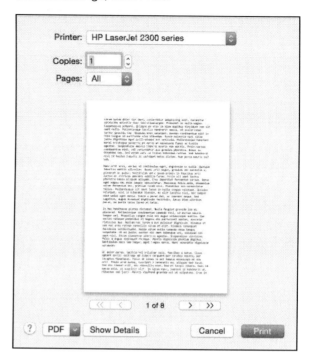

Otherwise, click Show Details to expand the dialog box.

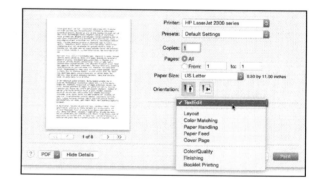

Choose preset settings or set new ones, and then click Print. Options vary by program and printer; some common ones are:

Printer
> Choose a printer (if you have more than one).

Presets
> Use this pop-up menu to save your print settings. Change the other settings in this dialog box (paper orientation, layout, colors, two-sided

printing, and so on), choose Save Current Settings as Preset from the Presets pop-up menu, and then name the preset ("Two-sided landscape", for example). The presets that you save appear in the Presets pop-up menu.

Copies
Set the number of copies to print.

Pages
Print all the pages or only a subset. Leave the From box empty to print from the start of the document; leave the To box empty to print to the end. Specify physical page numbers (1, 2, 3,…), not logical ones (roman numerals, for example).

Paper Size
Choose a standard paper size or choose Manage Custom Sizes to define odd sizes.

Orientation
Choose portrait (tall) or landscape (wide).

PDF
Set PDF options. PDF (Portable Document Format) is a standard file format for digital documents; it renders even complex documents faithfully on every modern operating system without font, layout, viewing, or printing problems. The PDF pop-up menu lets you save any document as a PDF file (instead of printing it). Other options let you preview or send PDFs, or add them to your iBooks library. Spotlight search indexes the content of PDF files. See also "Preview" on page 135.

Supplies
Open the printer manufacturer's website to a page shilling ink and printer supplies.

Additional Printing Options

Use the options pop-up menu (on the divider line) to change settings unique to the printer and program that you're using. Some common choices are:

Layout
Print multiple shrunken page images on a single sheet of paper.

Color Matching
Set the color-matching system of a color printer: ColorSync (page 124), your printer manufacturer's, or none.

Paper Handling
Set the pages to print and their printout order. The Odd and Even options can be used for double-sided printing. The Reverse option flips the printed stack. For multiple copies, clear the "Collate pages" checkbox to print pages 1, 2, 3, 1, 2, 3, or select it to print pages 1, 1, 2, 2, 3, 3.

Paper Feed
Choose which pages come from which tray of a multitray printer. These options are typically used to print the first page on letterhead and the remaining ones on blank paper.

Cover Page
Set an optional cover sheet to accompany the printout.

Scheduler
Delay printing until a specific time of day. These options are usually used to print long documents at low-traffic times.

Other settings
Other printer-specific and program-specific settings include color options, print quality (resolution), media type, paper path, paper type, and booklet printing.

Summary
Show a text summary of your current print settings.

Tip: If you're technically inclined, open a web browser and go to the address http://127.0.0.1:631. You land on the web interface for **CUPS** (Common Unix Printing System), macOS's underlying printing technology. From this administration page, you can access older printers that don't have macOS drivers, print test pages, manage networked printers and print jobs, stop printers, and more. If the CUPS web interface is disabled, run the indicated Terminal command to enable it.

Controlling Printouts

When you print a document, it's intercepted by an intermediary program, called a **print spooler**, on its way to the printer. The print spooler holds your documents (on drive or in memory) until your printer can accept them. The delay is usually short but can be substantial for large graphic files. The spooler puts each document in a **print queue**, where it waits its turn to be printed. You can pause or resume printing, change the printer for pending printouts, or cancel specific print jobs. Spooling occurs in the background, so you can keep working in your program—or even quit the program—and documents still print. You can use the print queue to print a document without opening its program.

To manage the print queue: If printing is in progress, click the printer's icon in the dock; otherwise, choose > System Preferences > Printers & Scanners. Select the printer, click Open Print Queue, click a printout (or Command-click multiple printouts) in the queue, and then use the toolbar buttons and Jobs menu to delete, hold (pause), or resume printouts. You can't reorder printouts by dragging but you can drag them to print queues in other printer windows.

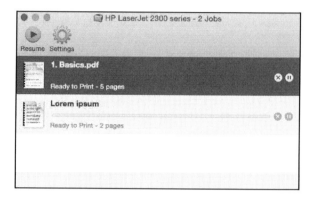

To print a document by using the print queue: Drag the document's icon from the desktop or a Finder window to the print queue or to the printer icon in the dock or on the desktop.

 To remove a printer icon from the dock: Right-click (or click-and-hold) the icon and then choose Quit. To autoremove the icon when all printouts finish, choose Auto Quit (if present).

Sharing a Printer

You can share a printer connected to your computer with other Macs on the same (wired or wireless) network. Your computer (with the attached printer) must be turned on for others to print. Everybody's print jobs go through your copy of macOS, draining your system resources. Windows users who have installed Bonjour (which comes with the Windows version of iTunes) can use a Mac's shared printer.

To share a printer: On the Mac connected to the printer, choose > System Preferences > Sharing. Turn on Printer Sharing and then select the checkbox for each printer that you want to share. To restrict a printer to certain users, select the printer and then click (+) or (–). You can also turn on printer sharing in > System Preferences > Printers & Scanners.

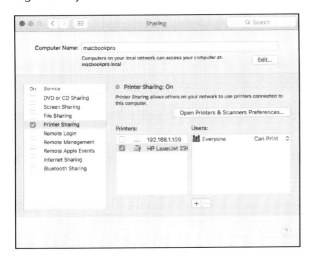

To use a shared printer over a network: Open a document to print and then choose File > Print (Command+P). In the Print dialog box, choose Add Printer from the Printer pop-up menu. Select the shared printer in the list and then click Add. The shared printer appears in the Printer pop-up menu from now on.

Faxing

Computer-based faxing conserves paper, saves money on ink and paper, and generates cleaner, more-legible faxes than ones sent via fax machine. Unfortunately, macOS doesn't support native faxing or even Apple's own (discontinued) USB modem. If you need to send or receive faxes, you have these options:

- Sign up for a service like eFax (*efax.com*) or Faxaway (*faxaway.com*), which let you send and receive faxes online.

- Buy a non-Apple analog (fax) modem, some of which work fine—try Zoom (*zoomtel.com*) or USRobotics (*usr.com*), for example. The modem comes with its own software and instructions.

Fonts

A **font** is a collection of letters, numbers, symbols, and other characters that describes a certain typeface, along with size, spacing, and other qualities. macOS includes many **OpenType** (.otf) and **TrueType** (.ttf) fonts, which look smooth and clear in all sizes, onscreen and in print. macOS also supports **PostScript Type 1** fonts but not the old OS 9 bitmapped fonts. Installed fonts appear on all Font menus and in font lists. You can install and manage fonts by using Font Book. Other tools—the Fonts, Typography, and Characters panels—let you apply fonts within documents, typeset text, and insert special characters.

Font Locations

Where a font is installed determines who can use it:

- User fonts, located in ~/Library/Fonts (~ denotes the home folder), are available only to the user who installs them.

- Computer fonts, located in /Library/Fonts, are available to all users and must be installed by an administrator.

- System fonts, located in /System/Library/Fonts, are used by macOS itself in the user interface— don't touch them.

- Application-specific fonts, located in /Library/ Application Support/*product_name*, appear when you install certain programs (Adobe and Microsoft products, for example).

Tip: If you're on a network, your administrator can make additional fonts available on a network server.

Font Book

Use Font Book to install, uninstall, find, group, preview, and disable fonts. Font Book organizes fonts into libraries and collections. **Libraries**, which appear at the top of the Collection (leftmost) column, group fonts by folder location or language (All Fonts is a library, for example). **Collections**, listed under libraries, assign fonts to user-defined groups (Fixed Width is a collection, for example). Font Book comes with built-in libraries and collections, and you can create your own. A typeface has variations (regular, italic, bold, condensed, and so on), each contained in a separate font file. You can disable fonts (without uninstalling them) to keep your font menu uncrowded. Font Book supports full-screen view.

To open Font Book: Do any of the following:

- Choose Applications > Font Book.

- Double-click a font file.

- Click ⚙ˇ > Manage Fonts in the Fonts panel or Characters panel.

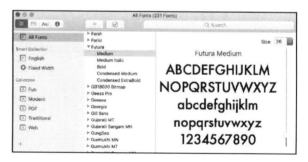

To set up Font Book: In Font Book, choose Font Book > Preferences and then set the following options:

Default Install Location
    Set the default library for installed fonts. Choose Computer if you want fonts that you install to be available to everybody (/Library/Fonts). Choose User if you want them to be available to only you (~/Library/Fonts).

Resolve duplicates by moving files to the Trash
    Prevent Font Book from installing duplicate fonts.

Automatic font activation

Autoenable (with optional warning) any disabled fonts when you open a document that uses them.

To install a font: Insert the disc that contains the new font, or copy or download the font to your drive, and then do any of the following:

- Drag the font file to a Fonts folder.

- Double-click the font file and then click Install Font in the font preview window.

- In Font Book, choose File > Add Fonts (Command+O) or click (+) in the toolbar.

- Drag font files to a library or collection in Font Book.

To remove a font: Do any of the following:

- In Font Book, select the font in the Font column and then choose File > Remove "*name*" or press Delete.

- In Finder, drag the font file out of its Fonts folder (typically /Library/Fonts or ~/Library/Fonts).

Tip: You can't remove critical system fonts. If your system fonts become corrupted, choose File > Restore Standard Fonts.

To preview or print fonts: Select a library or collection in the Collection column. In the Font column, select a font to see a preview in the rightmost column. Use the mouse or the four arrow keys to move up and down the font list or expand and collapse the font variations (regular, italic, bold, and so on). Click the toolbar buttons ▤ ⦙⦙⦙ Aa ❶ to see different font views or technical information. To change the preview size, use the Size box or the slider on the right of the preview column. Use the View menu to determine which characters are displayed—Sample, Repertoire (all characters), or Custom. To print a font reference sheet, choose File > Print (Command+P).

To create a library: Choose File > New Library (Option+Command+N), and then type a name for the library.

To add fonts to a library: In the Collection column, select the target library. Choose File > Add Fonts (Command+O) or click (+) in the toolbar. Select the folder that contains the fonts that you want to add, and then click Open. Adding a font to a library doesn't move or copy font files.

To create a collection: Choose File > New Collection (Command+N) or click + under the Collection column, and then type a name for the collection.

Tip: You can also create a **smart collection** (File > New Smart Collection) that self-updates to display fonts based on search criteria.

To add fonts to a collection: In the Collection column, select All Fonts or a library or collection that has the fonts you want to add. Drag the desired fonts from the Font column to the target collection. Adding a font to a collection doesn't move or copy font files.

To remove fonts from a library or collection: In the Collection column, select the library or collection that you want to change. In the Font column, select the target font(s), and then choose File > Remove *"name"* or press Delete. Removing fonts from a built-in library moves the font files to the Trash (they're gone from your system). Removing fonts from a user-created library leaves the font files untouched but invisible to programs (they can be reinstated later). Removing fonts from a collection removes them from that collection but not from Font Book (they're still available to programs).

To delete a library or collection: In the Collection column, select the target library or collection, and then choose File > Delete *"name"* or press Delete. Deleting a library or collection doesn't delete font files. Deleting a library makes its fonts unavailable to programs (you can't delete built-in libraries). Deleting a collection doesn't affect font availability. (It may be more convenient to disable, rather than delete, a font, library, or collection.)

To disable a font: In the Collection column, select All Fonts or a library or collection that has the font that you want to disable. In the Font column, select the target font, and then choose Edit > Disable *"font_name"* (Shift+Command+D). To enable the font, repeat these steps. Disabling a font in a collection hides it in the Fonts column when that collection is selected. Disabling a font in a library makes it unavailable to programs.

To disable a library or collection: In the Collection column, select the target library or collection, and then choose Edit > Disable *"collection_name"* (Shift+Command+E). To enable the library or collection, repeat these steps. Disabling a library disables all its fonts. Disabling a collection turns off its fonts in the Fonts column. Fonts in a disabled collection are disabled if they appear only in that collection.

To resolve duplicate-font conflicts: In the Collection column, select All Fonts. In the Font column, select any font (or font variant) marked with a yellow triangle ⚠, and then choose Edit > Look for Enabled Duplicates (or Resolve Duplicates).

To validate a font: In the Collection column, select All Fonts or a library or collection that has the font you want to validate. In the Font column, select the target font, and then choose File > Validate Font.

To open the Fonts, Typography, and Characters panels: Look for a program's Font and Special Characters commands. In TextEdit, for example, choose Format > Font > Show Fonts (Command+T). To show the Typography panel, click ✿ ⌄ > Typography in the Fonts panel. To show the Characters panel, choose Edit > Emoji & Symbols (Ctrl+Command+Spacebar). These panels also are available in Notes, Photos, Mail, Pages, Keynote, Numbers, and many other programs.

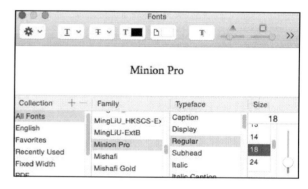

CHAPTER 7

Networks & Sharing

You create a **network** when you connect two or more computers to exchange data or share equipment. Users on a network can:

- Copy, open, and edit files and folders on computers across the network

- Share files by designating drives and folders as shared network resources

- Send brief onscreen messages to each other

- Share the same contacts list, calendar, database, or iTunes library

- Play games over the network

- Share printers, scanners, backup drives, and other devices

- Share screens to collaborate or get help

- Share an internet connection (page 175)

- Connect to the network remotely by using the internet as a conduit (page 176)

Setting up a network is usually easy, thanks to macOS's built-in tools (but the hassle of buying and installing network hardware remains). You can add macOS and Windows computers to your network.

This book covers small local (peer-to-peer) networks, common in homes and small businesses with ten or fewer computers, not large workplace or school networks maintained by full-time administrators.

Setting Up a Network

Before you can set up macOS's network software, you must install and configure network hardware. Your choice of network depends on your budget, the proximity of the computers to be networked, and your inclination to lay cable. Most people connect their computers using one of two types of standard connections: Ethernet or wi-fi.

Tip: To get information about or troubleshoot an existing network, choose Applications > Utilities > Network Utility.

Ethernet Networks (IEEE 802.3)

An **Ethernet** network is cheap, fast, secure, and reliable, and it imposes few limits on where the networked machines are placed. To create an Ethernet network, you'll need three components along with your computers:

Network adapter
Each computer must have a network adapter that provides a physical connection to the network. An adapter has an RJ-45 jack that you connect an Ethernet cable to. If your computer has no built-in Ethernet jack, buy a network interface card (NIC) or a USB plugin network adapter.

Ethernet cables
The cables used in Ethernet networks are a little thicker than telephone cables, and the **RJ-45 connectors** at each end are wider than ordinary phone (RJ-11) connectors. You can buy Ethernet cables—called 10BaseT, 100BaseT, CAT5, CAT5e, CAT6, or twisted-pair cables—of common lengths with attached connectors. For custom lengths, you (or someone at the store) can cut the cable off a spool and attach connectors. Or you can join two lengths by using an RJ-45 female/female coupler. A connection's length shouldn't exceed 100 meters (328 feet). If you're drilling through walls to lay cable, consider hiring an installer (or using a wireless network).

Hub/router
On an Ethernet network, you connect each cable from a computer's network adapter to a central connection point called a **hub**—a small box with a row of five to eight or more jacks (called **ports**) that accept RJ-45 connectors. Small green lights on the hub glow or flicker to signal an active connection. Computers communicate through the hub, so there's no direct connection between any two machines. One port (an **uplink** port) connects to a router, broadband modem, or another hub to expand the network. The other ports are numbered, but it doesn't matter which port you plug which cable into. You can also connect shared devices, such as printers, to the hub. If you have an internet connection, use a **router** instead of an ordinary hub to share the connection.

Wi-Fi Networks (IEEE 802.11)

Wireless networks are versatile and don't require cables. The wireless standard is called **wi-fi** or 802.11 (say *eight-oh-two-eleven*).

Each computer on a wireless network needs a wireless network adapter. Every laptop has a built-in wireless adapter. For a desktop computer, you may need to install a wireless adapter card. Wireless networks transmit and receive radio waves over a range of about 150 feet (through walls). To share a broadband internet connection, you need a **base station** (also called an **access point**). You can use any base station (Linksys, Belkin, and so on) but Apple's AirPort base stations are easiest to set up by using AirPort Utility (page 121). The base station, in turn, must be connected physically to a network and internet connection.

Tip: If an old-style analog modem is built into your base station, then you can plug the base station into a phone jack and go online via dial-up connection (page 174). Nearby wireless Macs can go online by remotely triggering the base station to dial.

To stop neighbors or passersby from stealing your internet bandwidth and eavesdropping, turn on the password or encryption option—usually labeled WPA or WPA2. (Don't use WEP, an older and easily broken protocol.) Also, change the default router password. Other security methods—hiding or changing the SSID, disabling DHCP, and restricting MAC addresses—are less effective than encryption.

Wireless equipment comes in these flavors: 802.11a, 802.11b, 802.11g, 802.11n, and 802.11ac. These protocols vary by compatibility, band, range, and speed. To make a long story short, buy only *g*, *n*, or *ac* equipment (*ac* being the latest standard). Note that faster wireless equipment doesn't make your internet connection faster (Chapter 8).

Ad-Hoc Networks

You can create a wireless **ad-hoc** ("computer-to-computer") network between two or more wi-fi–equipped computers without using a base station. This type of network lets you share files and play multiplayer network games easily. See also "AirDrop" on page 158.

To create a wireless ad-hoc network:

1   Click 🛜 in the menu bar and then choose Create Network.

2   Name the network and select a channel.

To join an ad-hoc network:

- Move within range of the host computer, click 🛜 in the menu bar, and then choose the ad-hoc network name (or choose from the Network Name pop-up menu in the Wi-Fi pane of Network preferences).

To connect only two Macs (your laptop and your desktop computer, for example), you can set up a simple wired network. No hub, router, or crossover cable is needed.

To create a wired ad-hoc network:

- Run a standard Ethernet cable between the Ethernet jacks of two computers.

Either way—wired or wireless—your Macs belong to the same ad-hoc network. If you share folders on one Mac, its name ("Joe's MacBook" or whatever) appears in the Finder sidebar of the other Mac. Click it to see its contents.

FireWire Networks (IEEE 1394)

You can form a simple "IP over FireWire" network if your computers all have FireWire (IEEE 1394) jacks, which usually are used to capture digital video from camcorders. (You can buy a 1394 adapter to get these jacks.) Just hook together the computers with 6-pin-to-6-pin IEEE 1394 cables. There's no need to buy a hub or router. FireWire networks usually have only two computers, but you can chain more than two if each has two free FireWire ports. The computers have to be close; 1394 cables can't be more than 15 feet (4.5 meters) long. And you can't use this arrangement to share a printer or DSL/cable modem.

To set up a FireWire network:

1   Connect two Macs with a FireWire cable.

2   Choose > System Preferences > Network.

3   Select FireWire in the network connection services list (click 🔒 if the settings are dimmed). If FireWire isn't listed, click (+), choose FireWire from the Interface pop-up menu, and then click Create. You typically don't have to enter the DNS and search domain addresses.

4   Click Apply.

File Sharing

After you set up a wired or wireless network, you can turn on file sharing, one of the most useful network features. File sharing lets you drag files across different Mac or Windows computers on the network, exactly like you drag files back and forth between the local folders and drives on your own computer.

macOS offers three ways to share files, each of which caters to different security and flexibility needs. Public-folder sharing (simple) and any-folder sharing (more flexible but more complex) let people on the same computer or network share files, folders, and drives among themselves. AirDrop (the easiest method) lets you share quickly and wirelessly with other nearby AirDrop users.

The Public Folder

A simple way to share files is to put them in your Public folder. Everyone with a user account on your Mac or on the same network can access your Public folder, no password needed. You can't choose who can access it—either everyone can or no one can. You must move or copy files to the Public folder—aliases won't work. Every user account has its own Public folder in its home folder.

To share your Public folder: Choose > System Preferences > Sharing and then select the File Sharing checkbox. All files and folders that you put in your Public folder become available to all users locally and over the network.

The Drop Box folder, located within your Public folder, lets others securely give *you* files. People can drop files and folders into your Drop Box, but they can't actually open it. This folder, too, is available both locally and over the network. (Don't confuse the Drop Box folder with the online Dropbox service.)

Tip: If you like, you can edit the Computer Name in the Sharing panel. Your Mac will appear on the network with this name. Use a descriptive name, such as Ken's MacBook Pro.

Any-Folder Sharing

 Using the Public folder can be inefficient. If you're sharing hundreds of photos, for example, it's wasteful to store copies in both your (unshared) Pictures folder and your Public folder. If you create or update files frequently, it's cumbersome to keep copying them to your Public folder.

Use any-folder sharing to share files and folders directly from the location where they're stored (typically, in your Documents, Pictures, or Music folder). You can set sharing permissions for individual users rather than for everyone on your network, giving some people more or less access (or no access).

To share any folder by using the Info window: Choose > System Preferences > Sharing and then select the File Sharing checkbox.

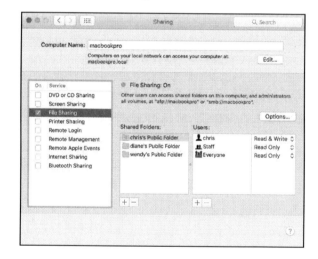

In Finder, select the folder or drive that you want to share and then choose File > Get Info (Command+I). In the Info window, expand the General panel and then select "Shared folder". (Type your administrator password, if prompted.) Expand the Sharing & Permissions panel (click 🔒 if the settings are dimmed).

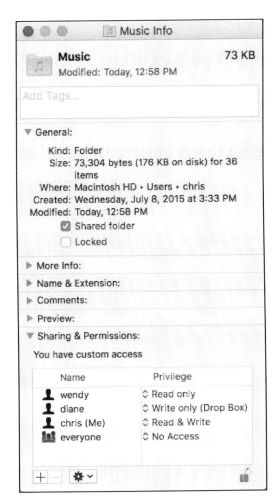

Select an existing user or group. Or add a new user: click (+), click New Person, type a name and password for the account, click Create Account, select the user in the list, and then click Select. To add an address-book contact, click Contacts, select the contact, click Select, assign a password to the new sharing account, and then click Create Account.

To choose a permission for yourself or another user, select from the pop-up menus in the Privilege column:

Read & Write
Lets a user add or delete a file, or open a file and change its contents.

Read Only
Lets a user open a file to see or copy its contents, but not change, move, or delete the original file.

Write only (Drop Box)
Lets a user copy files to the shared folder, but not see or change the folder's contents. Only the drop box's owner can open it to take out files.

No Access
Blocks all access. Users can see the folder or drive icon but can't open, change, or copy it. No Access is available only to the "everyone" group, which refers to everyone who's not specifically listed in the Name column.

To apply the same permissions to every item contained in the selected folder or drive, click ⚙ > "Apply to enclosed items".

To change the item's owner, select the new owner in the Name column, and then click ⚙ > "Make '*name*' the owner".

To remove a user or group, select the user or group in the Name column, and then click (–). The entry Everyone refers to everyone who's not specifically listed in the Name column.

To share any folder by using the Sharing preferences panel: Choose > System Preferences > Sharing and then select the File Sharing checkbox. The permissions table works the same way as it does in the Info window, except that the extra column, Shared Folders, shows all shared folders and drives in a master list (you can drag items from the desktop or a Finder window to this list). Use the (+) or (–) buttons to add or delete folders and users in the list (you can also turn off sharing for Public folders here).

To share with Windows users: Choose > System Preferences > Sharing, and then select the File Sharing checkbox. Click Options and then select "Share files and folders using SMB". (Windows uses the SMB—Server Message Block—protocol). Select the On checkbox for each account that will share files with a Windows computer.

To connect to a shared folder: In a Finder window, choose Go > Network (Shift+Command+K) to show the computers that you can access. To connect as a registered user, select the computer's icon, and then click Connect As in the connection bar near the top of the window. (Alternatively, you can connect as a no-login guest to access only Public folders.) Double-click a computer icon or click its name in the sidebar (if necessary, choose Finder > Preferences > Sidebar, and then select items under Shared). Use shared drives, folders, and files as you would any other Finder items (subject to their read–write permissions). To disconnect from a computer, click ⏏ next to its name in the Finder sidebar. To connect to an internet or unlisted server (by, say, WebDAV, DNS, NFS, FTP, or IP address), choose Go > Connect to Server (Command+K). You can also navigate to shares from within the Save and Open dialog boxes. To wake a sleeping computer for network access, see "Energy Saver" on page 74.

To get information about or troubleshoot a network: Choose Applications > Utilities > Network Utility.

AirDrop

AirDrop lets you quickly and wirelessly exchange files with other nearby AirDrop users on Macs and iOS devices, without any setup, passwords, special settings, or base stations. You don't need an internet connection or a wi-fi network, so AirDrop works on planes, trains, boats, and beaches.

To see other people nearby who are using AirDrop, do any of the following in a Finder window:

- Click the AirDrop icon in the sidebar. (To show or hide this icon, choose Finder > Preferences > Sidebar.)
- Choose Go > AirDrop.
- Press Shift+Command+R.

The user pictures and device names of those near you appear in the AirDrop window. To send a file to someone, drag it to that person's picture.

Alternatively, right-click the file's icon, choose Share > AirDrop from the shortcut menu, click the destination device's icon, and then click Send.

After the recipient accepts the file, it's transferred directly to their Downloads folder.

If someone sends a file to *your* Mac, it appears as a notification. Click Accept to download the file to your Downloads folder.

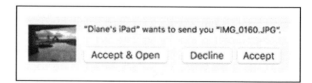

You can receive files even when AirDrop isn't selected in Finder, and choose to make yourself available to ("discovered by") everyone or only your contacts—or to no one if you want to turn off AirDrop.

If you send something to *yourself*—from your iPhone to your Mac, for example—then the receiving device accepts the transfer automatically. The incoming file goes directly into your Downloads folder without your confirmation. (You still get a notification that the transfer completed.) Both devices must be signed into the same Apple ID.

If you receive a file on an iPhone, iPad, or iPod touch, then the file opens automatically in the appropriate app (a webpage in Safari, a photo in Photos, a location in Maps, and so on). In some cases, your iOS device will instead offer you a list of installed apps that can open the file. If no installed app can open the file, iOS may display an App Store link to an app that *can*. If iOS draws a complete blank, it rejects the incoming file altogether.

You can also use AirDrop right from the application you're using: click the Share button 🔼 or Share menu in an app and then choose AirDrop. Depending on the app you're using, you can share text, documents, links, photos, contacts, locations, or videos. Apps that support sharing include Safari, Notes, Preview, Finder, Maps, iBooks, Photo Booth, Contacts, Photos, QuickTime Player, and Quick Look. To share selected text from TextEdit or Notes, right-click the selection and then choose Share. Many non-Apple apps can share via AirDrop, too—look for a Share button 🔼.

AirDrop encrypts files for transfer and creates a private firewall between you and the other person. AirDrop can also use an Apple ID (*appleid.apple.com*) to verify the identity of the person trying to send you a file. If senders are in your Contacts list and are signed in with their Apple IDs, then their names will appear under their photos in AirDrop. To cancel an incoming transfer, open the Downloads folder or stack and then click the × that appears on the incoming file's icon. AirDrop uses wi-fi to transfer files (to turn on wi-fi, choose > System Preferences > Network > Wi-Fi > Turn Wi-Fi On).

Troubleshooting AirDrop

If AirDrop isn't working, check the following:

- Both the sending and receiving devices must be turned on (awake) and within 30 feet (9 meters) of each other.

- Both devices must have Bluetooth and Wi-Fi turned on.

- Make sure that your recipient has AirDrop turned on. If AirDrop is restricted to "Contacts Only", then have the recipient either change the restriction to "Everyone" or add you to his Contacts list.

- AirDrop's Mac system requirements are listed in the Apple support article "Use AirDrop to send content from your Mac" at *support.apple.com/HT203106*. iOS system requirements are listed in "How to use AirDrop with your iPhone, iPad, or iPod touch" at *support.apple.com/HT204144*.

- If your newer Mac can't see a nearby older Mac, click "Don't see who you're looking for?" in an AirDrop window and then click "Search for an Older Mac". Note that when your Mac sees older Macs, it can't see newer ones—and vice versa.

- AirDrop won't work if "Block all incoming connections" is turned on in Firewall (> System Preferences > Security & Privacy > Firewall pane).

Accessing Shared Files

After setting up Public folder or any-folder sharing on your network, users can connect to computers and resources across the network to access shared files. People can connect by using the Finder sidebar (simple) or the Connect to Server command (more flexible but more complex).

Connecting via the Finder Sidebar

From your Mac, you can use the Finder sidebar to access shared files on another computer on the network.

Open any Finder window. In the Shared category of the sidebar at the left side of the window, icons for all the computers on the network appear, bearing whatever names they've been given in > System Preferences > Sharing.

If a particular Mac isn't listed here, then:

- It might be turned off.

- It might not be on the network.

- It might have File Sharing turned off.

- It might not have the correct file-sharing protocol turned on. To check, choose > System Preferences > Sharing, click Sharing, and then click Options. Networked computers can't see each other if they don't have at least SMB or AFP in common.

Tip: A Mac that's asleep still appears in the sidebar. You can access it from across the network if, on the sleeping Mac, "Wake for Wi-Fi network access" is turned on in > System Preferences > Energy Saver > Power Adapter tab.

If *no* computers are listed in the sidebar, then *your* computer:

- Might not be on the network.

- Might have Connected Servers and Bonjour Computers turned off in Finder > Preferences > Sidebar.

Tip: The same items listed in the sidebar also appear in the standard Open and Save dialog boxes that most applications use, making the entire network available for opening and saving files.

Large Networks

If the sidebar lists many computers, or if you're on a large organizational network that groups users into **workgroups,** then an "All" icon might appear in the sidebar. Click it to list all the network computers and resources that are visible to your Mac, including individual Mac, Windows, and Unix computers, and network zones (clusters of networked computers).

Windows Computers

To access a Windows computer, click the icon of the **workgroup** (computer cluster) that contains the target Windows computer. The default workgroup name is WORKGROUP or MSHOME, but workgroups can have almost any name that's 15 or fewer letters in length with no punctuation. Double-click workgroup icons until you see the icons of individual computers.

Other Networking Protocols

macOS can recognize servers that use the SMB/CIFS, NFS, FTP, and WebDAV protocols running in macOS Server, Unix, Linux, Windows servers (Windows NT or later), and Novell NetWare. However, the sidebar lists only the shared computers on your **subnet** (your local network).

Connecting to Another Computer

In the sidebar, click the computer whose files you want to access. The main window shows the Public folder icons for each account holder on that computer, as well as any other folders they've shared with you. If you have an account on the other computer, a folder containing your files also appears. You're now connected as a **guest.** If you can't connect, on the remote Mac, make sure that "Allow guests to connect to shared folders" is turned on in > System Preferences > Users & Groups.

Accessing Another User's Files

To access files that another user has shared with you, double-click that user's Public folder. Because you're only a guest, you don't have to type a password. In addition to the Public folder, you might see other folders that the account holder has specifically shared.

Inside the Public folder is the Drop Box folder, which lets you privately *give* files and folders to the other user. You can drop your own files onto the Drop Box folder, but you can't open it to see what other people have put there.

Files in the Public folder were put there by the account holder for you and other network users. You can't change the contents of the other user's Public folder, but you can open those files or copy them to your Mac.

Tip: If you click a computer icon in the sidebar and get a "Not Connected" or "Connection Failed" message, then your Mac may not be visible from the other Mac. Try this: on the remote Mac, choose > System Preferences > Sharing, click File Sharing, click Options, turn off "Share files and folders using SMB", and then close System Preferences. If that doesn't work, try restarting the remote Mac to affect the SMB change.

Accessing Your Own Files

You can log in to your account on another Mac on the network even while somebody else is using that Mac in person.

To access your own home folder on another Mac on the network:

1   Click the other Mac in the Finder sidebar and then click the Connect As button near the top of the window.

2   In the "Connect As" dialog box, type your account name and password for the remote Mac that you're connecting to (that is, the same name

and password you'd use to log in if you were actually seated at the remote Mac).

You can turn on "Remember this password in my keychain" to speed up this process in the future. Even if you don't have the Mac memorize your password, you can connect to the other Mac repeatedly during this particular session, without having to retype your password.

3   Click Connect.

The other Mac's icon appears in the sidebar, and its contents appear in the main window. To make the other Mac's icon appear on your desktop as well, turn on "Connected servers" in Finder > Preferences > General.

Now you can:

- Open files, copy them, and otherwise manipulate them as though they were files on your own hard drive.

- Edit or delete files if you have sufficient permissions.

- Use Spotlight to find files on the network drive. If the remote Mac is running OS X 10.5 (Leopard) or later, then you can search for words inside its files; otherwise, you can search for text in only the filenames.

Tip: When you delete a file from another Mac on the network, either by pressing the Delete key or by dragging it to the Trash, a message lets you know that you're about to delete that item permanently. It won't land in the Trash.

Account Types and Folder Visibility

The folders that you can access on a remote Mac depend on what type of user account you have on that Mac:

- **Guest account.** You can access only other users' Public folders, and any other folders with sharing turned on.

- **Standard account.** You can access only other users' Public and Drop Box folders, your own home folder, and any other folders with sharing turned on.

- **Administrator account.** You can access other users' Public and Drop Box folders, your own home folder, the drive to which you're connected, and any other drives connected to that Mac. You can view and edit the contents of the Applications, Library, Desktop, and Users/Shared folders. You can also see what folders are in other users' home folders, but you can't open them or change their contents.

- **Root user.** Unix-savvy superusers can move or delete any file or folder anywhere, including critical system files.

Tip: In OS X 10.11 (El Capitan) and later, System Integrity Protection, also called "rootless", prevents the user or any process from modifying the contents of system-protected folders, including /System, /bin, /sbin, and /usr (except for /usr/local). Not even administrators can add to these folders or edit files that they contain, and root users can't use the **sudo** command in protected directories.

Connecting via Connect to Server

The Finder sidebar provides an easy way to access computers on a network, but it has limits. You can't use it to type in a drive's network address, for example, meaning you can't access any shared drive on the internet (an FTP site, for example), or anywhere beyond your local network.

Fortunately, the more flexible Connect to Server command can connect to just about every type of networked drive. In Finder, choose Go > Connect to Server (Command+K). In the Connect to Server dialog box, type the address of the shared drive.

For example, you can connect to the following:

- **A Mac on your network.** Type the IP address of the Mac that you want to access and then click Connect to log in. Or type its Bonjour name formatted like *afp://office-macbook.local/*. After you enter your account password, and are connected, select the volumes (shared drives or folders) that you want to mount (access).

To see your Mac's IP address, choose > System Preferences > Network. Then look for a message like "Wi-Fi is connected to Arbor Network and has the IP address 192.168.1.78".

To see your Bonjour address, choose > System Preferences > Sharing. Click File Sharing. Near the top of the window, look for the computer name with a ".local" suffix (Mikes-Laptop. local, for example).

- **A Mac on the internet.** A Mac that has a static (permanent) IP address can be a server, to which you can connect remotely from anywhere via the internet.

- **A Windows PC.** Type the Windows PC's IP address or computer name, formatted like *smb://192.168.1.68* or *smb://Kitchen-Dell* (if you know the name of the shared folder, add it after a slash, like *smb://192.168.1.68/mysharedfiles*). Then click Connect. After a few seconds, type your Windows account name and password, choose the name of a shared folder, and then click OK. The PC's icon appears in the Finder sidebar and the shared folder's contents appear in the window.

- **An NFS server.** To connect to a Unix server, type the path of a shared directory formatted like *nfs://server-name/path-name*, where *server-name* is the computer's name or IP address, and *path-name* is the folder path to the shared item.

- **An FTP server.** FTP servers are drives on the internet that store the files used by websites. Type the FTP address of the server, formatted like *ftp://www.apple.com*. If the site allows anonymous (guest) access, a Finder window opens, showing the FTP site's contents. Otherwise, type your name and password for the FTP site (you can skip this step by embedding your name and password in the FTP address: *ftp:// your-name:your-password@www.apple.com*).

- **A WebDAV server.** WebDAV servers are web-based shared drives. Type the address of the server, formatted like *http://server-name/ path-name.*

As with sidebar connections, the Connect to Server command displays each connected computer or drive as an icon in the Finder sidebar, and in the standard Open and Save dialog boxes that most applications use.

Tip: After you type an address in the Connect to Server dialog box, you can click (+) to add it to the list of Favorite Servers. The next time that you want to connect, double-click the address. To reconnect to a server that you've accessed recently, click the clock icon and then choose it from the pop-up menu.

Disconnecting

When you're finished using a shared network drive or folder, you can disconnect from it: click the other computer's icon in the Finder sidebar and then click Disconnect at the top of the window. Alternatively, click ⏏ next to its name in the sidebar.

To see whether other people on the network are accessing *your* Mac, choose > System Preferences > Sharing > File Sharing > Options and then look for "Number of users connected: *n*".

If nobody is connected to your Mac over the network, then *n* will be zero; otherwise, *n* will be one or more. Having other users connected to your Mac isn't usually a security risk, since you control what they can see on your computer. Nor will multiple connections slow down your Mac noticeably as you work. But if you want to kick everyone else off your Mac, choose > System Preferences > Sharing and then turn off File Sharing.

If nobody is connected to your Mac, then your Mac stops sharing its files immediately. If anyone is connected to your Mac (from a Mac), then your Mac opens a dialog box that lets you send a message to every connected Mac user, warning them that they're about to be disconnected from your Mac (and giving them some time to wrap up their related work).

Bonjour

In the Connect to Server dialog box, and elsewhere in macOS, you can connect to another Mac, server, or printer by typing its IP address, which identifies it uniquely on the network (192.168.1.68, for example).

Fortunately, **Bonjour** spares you from having to memorize or write down IP addresses. Bonjour is an underlying macOS networking technology that lets networked devices detect each other on the network automatically and recognize each other's capabilities. With Bonjour, each device announces its own presence on the network. (Without Bonjour, you must specifically connect to each piece of equipment on the network by address or name.)

Bonjour works in the background, silently making network life easier. For example, Bonjour:

- Makes shared Macs' names appear in the Finder sidebar's Shared list

- Lists the names of available network-aware printers in the Print dialog box

- Populates your Bonjour buddy list in Messages automatically with the names of everyone who's on the same network

- Makes other Macs' names appear in the iTunes program so that you can listen to their music from across the network

The Shared Folder

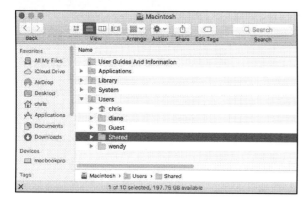

You can share files with other users on your computer (without a network) by using the Shared folder.

To share across accounts: Open the Shared folder, in the Users folder on your system drive. The Shared folder is a single folder available to every account on the Mac (it doesn't belong to any particular user). Each user, administrator or not, can add, open, or delete files without restriction.

Tip: If your family members all share the same Mac but have different accounts, and you all want to listen to the same music collection (MP3 files) by using the iTunes application, then move all the audio files into a new folder (named Music or whatever) and then move that music folder into the Shared folder, where it's available to everybody. Each account holder can log in, open iTunes, choose iTunes > Preferences > Advanced, and then click Change to choose the shared music folder.

Screen Sharing

You can connect to another computer on your network and show that computer's screen on your own display, controlling the other computer as if you were sitting in front of it—opening its programs and documents; moving, copying, renaming, or deleting files and folders; rearranging windows; using keyboard shortcuts; and even restarting or shutting down. You can also share your own screen with others on your network. Nobody can share your screen or take control of your Mac without your explicit permission.

Screen sharing is useful for accessing your own computer from afar, collaborating on projects, and giving technical support. macOS uses the standard VNC (Virtual Network Computing) remote-control protocol.

Setting Up Screen Sharing

To set up screen sharing, choose > System Preferences > Sharing, and then select the Screen Sharing checkbox.

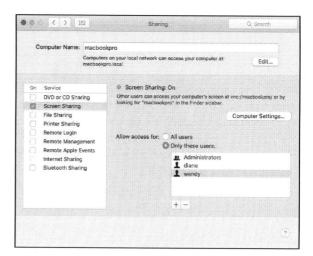

Select an "Allow access for" option:

- **All users.** Select "All users" to let anyone with a user account on your Mac share your screen and take control anytime they like, even when you're not at your computer. Users must type the same name and password they'd use if they were sitting at your Mac.

- **Only these users.** Select "Only these users" to restrict screen sharing to specific users. To add a user, click (+) and then select a user from Users & Groups, Network Users, or Network Groups. To delete a user, select the user in the list and then click (−). If you select "Only these users" but leave the user list empty, then only people who have administrator accounts on your Mac can share your screen.

Click Computer Settings to set the following options:

- **Anyone may request permission to control screen.** Let anyone on your network request to share your screen. When this setting is turned on, other users must request permission to see your screen. To grant it, click OK on the screen, in person, so that you can watch what they do.

- **VNC viewers may control screen with password.** Set the password needed by third-party VNC viewers to control your screen. (Don't bother setting a password if you share by using only macOS's built-in screen sharer.)

Sharing Another Computer's Screen

To share another computer's screen, in a Finder window, click the computer whose screen you want to see in the sidebar's Shared section, and then click Share Screen near the top of the window.

Sign in in one of the following ways:

- **By requesting permission.** Send the other Mac's current user a message asking whether you can share their screen. If that person grants permission, then the other Mac's screen image appears on your screen.

  To grant permission, the other Mac's user must first turn on "Anyone may request permission to control screen" in > System Preferences > Sharing > Computer Settings.

  To request permission, select the other Mac in the Finder sidebar, click Share Screen near the top of the window, select "By requesting permission", and then click Connect.

The other Mac's user receives an onscreen message and, if he clicks Share Screen, then the other Mac's screen image appears on your screen.

- **Registered user.** If nobody is at the other Mac to grant permission, but you have an account on the other Mac, then you can choose "Registered user".

- **Using an Apple ID.** If nobody is at the other Mac to grant permission, and you *don't* have an account on it, then you can sign in by using your Apple ID, provided the other Mac's user has preapproved you in the "Only these users" list. You must be in the other user's Contacts list with the email address that you use as your Apple ID. Both users must register their Apple IDs on their own computers in > System Preferences > Users & Groups.

If you sign in with the same account that's already logged into the other Mac (if they're both your Macs, for example), then the other Mac's screen image appears on your screen immediately. But if you connect by using a different account, then the Select Display dialog box opens.

Select a display option:

- **Ask to share the display.** View or control the screen that's in use now by whomever is using the other Mac.

- **Connect to a virtual display.** Take control of your account on the other Mac without disturbing whomever is now using it. The other person will see an ⊞ icon in the menu bar while you're connected.

Tip: To connect by using an IP address or DNS name, in Finder, choose Go > Connect to Server (Command+K), and then type *vnc://ip_address* or *vnc://name.domain*. (To see a computer's name or address, choose > System Preferences > Sharing > Screen Sharing.)

Screen Sharing Tips

- You can drag icons to transfer files between computers.

- You can copy and paste content between computers. To place what's on your clipboard onto the other Mac's clipboard, choose Edit > Send Clipboard, or choose Edit > Get Clipboard to do the reverse. These commands also have corresponding toolbar buttons.

- To show or hide the Screen Sharing toolbar, choose View > Show Toolbar. To customize the toolbar, right-click it.

- If you want only to watch what the other person is doing without controlling the screen, choose View > Switch to Observe Mode, or click the corresponding toolbar button. In Observe Mode, your cursor turns white and your mouse and keyboard actions have no effect on the other screen.

- To expand the Screen Sharing window to full screen, choose View > Enter Full Screen (Ctrl+Command+F) or click the green button in the window's top-left corner. To restore the window to its previous size, move the pointer to the top edge of the screen and then, when the menu bar appears, click the green button.

- To see the other screen at actual size, choose View > Turn Scaling Off, or click the corresponding toolbar button. If the other computer's display is the same size as yours or larger, then you must scroll the Screen Sharing window to see the entire image.

- Choose View > Full Quality to trade off the speed at which the screen updates for the image sharpness when you do something that creates a sudden change in the screen image (such as quitting a program or scrolling rapidly).

- Pressing Command+Q doesn't quit Screen Sharing—it quits whatever application is running on the other Mac. To quit Screen Sharing, choose Screen Sharing > Quit Screen Sharing.

- Screen Sharing is actually an app in the folder / System/Library/CoreServices. You can double-click it and then type the public IP address or domain name of the computer that you want to connect to.

- To share your screen over the internet, you can use the Messages application. No accounts, passwords, or setup are needed beyond initiating a Messages chat. OS X 10.5 (Leopard) or later is required on both Macs.

- If you use iCloud (page 78), then you can click Back to My Mac in the sidebar to connect (over a local or remote network) to the computer where you've registered in the iCloud preferences panel. For details, read the Apple support article "Set up and use Back to My Mac" at *support.apple.com/HT204618*.

CD & DVD Sharing

You can let other network users use the disc in your CD/DVD drive.

To share a CD or DVD: Choose > System Preferences > Sharing, select the DVD or CD Sharing checkbox, and then set the sharing options.

Bluetooth Sharing

You can transmit files wirelessly to and from Bluetooth devices (page 64).

To share over Bluetooth: Choose > System Preferences > Sharing, select the Bluetooth Sharing checkbox, and then set the sharing options. In the Bluetooth menu , choose the Send or Browse command to invoke Bluetooth File Exchange (page 122).

Facebook Integration

Facebook (*facebook.com*) is the dominant social-networking service. It's available systemwide in macOS.

- To sign in to your Facebook account, choose > System Preferences > Internet Accounts > Facebook.

- You can use share sheets to post photos, links, and comments straight to Facebook from Safari, Preview, Photo Booth, Photos , Notes, TextEdit, Quick Look, and more.

- To get Facebook notifications in Notification Center, choose > System Preferences > Notifications > Facebook. Click Options to specify which types of Facebook notifications to show (friend requests, comments, wall posts, and so on).

- Facebook posts can pick up your approximate location by using Location Services (page 184). Click the location indicator in the Facebook share sheet to add a location to your post.

- Facebook friends appear in Contacts with profile photos and up-to-date information.

- Facebook is integrated with Game Center.

Twitter Integration

Twitter (*twitter.com*) is a popular third-party micro-blogging service. It's available systemwide in macOS.

- To sign in to your Twitter account, choose > System Preferences > Internet Accounts > Twitter.

- You can send **tweets**—140-character messages—with attachments from several apps, including Safari, Preview, Photo Booth, Photos, Notes, TextEdit, Quick Look, and more. To tweet a link or photo, click the Share button and then choose Twitter. To tweet selected text, right-click the selection and then choose Share > Twitter. While you're composing a tweet, the number at the bottom of the Tweet window shows the number of characters remaining that you can enter (up to 140). Attachments use some of a tweet's characters.

- To get notifications for direct messages and mentions, choose > System Preferences > Notifications > Twitter.

- Tweets can pick up your approximate location by using Location Services (page 184).

- To add a Twitter field to a contact, open Contacts, select the contact, and then choose Card > Add Field > Twitter.

Share Sheets

A **share sheet** is a menu that appears when you click the Share button ⬆ or Share menu in an application that supports sharing. Share sheets let you share quickly and easily, with no need to switch apps or drag files. You can share via Mail, Messages, AirDrop, and other built-in apps, or post straight to Twitter, Facebook, Vimeo, Flickr, and other social networks (to sign in to your accounts, choose > System Preferences > Internet Accounts). Third-party developers can also add their apps and services to share sheets. To select and reorder items in share sheets choose > System Preferences > Extensions > Share Menu.

Depending on the app you're using, you can share text, documents, links, photos, contacts, locations, or videos. Apps that support sharing include Safari, Notes, Preview, Finder, Maps, iBooks, Photo Booth, Contacts, Photos, QuickTime Player, and Quick Look. To share selected text from TextEdit or Notes, right-click the selection and then choose Share.

AirPlay Mirroring

You can use **AirPlay**, Apple's wireless file-streaming technology, to mirror (duplicate) whatever is on your Mac's screen—videos, apps, games, photos, presentations, websites, anything—to a high-definition TV (HDTV), up to 1080p HD. AirPlay also lets you use an HDTV as a full-fledged display, complete with dock and menu bar—so while you're, say, running a slideshow on your TV, you can send email or chat on your Mac. You need an Apple TV (second generation or later, *apple.com/tv*) that's on the same wireless network as your Mac—macOS detects the Apple TV automatically. Click the AirPlay icon ◢ on the menu bar and then select Apple TV to start mirroring. If the AirPlay icon isn't visible, choose > System Preferences > Displays > Display pane > "Show mirroring options in the menu bar when available". You can also use the AirPlay Display menu in the Display pane to invoke AirPlay mirroring.

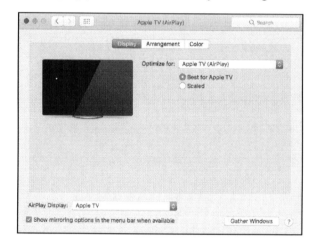

AirPlay mirroring scales your Mac's desktop image to fit your HDTV screen. For a sharp HDTV image, choose the best resolution for your Apple TV in the Display pane. For privacy, signals between your Mac and your Apple TV are encrypted. AirPlay mirroring requires a 2011 or newer Mac.

Tip: AirPlay mirroring sends audio (as well as video) from your Mac to your Apple TV. You can use the audio feature independent of AirPlay mirroring by selecting your Apple TV in Sound preferences.

Continuity

Continuity is Apple's umbrella term for wireless integration between Macs and iOS devices (iPhones, iPads, and iPod touches). Continuity encompasses several features and technologies, and requires OS X 10.10 (Yosemite) or later on the Mac side and, for most features, iOS 8 or later on the iDevice side. For an overview, see Apple's Continuity webpage at *apple.com/macos/continuity*.

To set up Continuity on your various devices, read the Apple support article "Use Continuity to connect your iPhone, iPad, iPod touch, and Mac" at *support.apple.com/HT204681*.

Handoff

Handoff lets you transition easily between devices while continuing to work on the same task. Suppose that you're composing an email on your iPhone on the way to work. When you arrive at the office, you can complete the email on your Mac and send it. Handoff makes the transition from iPhone to Mac frictionless by eliminating the usual steps of saving a draft of the outgoing message on a server, launching Mail on the Mac, syncing with the server, and finding the saved draft. Instead, when you log in to your Mac, Handoff places a Mail icon to the left of the dock (or on top, if your dock is on the side of the screen). A similar icon also appears in the Command+Tab application switcher. Clicking or selecting the icon opens Mail and displays a message that you were composing on your iPhone, with the insertion point blinking where you left off.

- Handoff works only when two devices are near each other. If you're composing an email on your iPhone in Hawaii, a Handoff icon won't appear on your office Mac in San Francisco. Devices discover each other by using Bluetooth Low Energy (BTLE), with a range of at most a few hundred feet.

- Handoff works between any combination of Macs and iOS devices (between two Macs, for example, or between an iPhone and an iPad) that are logged in to the same iCloud account. All communication is local; your data never appear on Apple's servers.

- Applications must support Handoff explicitly.

- The two applications involved in a handoff don't have to be the same on both devices, but they must be from the same developer. Only apps sold through the App Store or signed with a registered Apple Developer ID can support Handoff. A single developer can create a suite of cooperating iOS and macOS applications.

- Handoff works with Mail, Messages, Safari, Maps, Reminders, Calendar, Contacts, Notes, Keynote, Numbers, and Pages.

- Handoff works between iOS apps and Safari on macOS. You can start an activity by using an app on your iPhone, for example, and then pick it up on the app's corresponding website in Safari on your Mac.

- To toggle Handoff on your Mac, choose > System Preferences > General > Allow Handoff. Handoff requires a 2012 or newer Mac. To use Handoff, read "Pick up where you left off with Handoff" at *support.apple.com/kb/PH21868*.

iPhone Calls

You can pick up a phone call to your iPhone from your Mac, initiate a phone call from your Mac, or hand off an ongoing Mac phone call to your iPhone. iPhone calls require an iPhone with iOS 8 or later.

When you receive a call on your iPhone, that incoming call also rings on your Mac (even if your phone is charging or in another room). A notification on your Mac displays the caller's name, number, and, if available, profile picture. If you've set up a particular ringtone for the caller on your iPhone, then that same ringtone sounds on your Mac. Click the notification to answer, and your Mac acts as a speakerphone. You can have a phone conversation and work on your Mac at the same time.

When you make a phone call from your Mac, it's relayed through your iPhone using your existing phone number. You can dial a phone number anywhere that you see it on your Mac: Contacts, Calendar, Mail, Messages, Spotlight, Safari, or any document. You can also start a call from your FaceTime call history or type the digits on the keyboard.

SMS/MMS Messages

You can use your Mac and iPhone to send and receive SMS or MMS messages. SMS/MMS messages differ from Apple's iMessage messages. SMS/MMS is a worldwide standard that works on all mobile phones; iMessage is proprietary and works on only Apple iOS devices and Macs. SMS (Short Message Service) messages contain only text. MMS (Multimedia Messaging Service) messages can include pictures, video, or audio in addition to text. In the Messages app on your Mac or iOS device, SMS/MMS messages appear in green bubbles and iMessages appear in blue bubbles. SMS/MMS requires an iPhone with iOS 8.1 or later.

With Continuity, SMS/MMS messages are synchronized across all your devices: messages that appear on your iPhone also appear on your Mac. When someone texts you—regardless of what phone they use—you can reply from your Mac or iPhone. You can also start an SMS/MMS (or iMessage) conversation on your Mac by clicking a phone number in Contacts, Calendar, Mail, Messages, Spotlight, Safari, and so on.

AirDrop File Sharing

Use AirDrop (page 158) to quickly and wirelessly send files to other nearby AirDrop users, without any setup, passwords, special settings, or base stations.

Instant Hotspot (Tethering)

If no wi-fi signal is available, your Mac can go online by tethering to the personal hotspot on your iPhone when they're near each other. Your iPhone shares its cellular internet connection with your Mac. For details, see "Cellular Connections (Tethering)" on page 174.

Apple Pay

Apple Pay is Apple's mobile payment and digital wallet service that lets you make secure payments by using a compatible iPhone, Apple Watch, iPad, or Mac. To use Apple Pay on your Mac, look for Apple Pay on a participating website in Safari, then complete your purchase with Touch ID on your iPhone or by double-clicking the side button on your Apple Watch. For details about Apple Pay, visit the Apple Pay website at *apple.com/apple-pay*.

Auto Unlock with Apple Watch

You can log in to or unlock your Mac automatically when you're wearing your Apple Watch, with no need to type your user name or password. Your Mac, Apple Watch, and iPhone must all be logged in to the same iCloud account, and two-factor authentication (page 183) must be turned on. To unlock your Mac, your Apple Watch must be unlocked and within range of your Mac (about three meters). After you unlock your watch, it stays unlocked for as long as you're wearing it, and it locks instantly when moved out of range of your Mac. You need both your iPhone and your Apple Watch to unlock your Mac (neither device alone will unlock it). To turn Auto Unlock on or off, choose > System Preferences > Security & Privacy > General > "Allow your Apple Watch to unlock your Mac".

Universal Clipboard

Use the universal clipboard (page 34) to copy and paste content between Macs and iOS devices.

Internet Connections

As an individual, you can't connect to the internet directly. You must pay a go-between **ISP** (**internet service provider**) and rely on it to provide setup instructions, turn on your service, equip and maintain dependable connections, and help you when things go wrong.

You can also connect to a computer or network remotely. You can, for example, connect from your laptop or home machine to an unattended, distant machine in your office or at school to access its files and resources.

If you upgraded from an earlier version of macOS, your existing connections were preserved and should work fine.

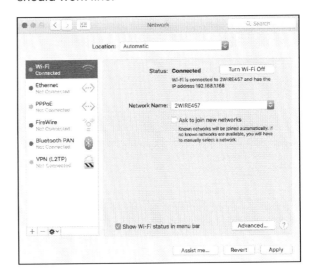

Connection Order

Connections are managed in the Network panel of System Preferences. The network connection services list shows the ways that your computer is set up to connect to the internet or other network (a remote office or school network, for example): Ethernet (wired), Wi-Fi (wireless), External Modem (dial-up), Bluetooth, FireWire, VPN, and so on. A colored dot shows each connection's status: green means turned on and connected to a network; yellow means working, but not connected; and red means the connection isn't set up yet.

The order of connections in the list is the sequence that macOS uses to go online when you open a browser or any program that needs internet or network access. macOS tries the first connection method; if that doesn't work, it tries the second, and so on. macOS can maintain multiple connections simultaneously—if a connection dies while you're using it, macOS switches automatically to the next. Laptop users usually sort the sequence by decreasing connection speed (or decreasing security): Ethernet, Wi-Fi, External Modem.

To set the order of connections: Choose > System Preferences > Network. Click ⚙▾ > Set Service Order. Drag the items up and down in the services list into priority order.

Broadband Connections

Broadband (DSL, cable, fiber, or office-network) connections are fast, always on, and easy to set up. Most broadband connections autoconfigure by using **DHCP** (Dynamic Host Configuration Protocol), so require no setup from you beyond plugging in an Ethernet cable or choosing a wireless network from the 🛜 menu (see also "Setting Up a Network" on page 154). For PPPoE connections, your ISP will give you an account name and password.

To create an Ethernet (wired) connection: Choose 🍎 > System Preferences > Network. Click (+) and then choose and name a new Ethernet service.

To create a wi-fi (wireless) connection: Choose 🍎 > System Preferences > Network. Click (+) and then choose and name a new Wi-Fi service.

To configure an Ethernet connection: Choose 🍎 > System Preferences > Network. Click Ethernet in the services list. Select from the Configure pop-up menu and (if you're not using DHCP) type the IP addresses provided by your ISP or administrator. When you're done, click Apply in the Network panel. (Alternatively, you can set up a connection by stepping through a series of interview windows: click "Assist me" at the bottom of the Network panel.)

To configure a wi-fi connection: Choose 🍎 > System Preferences > Network. Click Wi-Fi in the services list. Select a wireless network name, turn on the Wi-Fi menu 🛜, and set the other options. When you're done, click Apply in the Network panel. (Alternatively, you can set up a connection by stepping through a series of interview windows: click "Assist me" at the bottom of the Network panel.)

To configure a PPPoE connection: Choose 🍎 > System Preferences > Network. Click Ethernet in the services list and then choose Create PPPoE Service from the Configure pop-up menu. Alternatively, click (+), choose and name a new PPPoE connection, and then click it in the services list to configure it.

To remove a broadband connection: Choose 🍎 > System Preferences > Network. Click the target connection in the services list and then click (−).

To connect to a wireless network: In the menu bar, choose 🛜 > *network_name* (or choose from the Network Name pop-up menu in the Wi-Fi pane of Network preferences). If the network is secured (denoted by 🔒), type a password. To join a closed (hidden) network, choose Join Other Network and then type the network name.

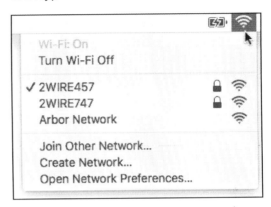

Troubleshooting Wireless Connections

Common wireless connection problems include:

- A network's signal strength is strong enough to appear in the 🛜 menu but too weak to support an actual connection (move closer).

- A wireless router broadcasts its presence even when its internet connection is down.

- A network is restricted to only certain machines (by MAC address).

- A commercial network requires a credit-card payment.

To see wireless network diagnostics quickly: Hold down the Option key and click the 🛜 menu. Network diagnostics are shown in gray text under the name of the active network. The BSSID is the MAC (Media Access Control) address of the wireless access point. To see your Mac's MAC address ("Wi-Fi Address"), choose 🍎 > System Preferences > Network > Wi-Fi > Advanced > Wi-Fi pane. Some administrators secure networks by restricting access to only certain MAC addresses.

To manage wireless networks: Choose 🍎 > System Preferences > Network, click Wi-Fi in the services list, and then click Advanced > Wi-Fi pane.

Cellular Connections (Tethering)

If you have an iPhone, Android phone, or other smartphone, you may be able to get your Mac online via **tethering**: your phone acts as an internet hotspot for your laptop, relying on the cellular network for its connection. The phone connects to your laptop either with a USB cable or wirelessly (wi-fi or Bluetooth). You can get online almost anywhere there's cellphone coverage, but the connection isn't always fast, and you have to pay your cellular carrier an extra fee.

On an iPhone, for example, choose Settings > General > Network, turn on Personal Hotspot, assign a private hotspot password, and then choose a connection type (wi-fi, for example). On your Mac, choose your iPhone's name from the 🛜 menu and then type your hotspot password (which your Mac memorizes). The menu icon changes to ⊂⊃ while you're tethered. Tethering drains your phone's battery quickly (usually within about 3 hours). When connected to your personal hotspot, your Mac displays the signal strength and battery life of your iPhone at the top of the 🛜 menu. After you finish browsing, the hotspot deactivates automatically to preserve battery life.

Cellular carriers also offer USB sticks or pocket routers that act as mobile wi-fi hotspots. To get online, insert the USB stick or turn on the pocket router, then wait about 15 seconds for the cellular signal. Your cellular provider might provide you with a proprietary (and typically poorly written) program to make the internet connection, but you may not need it—try using the 🛜 menu instead.

Dial-Up Connections

Each time that you connect to the internet or a remote network via dial-up, your analog modem dials your ISP or network over a standard phone line. Dial-up connections are slow compared with broadband, but they're a good choice for frequent travelers, because big ISPs provide local access numbers over large geographic areas. In some areas, dial-up is your only choice. You need an analog

Bluetooth or USB modem. macOS doesn't support Apple's (discontinued) USB modem, so you must use a non-Apple modem that supports macOS (try Zoom or USRobotics). The modem comes with its own software and instructions.

To create a dial-up connection: Connect the modem. Choose > System Preferences > Network. Click (+) and then choose and name a new External Modem (or Internal Modem) service.

To configure a dial-up connection: Connect the modem. Choose > System Preferences > Network. Click External Modem in the services list. Type the local access number, user name, and password provided by your ISP or administrator. Turn on the modem menu 📞.

You can use the Configuration pop-up menu to add, rename, or delete multiple dial-up numbers. It's sensible to name a configuration after the ISP and access location ("AT&T San Francisco", for example).

You can prefix a number with dialing codes. Add a 9 to get an outside line, for example, or *70, to turn off call waiting (a comma pauses dialing for 2 seconds). Calling-card numbers are valid too.

Click Advanced to set other options. In the Modem pane, set model, dialing, and sound options. In the PPP pane, specify the idle-time before autodisconnect and the number of redials to a busy number. To autodial whenever you open your browser or email program, select "Connect automatically when needed" (otherwise, you must connect manually each time).

When you're done, click Apply in the External Modem pane of Network preferences.

(Alternatively, you can set up a connection by stepping through a series of interview windows: Click "Assist me" at the bottom of the Network panel.)

To remove a dial-up connection: Choose > System Preferences > Network. Click External Modem in the services list and then click (–).

To connect to a dial-up network: The modem will autoconnect if you turned on "Connect automatically when needed" when you configured the dial-up connection. To connect manually, choose a configuration in the ☎ menu, and then choose ☎ > Connect External Modem (or choose from the Configuration pop-up menu in the External Modem pane of Network preferences, and then click Connect).

To disconnect from a dial-up network: The modem will autodisconnect in some situations, depending on the options you chose in the PPP pane when you configured the dial-up connection. To disconnect manually, choose ☎ > Disconnect (or click Disconnect in the External Modem pane of Network preferences).

Network Locations

Network locations are for travelers who use different network settings in different places: Ethernet at work, wireless at home, dial-up when travelling, and so on. A "location" is actually a group of saved network settings that you can switch to easily.

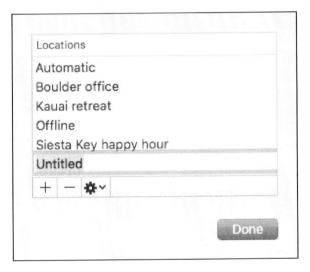

To set up a location: Choose > System Preferences > Network. Choose Edit Locations from the Location pop-up menu (near the top of the panel). Click (+), type a location name, and then click Done. You can click ⚙▾ to rename or duplicate an existing location, or (−) to delete one.

Back on the Network panel, click each network connection and then configure it (to disable it, click ⚙▾ > Make Service Inactive). Reorder the connections as needed (page 172).

To switch to a location: Choose > Location (this menu appears only after you set up more than one location), or choose > System Preferences > Network > Location pop-up menu.

Tip: If you have a laptop, create a location named Offline and make all its connections inactive. Choose this location when you're on an airplane or submarine or anywhere else where you don't want to go online.

Internet Sharing

To share one internet connection with every computer on a local network, you have two options:

Install a router

A **router** is a small box with one jack that connects to a hub and another jack that connects to a DSL, cable, or dial-up modem. A **router/hub** doubles as a hub, sharing the modem's bandwidth among multiple Ethernet ports that the network computers connect to. A slightly more expensive **router/switch** is faster than a router/hub and should be used when you're passing lots of data around the network (when playing network games or sharing music, for example).

Use Internet Sharing

Internet Sharing is a built-in macOS feature that acts like a software router. It's free but limited compared to a hardware router. You must designate one computer as the **host** (or **gateway**) through which all internet traffic passes. For broadband connections, the host must have two Ethernet adapters: one that connects to the DSL or cable modem and one that connects to a hub. Sharing also works with dial-up and Bluetooth cellphone connections. If the host is turned off, the other computers can't go online.

To share an internet connection:

1   On the host computer, choose > System Preferences > Sharing.

2   Turn *off* the Internet Sharing checkbox (if it's not already turned off).

3   Click the "Share your connection from" pop-up menu and choose the source of this host computer's internet connection.

4   In the "To computers using" list, select each port to indicate how the host will distribute (rebroadcast) the internet connection to the other computers. Choose a connection type different from the one in the preceding step (you can't get your signal via wi-fi and then share it via wi-fi, for example). The services that appear here mirror those that are turned on in > System Preferences > Network.

5   Turn on the Internet Sharing checkbox.

6   On each of the other Macs on the same network (but not the host), do the following:

   ▸   Choose > System Preferences > Network, select the network type that you chose in step 4 above, and then click Apply.

   ▸   Turn off Firewall in > System Preferences > Security & Privacy > Firewall.

VPN Connections

A **virtual private network (VPN)** lets you connect from your computer to a network securely and privately by using the internet as a conduit. VPNs overcome direct dialing's twin evils: slow speeds and high costs.

To create a VPN connection: Choose > System Preferences > Network. Click (+) and then choose and name a new VPN service. Ask your network administrator which VPN Type (tunneling protocol) to choose.

To configure a VPN connection: Choose > System Preferences > Network. Click VPN in the services list. Type the server address and account name provided by your administrator. You can use the Configuration pop-up menu to add, rename, or delete multiple VPN connections. Turn on the VPN menu . Click Authentication Settings to specify security settings. Click Advanced to set other options. When you're done, click Apply in the Network panel.

To remove a VPN connection: Choose > System Preferences > Network. Click the target connection in the services list and then click (−).

To connect to a VPN: Choose a configuration in the menu, and then choose > Connect VPN (or choose from the Configuration pop-up menu in the VPN pane of Network preferences, and then click Connect).

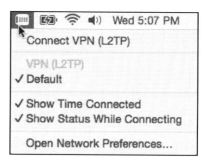

To disconnect from a VPN: The VPN will autodisconnect in some situations, depending on the options you chose in the Advanced > Options pane when you configured the VPN connection. To disconnect manually, choose > Disconnect (or click Disconnect in the VPN pane of Network preferences).

CHAPTER 9

Security & Privacy

MacOS's security and privacy features include major tools like Firewall, FileVault, Keychain Access, and Parental Controls, and smaller ones like Password Assistant and secure virtual memory.

You can also use secure login options (page 16), secure-erase a drive (page 109), restrict program installations (page 112), and use Private Browsing mode in Safari. When you try to do something potentially dangerous (like run a program downloaded from the internet), macOS will warn you or prompt you for an administrator password.

Firewall

A **firewall** is a piece of software or hardware that helps screen out hackers and malware that try to reach your computer over the internet. It's the most important security component on your computer or network; if you don't have one, attackers can compromise your computer minutes after you go online. macOS provides Firewall for free, but consider using a router too.

A router is a small box that distributes the signal from your modem (DSL, cable, or dial-up) to the computers on your network. A router has a built-in firewall and appears to the outside world to be a computer without programs and hard drives to attack or infect; it's the safest type of firewall, because it protects your entire network and is always on. Even if you're not on a network, you can put a router between your computer and your modem. If you're on a network, a router won't protect you from *other* computers on the network if one of them becomes infected because someone downloaded a virus. For that kind of protection, you need macOS's software Firewall on your individual computer. See also "Setting Up a Network" on page 154.

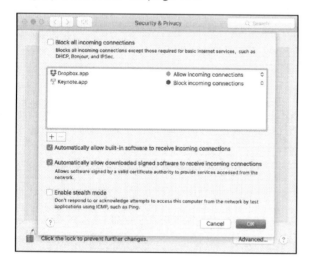

To turn Firewall on or off: Choose > System Preferences > Security & Privacy > Firewall pane > Turn On/Off Firewall (click if the settings are dimmed). Turn off Firewall only if you're using a router, a different firewall, or someone's shared internet connection.

To configure Firewall: Choose > System Preferences > Security & Privacy > Firewall pane > Firewall Options (click if the settings are dimmed), and then set the following options:

Block all incoming connections
Block everything but a few crucial network services (secure but limiting).

[List of services and applications]
Block all incoming signals except those sent to programs that you've approved (the most flexible choice). In the list, macOS's sharing features appear automatically above the divider line. To add a program, click (+), choose the program, and then click ◊ to set its limits. To delete a program, select it and then click (−).

Automatically allow built-in software to receive incoming connections
Trust the programs that come with macOS.

Automatically allow signed software to receive incoming connections
Trust well-known programs whose authenticity has been confirmed by a third-party certificate authority.

Enable stealth mode
Make your Mac invisible to automated cracker programs trolling the internet. macOS won't respond to "pings" (including those from you when you're travelling).

Tip: To see the Firewall log, choose Applications > Utilities > Console > appfirewall.log.

FileVault

FileVault automatically encrypts and password-protects your entire drive (including external USB and FireWire drives). After you set up FileVault, it runs in the background. Everything works like before, with no noticeable performance hit, except now your data are secured against laptop thieves, drive thieves, cops, and customs agents at border crossings. Your files are readable by only you and anyone with a master recovery key. Any shared folders in your home folder become unreadable by others on the network when you're not logged in. Time Machine (page 188) can copy an encrypted home folder only when you're logged out. FileVault uses standard XTS-AES encryption with 128-bit keys; if you forget your password and the master recovery key, your data are lost forever.

Tip: To quickly encrypt a (nonsystem) drive, right-click the drive icon in Finder or on the desktop and then choose Encrypt.

To set up FileVault: Choose > System Preferences > Security & Privacy > FileVault pane (click if the settings are dimmed). Click Turn On FileVault and then follow the onscreen instructions. During the process, an autogenerated key is added to the keychains (page 180) of assigned users, letting them unlock (decrypt) their FileVault-encrypted data by remembering only a login password. (Alternatively, you can use your iCloud password as the key.) You must give explicit permission to each user that you want to allow to log in to a FileVault-protected Mac. Any user with a passwordless account must set a password. Print, copy, or store the recovery key when it appears (in large type). The recovery key is a master password that lets an administrator access any account without knowing the account holder's password, or turn off FileVault for any account.

Tip: If FileVault is turned on, the Recovery HD partition (page 11) won't appear when you hold down the Option key during startup, but you can still hold down Command+R during startup to boot directly to it.

Keychain Access

Use Keychain Access to manage your passwords for secure websites, FTP sites, network servers, encrypted folders and volumes, and other secure items. macOS creates, maintains, and unlocks your default (login) keychain automatically, so passwords are available when they're needed to access secured items and locations. You can also store credit-card numbers, PINs, and other private data in secure notes on your keychain. Keychain Access remembers passwords only for programs that are keychain-aware. See also iCloud Keychain (page 80).

To open Keychain Access: Choose Applications > Utilities > Keychain Access.

To add a keychain item: Access a secure item or location normally, type your password when prompted, and then choose to save or remember the password (you may have to click an Options button). The password is added to your keychain and appears in Keychain Access.

Tip: To make Safari remember your login credentials for various websites in your keychain, open Safari, choose Safari > Preferences > AutoFill tab, and then select "User names and passwords". From now on, Safari will fill in saved user names and passwords automatically when you log in to memorized websites.

To add a password item manually: In Keychain Access, click (+) or choose File > New Password Item (Command+N). Type a name or URL in the Keychain Item Name box. Type a user ID or account name or number in the Account Name box. Type the password in the Password box (select Show Typing to reveal your password as you type, or click 🔑 for password help). When you're done, click Add.

To add a secure note: In Keychain Access, choose File > New Secure Note Item (Shift+Command+N). Type a name for the note in the Keychain Item Name box. Type the note in the Note box. When you're done, click Add.

To delete a keychain item: In Keychain Access, select the target item and then choose Edit > Delete or press Delete.

To inspect or control access to a keychain item: In Keychain Access, double-click the item, or select it and then click i . To see the text of password or secure note, click the Attributes tab and then select "Show password" or "Show note".

To control access to the item, click the Access Control tab and then choose one of the following options:

Allow all applications to access this item
> Lets any program access the item, without showing a confirmation dialog box.

Confirm before allowing access
> Shows a confirmation dialog box for every program that tries to access the item. "Ask for Keychain password" determines whether the confirmation prompts for a password. Click (+) or (–) to add or delete programs that can access the item without triggering the confirmation.

Click Save Changes, type the keychain password in the dialog box that appears, and then click Allow.

To use a keychain item: Access a secure item or location normally. If Access Control permits access to the item without confirmation, the item opens without showing a confirmation dialog box; otherwise, click one of the following buttons in the confirmation dialog box:

Always Allow
> Lets the keychain open the item and adds the item to the Access Control list to suppress this dialog box in the future.

Deny
> Prevents use of the keychain item; type a password to access the secure item.

Allow
> Lets the keychain open the item this time.

To manage keychains: To create a new keychain, choose File > New Keychain (Option+Command+N). To view a different keychain, click to show the Keychains list and then click the keychain. To lock or unlock a keychain, select it and then click the lock at the top of the Keychain Access window. Keychains are stored as files in ~/Library/Keychains (~ denotes your home folder). You can copy these files to other Macs.

Parental Controls

Parental Controls lets you manage how your children (or anyone) can use the computer. You can set limits on camera use, programs run (including games played), web access, store purchases, Mail and Messages communications, login hours, and more. You can also log a user's activities for later review. You, an Administrator, can apply these controls to only Standard user accounts, which then become Managed accounts in the Users & Groups panel.

To set up parental controls for an account: Choose ⌘ > System Preferences > Parental Controls (click 🔒 if the settings are dimmed). Select the account in the list and then click Enable Parental Controls. Set the desired restrictions in each pane (Apps, Web, and so on). To turn off all settings, click ⚙ > Turn off Parental Controls.

Remote Parental Controls

Parental Controls are useful in environments where multiple Macs on the same network are in use (in classrooms or crowded households, for example). You can adjust Parental Controls settings for Macs 1, 2, 3, and 4 while seated at Mac 5, for example. To do so, follow these steps:

1 Log in to the first remote Mac (not your Mac), choose ⌘ > System Preferences > Parental Controls, click 🔒, enter your password, and then click the name of the account that you want to manage remotely.

2 Click ⚙ > Allow Remote Setup.

3 Close System Preferences.

4 Repeat steps 1–3 for each account on each Mac on the network that you want to manage remotely.

5 Return to *your* Mac.

6 In Finder, choose Go > Connect to Server, and then click Browse.

   A list of the other Macs on the network appears.

7 Click one of the other Macs and then enter an administrator's name and password for that Mac.

8 Choose ⌘ > System Preferences > Parental Controls, click 🔒, and then enter your password.

   A section named Other Computers appears in the Users & Groups list.

9 Click the account name (on the other Mac) whose Parental Controls settings you want to change remotely and then enter the administrator name and password of the remote computer.

10 Repeat steps 6–9 for the other Macs and accounts that you want to manage remotely.

Password Assistant

Password Assistant helps you avoid creating easily guessed passwords (names, birthdays, dictionary words, and so on). It can generate secure passwords or rate ones that you make up. To open Password Assistant, click 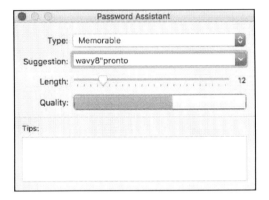 wherever you're supposed to create a password—in Users & Groups or Keychain Access, for example. To test your own password, type it in the Suggestion box; otherwise, use the Type pop-up menu and the Length slider to generate secure passwords. (FIPS-181 is a standard U.S. government password-generating algorithm.) The Quality bar shows password toughness.

Secure Virtual Memory

If you're running a lot of programs and hit the limits of physical memory (RAM), then macOS claims drive space and creates a **swap file** to use as virtual memory. By default, macOS encrypts swap files so that thieves can't pluck data and passwords off your drive. (In Mavericks (OS X 10.9) or earlier, you had to turn on secure virtual memory manually.)

System Integrity Protection

System Integrity Protection, also called "rootless", prevents the user or any process from modifying the contents of system-protected folders, including /System, /bin, /sbin, and /usr (except for /usr/local). Not even administrators can add to these folders or edit files that they contain, though they retain their access to the rest of the files on the drive. In Terminal, you can't use the sudo command in protected directories.

This feature makes Macs more resistant to attacks and malware, but it also limits what advanced users can do to their systems. To circumvent System Integrity Protection, restart your Mac, hold down the Option key during startup, and then choose Recovery HD when the list of startup partitions appears. In the Utilities menu, toggle System Integrity Protection. To check the status of System Integrity Protection, run the command csrutil status in Terminal.

Two-Factor Authentication

Two-factor authentication is a robust, optional security add-on for your Apple ID on macOS and iOS. When this feature is turned on, an enemy needs not only your password to break in, but also access to another of your devices. When you sign in to a new device or web browser with your Apple ID, you must verify your identity by typing your Apple ID password *and* a separate six-digit verification code. This code displays automatically on all the other macOS (El Capitan or later) and iOS (version 9 or later) devices that you're currently signed in to. Type the code on the new device.

You don't need to verify a device again unless you erase it, change your password, or remove it from your Apple ID's trusted device list. To see this list on your Mac, choose > System Preferences > iCloud > Account Details > Devices tab.

To set up two-factor authentication on your Mac, choose > System Preferences > iCloud > Account Details > Security tab > Set Up Two-Factor Authentication.

For details, read the Apple support article "Two-factor authentication for Apple ID" at *support.apple.com/ht204915*.

Tip: Two-factor authentication is built into OS X 10.11 (El Capitan) and later and iOS 9 and later. If you already set up your devices to use Apple's older two-step verification process on earlier versions of OS X and iOS, then you can continue to use that older process. (Two-factor authentication isn't the same process as two-step verification.)

Privacy Settings

To set miscellaneous privacy-related options, choose > System Preferences > Security & Privacy > Privacy pane (click 🔒 if the settings are dimmed).

Location Services

> Location Services lets apps and services use your physical whereabouts via the Mac's built-in positioning service, which determines your approximate location by using the data from nearby wireless hotspots. For example, Location Services lets your laptop determine its own time zone automatically, lets Maps and Siri determine your current location, and lets a weather website show your local weather the first time that you visit the site. The first time an app makes a request to use Location Services, macOS opens a location warning for that app, which you can allow or refuse. Your response sticks, and the request isn't shown again. You can turn off Location Services for some or for all apps and services.

Contacts, Calendars, Reminders

> Choose which apps and services can access your contacts, calendars, and reminders.

Twitter, Facebook, LinkedIn, and so on

> Choose which apps and services can access your social networking accounts (if you've created those accounts in > System Preferences > Internet Accounts).

Accessibility

> Choose which apps and services can control your computer's Accessibility features (page 63).

Diagnostics & Usage

> If you select these checkboxes, your Mac will quietly and automatically send anonymous data to Apple and third-party developers (via Apple) about your crashes, freezes, programs, hardware, peripherals, and so on. Don't bother; save the bandwidth.

CHAPTER 10

Maintenance & Backups

MacOS includes tools to keep your system running smoothly.

Software Updates

Apple regularly releases updates for macOS system software and other Apple programs. These updates include bug fixes, new features, security patches, version upgrades, and other improvements. All Apple software updates are available from the Updates section of the Mac App Store (page 121).

Tip: Updates for third-party programs downloaded from the App Store are also available from the App Store. If you didn't get a program from the App Store, check the developer's website for updates or use the program's built-in updater. See also "Installing & Removing Programs" on page 112.

 By default, macOS automatically checks for updates every day, but you can check manually at any time. If any updates are available, App Store sends a notification and adds a numbered badge, denoting the number of updates, to the App Store's dock icon and menu entry.

To open App Store, choose > App Store. Available updates are listed in the Updates pane. To learn more about an update, click its *More* link. You can update any single item by clicking Update next to its name, or you can update everything by clicking Update All at the top of the window. You're also free to ignore updates.

Tip: If you're on a large network, your network administrator might distribute updates via network server.

To set up software updates: Choose > System Preferences > App Store.

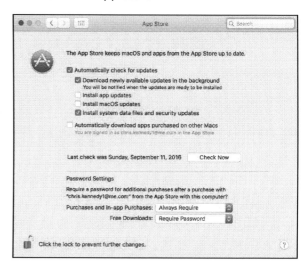

Set the following options (click if the settings are dimmed):

Automatically check for updates
> Check for updates automatically and periodically.

Download newly available updates in the background
> Download updates in the background without being asked. You'll still be notified before the updates are installed.

Install app updates
> Install downloaded app updates without asking you.

Install macOS updates
> Install downloaded macOS updates without asking you.

Install system data files and security updates
> Install downloaded critical system updates without asking you.

Automatically download apps purchased on other Macs
> Download apps (from the Mac App Store) that you bought on other Macs.

Show Updates
> Open the Mac App Store and see any available updates.

Check Now
    Check for updates manually.

Password Settings
    Choose whether a password is required for additional paid and free downloads from the Mac App Store.

Power Nap

While your Mac sleeps, Power Nap will silently and automatically:

- Get the latest mail, contact information, calendar events, reminders, notes, Photo Stream photos, and other iCloud updates (hourly). Mail and Notes must be open before your Mac sleeps.

- Synchronize iCloud documents (hourly).

- Update Find My Mac locations (hourly).

- Maintain certified VPN-on-demand connections.

- Let you lock and wipe your Mac remotely.

If your Mac is asleep and plugged in to an AC power outlet, Power Nap will also:

- Download and install Mac App Store software updates (hourly) and purchases (weekly).

- Make Time Machine backups (attempted hourly until a successful backup completes).

- Build the Spotlight search index.

- Update Mac Help.

- Let wireless base stations wake your Mac (Wake on Wireless).

Power Nap works whether your Mac is plugged into a power outlet or is using battery power (draining little power). Power Nap refreshes the data on your Mac silently; no fans or lights come on and the display remains dark (but the drive, processor, and networking hardware are all active).

To turn on Power Nap, choose > System Preferences > Energy Saver > "Enable Power Nap". For MacBooks, you can configure Power Nap independently in the Battery and Power Adapter panes.

Power Nap works only on Macs that have flash memory, including the MacBook Air (late 2010 or newer), MacBook (2015 or newer), MacBook Pro with Retina display, iMac (late 2012 or newer), and Mac Pro (late 2013 or newer). If you have a compatible Mac but don't see Power Nap settings, you may have to update your firmware (> App Store).

Time Machine

Time Machine

Eventually your drive will fail catastrophically, taking your data with it. Or you (or someone) will delete important files irretrievably. Time Machine protects your files by backing them up periodically and automatically to an external drive, a network drive, or another internal drive. (Apple also sells AirPort Time Capsule (*apple.com/airport-time-capsule*), a wireless drive that works seamlessly with Time Machine.) Time Machine remembers past versions of your files that you can go "back in time" to recover. By default, Time Machine keeps hourly backups for the past 24 hours, daily backups for the past month, and weekly backups until your backup drive is full. You can back up multiple Macs onto the same backup drive; each Mac's backup is stored in a separate folder on that drive. You can't back up to a CD or the startup drive.

You can exclude unnecessary files and folders from Time Machine backups to reduce the space needed on the backup drive. To configure backups, you use the Time Machine preferences panel. To restore backups, you use the Time Machine application. You can optionally encrypt backups.

To set up Time Machine: Connect or mount the backup drive. Choose > System Preferences > Time Machine > Select Backup Disk. In the window listing available drives, select the drive that you want to use for backups, and then click Use Disk. If necessary, move the Time Machine slider to On. For security, select "Encrypt backups". For quick access to Time Machine, turn on the Time Machine menu .

Tip: You can designate multiple backup locations and then switch among them. This feature lets you make separate backups at, say, home and work.

To exclude items from backup: Choose > System Preferences > Time Machine > Options. Click (+) or (–) to add or remove excluded items in the list. Choose whether to be warned when Time Machine starts replacing old backups with new ones because your backup drive is full.

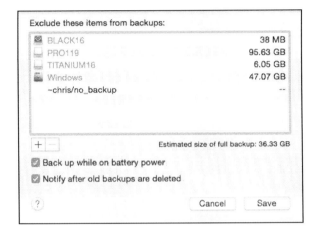

To check the status of Time Machine backups: Choose > System Preferences > Time Machine, or choose > Open Time Machine Preferences. Backup status appears in the Time Machine panel (if a backup is in progress, a progress bar appears). The first backup takes a long time. After that, backups are fast because only the changes ("deltas") to the original backup are recorded.

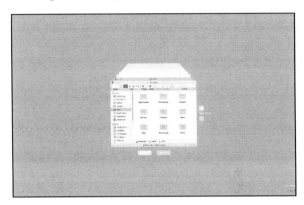

To restore a backed-up file: Open the drive or folder to restore. Choose Applications > Time Machine, or choose > Enter Time Machine. The Time Machine interface replaces the desktop. To navigate to the past version of the file that you want to restore, click the backward or forward arrows; click along the timeline on the right edge of the screen; or click the title bar of the window version that you want to see. Select the item that you want to restore, and then click Restore. Time Machine restores backups to their original location in Finder. If you open Time Machine when a Spotlight search window is active, you can browse backward through the search results.

Optimized Storage

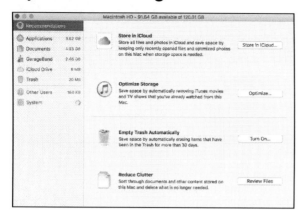

If you're running low on drive space, the Optimized Storage feature can help make room: choose > About This Mac > Storage tab > Manage. After analyzing your drive, macOS lists various manual and automated storage-management options. Click the items on the left (Recommendations, Applications, Documents, and so on) to review the suggestions for decluttering your Mac. You can make room by automatically storing infrequently used files in iCloud (page 78), for example, or delete duplicate or obsolete files such as used app installers, duplicate downloads, caches, and logs. You can also easily find and delete large apps and files, or ones that you don't use.

Target Disk Mode

Target disk mode turns one Mac (the target computer) into an external drive for another (the host computer). It's the fastest way to bulk-copy data and useful for transferring files from laptop to desktop or old Mac to new Mac. Each Mac must have a FireWire or Thunderbolt jack. You need a 6-pin FireWire 400 cable (older Macs), a 9-pin FireWire 800 cable, or a Thunderbolt cable (newer Macs).

To use target disk mode: Connect the target and host computers with a FireWire or Thunderbolt cable. On the target, choose > System Preferences > Startup Disk > Target Disk Mode, and then click Restart (click 🔒 if the settings are dimmed). After the target restarts, the target's drive will appear on the host's desktop, labeled with a FireWire icon 🔆 or Thunderbolt icon ⚡. After you finish copying files from target to host, eject the target drive normally from the host desktop, and then restart the target.

To use target disk mode (the old way): Disconnect all FireWire devices from the target and host computers. Turn off the target computer (if it's a laptop, keep it plugged in). The host computer needn't be turned off. Connect the computers with a FireWire or Thunderbolt cable. Start the target computer and immediately press and hold down the T key until the FireWire icon 🔆 or Thunderbolt icon ⚡ appears. The target's drive will appear on the host's desktop. After you finish copying files from target to host, eject the target drive normally from the host desktop, and then restart the target. This method is quicker because you don't have to open System Preferences and works when the host Mac can't start on its own.

CHAPTER 11

Switching from Windows

The following glossary lists Microsoft Windows terms and features and their macOS equivalents. Features with no macOS counterparts are marked N/A (Not Applicable).

Windows	macOS
About *Program* (Help menu)	About *Program* (Application menu)
Accessibility	Accessibility preferences
Accounts	Users & Groups preferences
Action Center	Notification Center and System Preferences
Active Desktop	Dashboard
Add Hardware	N/A
Add or Remove Programs	Drag-and-drop installation
Address Book	Contacts
Administrative Tools	Utilities folder
Adobe Reader/Acrobat	Preview
All Programs	Applications folder
Alt key	Option key
Alt+Tab	Command+Tab

Windows	macOS
Automatic Updates	App Store
AutoPlay	CDs & DVDs preferences
Backspace key	Delete key
Backup and Restore	Time Machine
BIOS	Firmware
BitLocker	FileVault
Blue screen of death	Spinning beachball of death
Bluetooth Devices	Bluetooth preferences
Calculator	Calculator
Calendar	Calendar
Camera and Scanner Wizard	Photos and Image Capture
Character Map	Keyboard Viewer and Characters panel
Clipboard	Clipboard
Close	Close
Color Management	ColorSync Utility
Command Prompt	Terminal
Computer folder	Computer folder
Computer Management	Utilities folder

Windows	macOS
Contacts	Contacts
Continuum	N/A
Context menu	Shortcut menu
Control Panel	System Preferences
Cortana	Spotlight and Siri
Ctrl key	Command key, usually
Ctrl+Alt+Delete	Option+Command+Esc or Apple menu
Cut, copy, and paste	Cut, copy, and paste
Date and Time	Date & Time preferences
Default Programs	Open With
Delete key	Forward Delete key
Desktop	Desktop
Desktop Background	Desktop preferences
Desktop Gadgets	Widgets
Desktop Slideshow	Desktop preferences
Device Manager	System Information
Devices and Printers	Sidebar
Directories	Folders
Disk Defragmenter	N/A (automated)
Display	Displays preferences
DOS Prompt	Terminal
Drive letters	Drive names
Ease of Access Center	Accessibility preferences
Edge	Safari
Eject	Eject key ⏏
End Task	Force Quit
Exit	Quit
Favorites	Sidebar
Fax/Fax and Scan	Fax
File Explorer	Finder

Windows	macOS
Firewall	Firewall
Folder Options	Finder > Preferences
Folders	Folders
Fonts	Font Book
FTP	Finder > Go > Connect to Server
Gadgets	Widgets
Games	Game Center
Help and Support	Finder > Help
Hibernate	Sleep
HomeGroup	Family Sharing
Indexing Options	Spotlight
Instant Viewer	Exposé
Internet Explorer	Safari
Internet Options	Safari > Preferences
Jump lists	Dock Exposé and Stacks
Keyboard	Keyboard preferences
Libraries	Smart folders
Logon and logoff	Login and logout
Mail	Mail
Maps	Maps
Maximize	Zoom and Full-Screen Apps
Menu bars	Menu bar
Messenger/Messaging	Messages
Modern/Metro apps	Widgets
Microsoft ID	Apple ID
Microsoft Security Essentials	N/A
Minimize	Minimize
Mouse	Mouse preferences
Movie Maker	iMovie

Windows	macOS
MSN Messenger	Messages
Music	iTunes
Multiple desktops	Spaces
"My" folders	Home folder
My Network Places	Sidebar
Network and Sharing Center	Network preferences
Network Connections	Network preferences
Network Setup Wizard	Network preferences > "Assist me"
Notepad	TextEdit and Notes
Notification area	Menu extras (status menus)
OneDrive	iCloud or iCloud Drive
Options	Preferences
Outlook	Mail and Calendar
Parental Controls	Parental Controls
Path	Path
People	Mail
Path separator: backslash (\)	Path separator: forward slash (/)
PC Settings	System Preferences
Peek	Exposé
Personal folder	Home folder
Personalization	General and Desktop & Screen Saver preferences
Phone and Modem	Network preferences (dial-up connections)
Photos/Photo Gallery	Photos and Image Capture
Picture and Fax Viewer	Preview
Power Options	Energy Saver preferences

Windows	macOS
PowerShell	AppleScript
Previous versions	Auto Save and Versions
Print Screen	Grab
Printers and Faxes	Printers & Scanners
Program	Application or app
Program Files	Applications folder
Programs and Features	Drag-and-drop installation
Properties	Info
Reader	Preview
Recycle Bin	Trash
Region and Language	Language & Region preferences
Remote Assistance	Screen sharing
Remote Desktop	Apple Remote Desktop (sold separately)
Ribbon	N/A
Right-click menu	Shortcut menu
Run command	Terminal
Safe mode	Startup options
ScanDisk	Disk Utility
Scanners and Cameras	Photos and Image Capture
Scheduled Tasks	Terminal launchd command
Screen Saver	Desktop & Screen Saver
Search	Spotlight
Settings	System Preferences
Shadow copy	Auto Save and Versions
Shake	N/A
Shortcut menu	Shortcut menu
Shortcuts	Aliases

Windows	macOS		Windows	macOS
Show Desktop	Exposé		User Accounts	Users & Groups preferences
Sidebar	Dashboard		Video	iTunes
Skype	FaceTime and Messages		Weather	Widgets
Snap and Snap Assist	Split View		Window Color	N/A
Snipping Tool	Grab		Windows Explorer	Finder
Sound Recorder	GarageBand		Windows Firewall	Firewall
Sounds	Sound preferences		Windows folder	System folder
Sounds and Audio Devices	Sound preferences		Windows Hello	N/A
Speech	Accessibility preferences		Windows Live ID	Apple ID
			Windows Live Mail	Mail
Speech Recognition	Dictation preferences		Windows Live Messenger	Messages
Stand By	Sleep		Windows Live Movie Maker	iMovie
Start menu or Start screen	Dock		Windows Live Photo Gallery	Photos and Image Capture
Startup folder	Login Items		Windows logo key	Command key
Sticky Notes	Stickies		Windows Mail	Mail
Sync Center	iCloud		Windows Media Center	Apple TV (sold separately)
System	Apple menu , System Information, Sharing preferences, and App Store		Windows Media Player	DVD Player, iTunes, and QuickTime Player
			Windows Messenger	Messages
System Information	System Information		Windows Mobility Center	Accessibility preferences
System Restore	Startup options			
System tray	Menu extras (status menus)		Windows Photo Viewer	Preview
Task Manager	Activity Monitor		Windows Search	Spotlight
Task Switcher	Exposé		Windows Store	Mac App Store
Task View	Spaces		Windows Update	App Store
Taskbar	Dock		WordPad	TextEdit or Notes
Taskbar and Start Menu	Dock preferences		ZIP files	ZIP files
Trackpad	Trackpad preferences			

CHAPTER 12

Keyboard Shortcuts

Keyboard shortcuts involve the modifier keys and other keys. On laptop keyboards, you may have to press the Fn key in combination with the function keys, depending on your setting for > System Preferences > Keyboard > Keyboard pane > "Use all F1, F2, etc. keys as standard function keys".

To change a modifier key: Choose > System Preferences > Keyboard > Keyboard pane > Modifier Keys. Choose an action from the popup menu next to the modifier key that you want to change. To return the keys to their original settings, click Restore Defaults. For a list of the symbols used for modifier and other keys, see "Menus" on page 26.

To change keyboard shortcuts: Choose > System Preferences > Keyboard > Shortcuts pane. Click a shortcut category in the list on the left. In the list on the right, use the checkboxes to toggle shortcuts. To assign or change keyboard shortcuts, click a shortcut's name and press Return (or double-click to the right of a shortcut's name), and then type the new keystroke (on laptop keyboards, you may have to hold down the Fn key when you assign the new shortcut). To add or remove custom shortcuts, click the App Shortcuts category, and then click (+) or (–). To return the shortcuts to their original settings, click Restore Defaults.

To see keyboard-shortcut conflicts: Choose > System Preferences > Keyboard > Shortcuts pane. A yellow warning triangle next to a shortcut category or a keyboard shortcut denotes a conflict.

Accessibility

To	Press
Show Accessibility controls	Option+Command+F5
Toggle zoom	Option+Command+8
Zoom in	Option+Command+=
Zoom out	Option+Command+-
Toggle smooth images	Option+Command+\
Toggle white-on-black (invert colors)	Ctrl+Option+Command+8
Increase contrast	Ctrl+Option+Command+.
Decrease contrast	Ctrl+Option+Command+,
Toggle Sticky Keys	Shift five times
Toggle Mouse Keys	Option five times
Toggle VoiceOver	Command+F5

Apple Menu

To	Press
Sleep	Option+Command+Eject ⏏
Restart	Ctrl+Command+Eject ⏏
Force-restart	Ctrl+Command+Power ⏻
Shut down	Ctrl+Option+Command+Eject ⏏
Open the Sleep/Restart/Shut Down dialog box	Ctrl+Eject ⏏
Log out after a cancelable delay	Shift+Command+Q
Log out immediately	Shift+Option+Command+Q
Change "About This Mac" to "System Information" and suppress cancelable delays	Hold down Option, and then click

Dashboard

To	Press
Toggle the dashboard	F12 (or F4 on older Macs)
Refresh the current widget	Command+R
Close or delete the current widget	Option

Dialog Boxes

To	Press
Move to the next/previous control	Tab/Shift+Tab
Move to the next control when a text field is selected	Ctrl+Tab
Move to the next item in a list, tab group, or menu	Arrow keys
Move sliders	Arrow keys
Move to a control next to the text field	Ctrl+arrow keys
Select the highlighted menu item	Spacebar
Click the default (highlighted) button	Return or Enter
Click "Don't Save"	Command+D
Click "Replace"	Command+R
Click the Cancel button	Esc or Command+dot (.)
Close a menu without choosing an item	Esc

Dock

To	Press
Toggle dock hiding	Option+Command+D
Activate the dock	Ctrl+F3 (press the arrow keys to select an icon, and then press Return to open it)
Resize the dock	Drag the divider
Reposition the dock	Shift-drag the divider
Open the dock shortcut menu	Right-click the divider
Open a dock icon's shortcut menu	Right-click the dock icon
See a program's open windows	Right-click (or click-and-hold) the program's dock icon
Add an open program to the dock	Right-click (or click-and-hold) the program's dock icon, and then choose Options > Keep In Dock
See an item in Finder	Command-click the item's dock icon
Switch to another program and hide the active one	Option-click the program's dock icon
Switch to another program and hide all other programs	Option-Command-click the program's dock icon
Quit a program	Right-click (or click-and-hold) the program's dock icon, and then choose Quit
Force-quit a program	Option-right-click (or Option-click-and-hold) the program's dock icon, and then choose Force Quit
Force-open a document in a program	Option-Command-drag the document's icon to the program's dock icon
To drag an actual item (rather than its dock alias)	Shift-drag its dock icon
To freeze dock icons while dragging an item to the dock	Command-drag

Finder

To	Press
Open Preferences window	Command+, (comma)
Hide Finder windows	Command+H
Hide other programs	Option+Command+H
Open a new Finder window	Command+N
Create a new folder	Shift+Command+N
Create a new smart folder	Option+Command+N

To	Press
Open a new tab	Command+T
Open the selected item(s)	Command+O
Change "Open With" to "Always Open With"	Option+File menu
Close the active Finder window	Shift+Command+W
Close all Finder windows	Option+Command+W
Close the active tab	Command+W
Open Info window	Command+I
Open Inspector window	Option+Command+I
Open Summary Info window	Ctrl+Command+I
Duplicate the selected item(s)	Command+D
Alias the selected item(s)	Command+L
Preview the selected item in Quick Look	Spacebar or Command+Y
Invoke full-screen Quick Look	Option+Spacebar or Option+Command+Y
Show a slideshow of the selected items	Option+Command+Y
Show the original of an alias	Command+R
Add the selected item(s) to the sidebar	Ctrl+Command+T
Toggle to the sidebar	Option+Command+S
Add the selected item(s) to Favorites	Shift+Command+T
Move the selected item to the Trash	Command+Delete
Eject a CD or DVD	Command+E
Find (Spotlight window)	Command+F
Find by name (Spotlight window)	Shift+Command+F
Undo	Command+Z
Cut/Copy/Paste	Command+X/C/V
Select All	Command+A
Deselect All	Option+Command+A
View as Icons/List/Columns/Cover Flow	Command+1/2/3/4
Change "Clean Up Selection" to "Clean Up" and "Arrange By" to "Sort By"	Option+View menu
Toggle the toolbar	Option+Command+T
Toggle the View Options panel	Command+J
Go back	Command+[
Go forward	Command+]

To	Press
Open the parent (enclosing) folder	Command+↑
Open the parent (enclosing) folder in a new window	Ctrl+Command+↑
Open the All My Files folder	Shift+Command+F
Open the Documents folder	Shift+Command+O
Open the Desktop folder	Shift+Command+D
Open the Downloads folder	Option+Command+L
Open the home folder	Shift+Command+H
Open the Library folder	Option+Window menu > Library
Open the Computer folder	Shift+Command+C
Open the AirDrop folder	Shift+Command+R
Open the Network folder	Shift+Command+K
Open the Applications folder	Shift+Command+A
Open the Utilities folder	Shift+Command+U
Open a specified folder by typing its path	Shift+Command+G
Connect to a server	Command+K
Minimize the active window	Command+M
Minimize all Finder windows	Option+Command+M
Change "Minimize" and "Zoom" to "Minimize All" and "Zoom All"	Option+Window menu
Cycle forward or backward through Finder windows	Command+` or Shift+Command+`
Cycle forward or backward through tabs	Ctrl+Tab or Shift+Ctrl+Tab
Toggle to tab bar	Shift+Command+T
Open the Help search box	Shift+Command+?

Folder Navigation & Icons

To	Press
Expand/collapse the selected folder (list view)	→/← or click ▶/▼
Expand/collapse the selected folder and its sub-folders (list view)	Option+→/← or Option-click ▶/▼
Open a folder in a new window	Command-double-click

To	Press
Open a folder in a new window, closing the current window	Option-double-click
Open the parent folder	Command+↑
Open the parent folder in a new window, closing the current window	Option+Command+↑
Open the selected folder in a new window, closing the current window	Option+Command+↓
Activate the desktop	Shift+Command+↑
Go back/forward a folder	Command+[and Command+]
Align icons	Command-drag
Copy (instead of move) an item	Option-drag
Move (instead of copy) an item	Command-drag
Alias an item	Option-Command-drag
Copy an item	Select it, press Command+C, open the new location, and then press Command+V
Open the selected icon	Command+↓ or Command+O
Select the next icon	Arrow keys
Select an icon by name	The first letter of its name
Select the next/previous icon	Tab/Shift+Tab
Add to the selection (icon view)	Shift-click
Select adjacent icons (list view)	Shift-click
Select or deselect nonadjacent icons	Command-click
Select the icon's name (to rename)	Return
Preview the selected icon in Quick Look	Spacebar or Command+Y
Invoke full-screen Quick Look	Option+Spacebar or Option+Command+Y
Show a slideshow of the selected icons	Option+Command+Y
Open a spring-loaded folder immediately during a drag	Spacebar
Scroll in any direction (list or icon view)	Option-Command-drag
Move an item from or to the System folder	Command-drag

Frozen Programs

To	Press
Stop a process	Command+dot (.)
Force quit	Option+Command+Esc
Turn off your computer	Power button ⏻
Force shut down	Shift+Option+Command+Power ⏻
Force restart	Ctrl+Command+Power ⏻

Menus

To	Press
Activate the menu bar	Ctrl+F2
Activate menu extras (status menus) in the menu bar	Ctrl+F8
Rearrange or remove menu extras	Command-drag them
Reveal extra information or commands when you click a status menu	Option
Navigate to a menu command	Arrow keys (or type a command name in the selected menu)
Choose a menu command	Return
Close a menu without choosing a command	Esc

Mouse Keys

To	Press
Turn Mouse Keys on or off	Option five times
Move up	8 (8)
Move down	2 (K)
Move left	4 (U)
Move right	6 (O)
Move diagonally	1 (J), 3 (L), 7 (7), 9 (9)
Click the mouse button	5 (I)
Hold down the mouse button	0 (M)
Release the mouse button	Dot (.)

Programs, Exposé, Spaces & Launchpad

To	Press
Activate the next/previous program	Command+Tab/Shift+Command+Tab
Cycle forward/backward through windows of the active program	Command+~/Shift+Command+~
Hide a program	Command+H, or Command+Tab to the program and then press H
Hide other programs	Option+Command+H
Open program preferences	Command+, (comma)
Switch to new program and hide the active one	Option-click a dock icon
Show all windows (Exposé/Mission Control)	F3 or Control+↑
Show all open windows of the active program (Exposé/Mission Control)	Control+↓
Show the desktop (Exposé/Mission Control)	F11
Show all spaces (Spaces/Mission Control)	F3 or Control+↑
Switch to a space (Spaces)	Ctrl+1/2/3/4/… or Ctrl+←/→
Show Launchpad	F4 (on newer Macs)
Quit a program	Command+Q, or Command+Tab to the program and then press Q

Screenshots

To	Press
Capture the whole screen as a file	Shift+Command+3
Capture the whole screen to the clipboard	Ctrl+Shift+Command+3
Capture part of the screen as a file	Shift+Command+4, and then drag
Capture part of the screen to the clipboard	Ctrl+Shift+Command+4, and then drag
Capture a screen object	Shift+Command+4, and then press Spacebar

Spotlight & Siri

To	Press
Open the Spotlight window	Command+Spacebar
Open a search window in Finder	Option+Command+Spacebar
Open the selected item in the results list	Return
Open the top hit in the results list	Command+Return
Jump to the previous/next category in the results list	Command+↑/↓
Display the selected item in Finder	Command-double-click the item
Get information about the selected item in the results list	Command+I
Clear the search text	Esc (once)
Cancel the search	Esc (twice)
Open the Siri window	Hold Command+Spacebar, hold Option+Spacebar, or press Fn+Spacebar (set in Siri preferences)

Startup

To	Press
Start normally	Power button ⏻
Start from a CD/DVD	Press and hold C
Start from the first drive/partition	Press and hold D
Reset the laptop display	Press and hold R
Start from a network server	Press and hold N
Start in target disk mode	Press and hold T
Start from an external drive/disc	Press and hold Shift+Option+Command+Delete
Start in 64-bit mode	Press and hold 6 and 4
Prevent automatic login	Press and hold Left-Shift when the spinning progress indicator appears
Suppress Login Items and Finder windows at login	Press and hold Shift after clicking the Log In button
Select a startup drive/partition	Press and hold Option
Force-boot macOS	Press and hold Command+X
Start in safe mode (safe boot)	Press and hold Shift at startup until the login screen indicates a safe boot

To	Press
Eject a CD/DVD at startup	Press and hold Left mouse button
Troubleshoot at startup	Press and hold Command+S (single-user command-line), Command+V (verbose Unix console), or Option+Command+P+R (reset NVRAM/Parameter RAM)
Reinstall (recover) macOS	Press and hold Command+R

Trash

To	Press
Move the selected item to the Trash	Command+Delete
Put back the selected item from the Trash	Command+Delete
Empty the Trash	Shift+Command+Delete
Empty the Trash without confirmation	Shift+Option+Command+Delete

Windows

To	Press
Activate the next/previous window	Ctrl+F4/Shift+Ctrl+F4
Activate window drawer	Option+Command+`
Cycle forward/backward through windows in the active program	Command+~/Shift+Command+~
Minimize the active window	Command+M or double-click the title bar
Minimize all windows	Option+Command+M
Move a window without activating it	Command-drag its title bar
Close/minimize/enlarge all windows in the active program	Option-click the close/minimize/zoom button
Scroll quickly	Click-and-hold in the scrollbar
Temporarily switch between "Scroll to here" and "Jump to page"	Option-click in the scrollbar
Activate the toolbar	Ctrl+F5
Rearrange toolbar controls	Command-drag
Activate a floating window	Ctrl+F6
Activate the sidebar or drawer	Option+Command+~
Jump to a folder in the folder path	Right-click (Command-click) the window title

Index

Printed in Great Britain
by Amazon